Unlocking the Scriptures for You

REVELATION

Lewis Foster

STANDARD
BIBLE STUDIES

STANDARD PUBLISHING
Cincinnati, Ohio   11-40116

Library of Congress Cataloging in Publication Data:

Foster, Lewis A.
    Revelation / by Lewis Foster.
      p. cm. — (Standard Bible studies)
    Bibliography: p.
    Includes index.
    ISBN 0-87403-607-0 :
    1. Bible. N.T.   Revelation—Commentaries.   I. Title.
II. Series.
BS2825.3.F63   1989
228'.07—dc19   89-4138
                              CIP

CONTENTS

Maps

Charts

PREFACE

The book of Revelation is a fitting climax and conclusion to the whole of the Bible. It sums up the struggle of God's people through the ages. It tells of God's victory in the end, and how He will share that victory with His children. It tells of Heaven, the end of time, and the beginnings of eternity.

In some ways, the Christians of the second century should have been able to understand the meaning of the writing better than we do. Hellenistic Greek was used everyday, and they were acquainted with its figures and idioms. They lived closer to the authorship of the book, and they could check with John and pass on the answers he gave them. Although the book has a message that is timeless, it was delivered to a people who were undergoing particular trials and persecutions, and Revelation had special significance to them.

On the other hand, since the message of Revelation is timeless, it fills a need for every generation from its initial publication to the end of time, including our own generation. In fact, the early centuries had no monopoly on correct interpretations or false interpretations. This book speaks of Heavenly scenes described in an earthly language, and this stretches the capability of any language, whether our own or one from another century. It tells of the future and, of necessity, employs prophetic terminology. It was read in those early times without any assurance that Jesus was going to delay His coming for thousands of years. Each generation must be lived out with the urgency that every day might be the last. Furthermore, the truths in Revelation continually take us across the threshold into a spiritual realm that lies beyond the view of physical eyes. Here the Christians at the close of the first century or the twentieth century are equally dependent on the time when John was taken by the hand and led into the very mysteries of Heaven, the future, and even eternity. Just because one crosses over from this world to the Heavenly kingdom in thought does not mean all tangible existence ceases, that no relationship exists between the two. Some insist too much upon the necessity of a literal fulfillment for every figure introduced in Revelation. Others go too far in presuming that, because it is figurative in language or spiritual in connotation, it therefore can have no literal, historical fulfillment. Each extreme leads to an unfortunate emphasis, and a cloud is cast over the main messages of the book of Revelation.

Christians today should be able to grasp more readily how the material in the Apocalypse of John is unfolded. All TV viewers have become accustomed to the use made of montages. In one corner of the TV, one may see a swimmer diving into the water; and right beside him, a golfer swings at his golf ball. Just below him, a basketball player pops up to make a basket. In another corner, a football player goes out for a pass, and then a hockey player comes speeding over the ice. By now the viewer is thoroughly convinced that a sports program is getting underway, but he does not become discouraged because he fails to identify the person involved in each of the actions, or he cannot locate the scene of the action, or he finds the relationship of the shots uncertain. The book of Revelation makes use of a series of montages. It does not give us a road map or a time table for the future. But it does give us full assurance of certain important truths:

(1) God knows how the whole of human existence is going to turn out.

(2) God is in control and will be victorious in the end.

(3) He will share His triumph with all God's people.

(4) But before this can come about, there will be great tribulations.

The purpose of the book of Revelation is to steel the nerve of God's followers so that they remain faithful to the end. Through warnings, Revelation brings fortitude for faithfulness. Through making known assured truths, it provides foundations for steadfastness. Through promises, it brings hope to the faithful. The purpose of this commentary on Revelation is to highlight these warnings, truths, and promises. Although the positions of major schools of interpretation will be acknowledged as texts are treated, this is not an attempt to compile what others have written on the subject. Nevertheless, I owe a great debt to what has been already written in the vast literature of the subject. My greatest debt, however, is to my father, who taught a college course in Revelation for many years. I have come to share his emphasis on the cyclical nature of the book, that is, that some parts travel through the same span of time as other sections. This present book, however, is not a defense of one particular approach to the interpretation of Revelation. Although the second coming of Christ is viewed as the heart of the message in the book of Revelation, decisions as to the time of His coming or the order of events before and after His coming will not be guaranteed. The emphasis of this commentary on Revelation is the exhortation given to all Christians in every age for faithfulness until Christ returns in His glory.

INTRODUCTION

Background

The book of Revelation is a letter originally sent to seven churches in the Roman province of Asia.[1] The Christians who first received this message lived in constant danger of persecution. Initial understanding of this writing must have been moved by the trials through which the early readers were living, even as our own day finds a message to us in our own predicament. Neither of these exhausts the depth of meaning intended by the divine mind who knows the past, present, and future. Thus, we would like to be aware of all three levels insofar as we can.

(1) We want to read the book of Revelation with a feel for the early setting of the first Christians who received this record of John's vision, but

(2) we are eager to apply it to our own situation today.

(3) The third level is a recognition that God's knowledge and intent penetrate far beyond the grasp of any one age.

The Occasion

Although the authorship and date of Revelation will receive fuller attention later,[2] conclusions can be noted here. John the apostle is accepted as the author. This identification was shared by such early Christian writers as Justin Martyr[3] and Irenaeus.[4] The

---

[1]Revelation 1:4-6.

[2]See below, Concluding Notes, pp. 325ff.

[3]Justin Martyr, *Dialogue With Trypho,* 8.

[4]Irenaeus, *Against Heresies,* 5,35.

end of Domitian's reign (A.D. 96) is the most likely time of writing. John himself was in exile on the Isle of Patmos, believers were daily facing hostile neighbors, and the temptation of compromising faith in Jesus was ever present. The need for reassurance was great. There were other needs as well. This book must serve as a conclusion to a span of writings extending back fifteen hundred years. It must also reach forward to the return of Christ and the culmination of all time. In addition, it must be meaningful and helpful to each succeeding generation between the writing and the end. The Apocalypse does just that.

One of the essentials to the proper understanding of Revelation is to stand some distance from the isolated action of the report and view the whole panorama of the picture. John's purpose in writing becomes evident. He wants to emphasize the presence of God and His ultimate victory. The people of God will be victorious with Him, but not without great tribulation.

The literary style of this book is different. This is not the genre of Gospels or Epistles. This is not the historian's format. This writing is the report of a vision, and its form is that of the direct revelation, the apocalyptic. Its example, however, is not found in the spurious works of the apocryphal, but from the genuine reports in such canonical works as Daniel and Ezekiel.

The Approach

The government of the United States has three branches: the Executive, the Legislative, and the Judicial. They serve as checks and balances on one another. The President must send his major plans for the approving vote of Congress, but Congress sends its decisions for the signature of the President. Both of these branches function, however, under the Supreme Court's interpretation of the Constitution of the United States. As one undertakes a study of the book of Revelation, he becomes conscious of three branches as well. They might be labeled as follows: interpretation, verification, and application. Each is helpful to the proper functioning of the other.

Interpretation

The immediate interpretation of a section in Revelation has to do with the understanding of that passage and its natural place in the book. This involves special attention to the exegesis of the words, a sensitivity to the context, and an awareness to the

intended meaning of the author. Both verse-by-verse consider-
ations and broader overviews of the scene from horizon to horizon must be included in such an approach to the Apocalypse. The
first question is, "What does it mean?"

Verification

Not long after a person undertakes the study of Revelation,
another question pops up: "How does it fit?" How do the details
in this book relate to information found in other books of the
Bible? After all, there is a divine harmony in Scripture, and this
should be one way to test what we thought was the natural way of
understanding this final book of the Bible. We may have been too
presumptuous in advocating a certain interpretation as being the
natural way to understand a passage, only to find it fails to be
verified when placed alongside passages in other parts of Scripture. Whereas a brief verse-by-verse treatment will be the heart of
the interpretation section of our approach, each chapter will also
include consideration of a special topic that will reach into other
books of the Bible to satisfy something like verification for the
interpretation of Revelation.

Since Revelation encompasses long segments of time, history is
also engaged in the verification of our understanding of it. Here
one must walk gingerly. Perhaps we are not viewing history cor-
rectly. Perhaps it has no connection with what we are studying in
Revelation at some point. We cannot escape the question, however, as to how the book of Revelation and history fit together.
First comes the meaning; then comes how it fits.

Application

A third question introduces itself. "What is the message for me
in these passages?" Scripture is never read and interpreted properly without an application. To satisfy this demand, each chapter
will in one way or another address three questions as a means of
arriving at a realization of meaning included for one's own life.[5]

---

[5]Although contemporary Biblical studies are prone to spend much time
in detailed theory concerning possible sources, literary form, and style
and structure, the questions asked here are a part of an approach to
interpretation known as factual criticism. See Lewis Foster, "Realges-
chichte: Old and New in Interpretation," *Journal of the Evangelical Theological Society* (28/2 June, 1985), pp. 153-68.

(1) What is true to life? In Revelation, we find certain themes that run throughout, and then we discover our own lives identify with these. We are involved. For example, the conflict of good and evil, the presence of the faithful and the unfaithful, the existence of principalities and powers beyond our physical sight. God is in control, and God will win out in the end.

(2) What is unexpected? Even though Revelation becomes more meaningful when we see how we identify with its message (true to life), we also profit by noting what is out of the stream of what we would expect. But, after all, we should not be too surprised at this since God is ultimately handling the scenario. His ways are different from the ways of men as high as the heavens are above the earth. We find the necessity of commitment, understanding, and perseverance as we face the unexpected. For example, if God is in control, why should God's people suffer tribulation? Why is punishment delayed for the ungodly? Why is Satan bound and then released for a time again? The book of Revelation is filled with the unexpected. But this is in itself part of the purpose of the book—preparing the Christian for the unexpected.

(3) What is the key message? When we are reading Revelation, finding the bottom line in each of the passages is an important part of understanding the meaning. If we can determine what the main thrust is, we have gone a long way toward making an application to our own lives. It should be a regular practice to identify the key message as we proceed from section to section. For example, "be faithful" is a common exhortation that echoes in innumerable passages. "Be ready" is another, and "be a witness of Jesus Christ" is another. The book is not primarily a warning to those living in the last generation to let them know when the time for the second coming has arrived. Rather, it is to serve as a warning to help steel the nerve of Christians in every age. They must endure and remain faithful, not being caught unaware by hardships too great for them to bear. "Be faithful, even to the point of death" (Revelation 2:10) is a key message that should be written over the whole book and applied to each Christian reader.

Schools of Interpretation

Such diverse interpretations of the book of Revelation have appeared that each one clamors for recognition at the outset. From the earliest record of the ways people understood Revelation, heated differences have been registered. Eusebius disliked

Papias because he took the thousand-year reign to be literal, upon this earth. Whereas some felt that the imperial power of Rome was the restraining force holding back the coming of the Antichrist, others felt that Rome *was* the Antichrist. In the Reformation period, the Reformers lost no time in agreeing with this latter identification—as one would quickly note in the introduction to the earliest editions of the King James Version (the seventeenth century). The editors identified Rome—not as the pagan Rome and its imperial power—but as the Roman Catholic Church and its papal power!

Present schools of interpretation can be summed up in five different groups:

Spiritual

This approach emphasizes the symbolism of Revelation as teaching spiritual lessons rather than expecting literal fulfillment. The prevailing lesson pertains to the constant warfare between good and evil, both in Heaven and on earth. This faces toward helpful reminders, but lends itself to easy error as well. To begin with, the fact that a teaching employs symbolic language does not necessarily mean that the fulfillment will not be literal. For example, Daniel's vision of four beasts was symbolic, but this did not mean there would be no literal kingdoms to fulfill the figurative language. When one is determined to spiritualize the truths, there is always the danger that more may be spiritualized than was originally intended. Such procedure cuts away the import of predictive prophecy and leaves the book of Revelation a picture book of self-evident principles on the conflict of good and evil.[6]

Preterist

This type of interpretation supposes that the descriptions in Revelation have to do with events that are either in the present with the writing or are already past rather than many of them in the future as they are pictured. (*Praeter* means "past.") Once again, this nullifies the predictive element of Revelation and leaves the ground covered exclusively in the realm of the Roman

---

[6]William Henry Simcox, *The Revelation of St. John the Divine* (Cambridge Bible for Schools and Colleges, 1898).

persecution of the church, emperor worship, and divine judgment on Rome, things that were already happening. Although the original recipients of this writing would no doubt see particular significance to their own times, it is difficult to believe that Revelation concerned only items that were confined to the first century and contained no message for all the generations that have followed. If so, this would be at variance with the stated purpose of the writing to tell of things to come.[7]

Futurist

Although this school recognizes the first-century setting of Rome versus the church in the first three chapters, it maintains that chapters 4-22 are an inspired look at the time immediately preceding the second coming. This might be accompanied with different tribulation theories, but is usually seen as assigning chapters 8-18 to the last seven years extending to the return of Christ. Then the new order of things is described: chapters 19-22. If this were true, it would leave all those centuries of Christians between the opening decades of the church and the final countdown for the second coming without a message in the book of Revelation.[8]

Historicist

Some view the book of Revelation as an allegorical panorama of the history of the (western) church from the first century to the second advent. This continuous-historical view was held in the Reformation period by Luther, Zwingli, and Knox.[9] It has become obvious, however, that the course of events cannot be in chronological order, continuous-historical, because by Revelation 6:12ff, one has already arrived at the final days (cf. Matthew 24:29ff). The whole of the following chapters could not be following this point in chronological order.

---

[7]See weaknesses considered by George Ladd, who himself is a modified futurist (*A Commentary on the Revelation of John* [Grand Rapids: Eerdmans, 1972], pp. 10ff.)

[8]See weaknesses cited by Merrill C. Tenney, *Interpreting Revelation* (Grand Rapids: Eerdmans, reprint 1980), pp. 137ff.

[9]Ibid.

Cyclical

This last group includes a number of variations. Such words as *spiral, concurrent, recapitulation,* and *historical cycles* are used to characterize it. In this approach, certain features are included as live possibilities. For instance, some events in Revelation can be concurrent. Some prophecies may have more than one fulfillment. The book may lead up to the end time and then drop back in a new cycle to approach the end again with other figures.

> In fact, the method and plan of the book seems to be, that we have again and again a series—most frequently a group of seven—of pictures that plainly symbolize the approach of the Judgment. Up to the penultimate (next to last) stage, everything would lead us to think the Judgment was immediately to follow: but the penultimate state itself is prolonged and expanded: and when at last it ends, and the series is complete, it is found to usher in, *not* the end of all things, but the beginning of a new series of events, still preparatory for the final Judgment.[10]

Those advocating such a view might be called cyclists. This is the approach favored in this commentary.

Millennial Views

Going hand in hand with the various schools of interpretation are the millennial views related to them. In only one passage of Scripture, Revelation 20:1-6, can one find reference to Christ's reign of a thousand years (the millennium). Seemingly the single most significant factor in one's interpretation of the whole book is where he locates this period of Christ's reign in time and place.

Amillennial

One might raise an objection at the outset to the label used to identify this group of interpreters. In the Greek, to use the letter *a* in front of another word is a way of negating what follows. For example, a theist believes in God, but an *a*theist does not believe in God. By this token, an amillennialist would not believe in the

---

[10]W. H. Simcox, *The Revelation,* p. lv.

millennium. This is not the true position of the amillennialist, however. Rather, he does not believe in this reign of Christ as an earthly kingdom established in Jerusalem. He locates Christ's rule in Heaven. As to the time of this reign, he considers the period of one thousand years to be a figurative number simply representing a long period of time. This enables him to identify the period as the time between Calvary and Christ's second coming, whenever that might be.

But Satan is to be bound in this period (Revelation 20:2, 3). This raises a difficulty in explaining Satan's activity of persecuting the church throughout its history, James's admonition to resist the devil (James 4:7), and Peter's warning that the devil prowls as a lion seeking someone to devour (1 Peter 5:8). To say that Satan is only bound by being on a leash and that his activity continues as usual puts a strain on the whole approach. This millennial interpretation is commensurate with the first of the general approaches listed above, the spiritual.

Postmillennial

The problem of the time of the millennium is easily stated. Is it before or after the second coming? But because of the names of the millennial views, one must be cautious to state the question properly: is the second coming before or after the millennium? In the postmillennial position, the second coming follows after the millennium. In this view, the gospel will be preached throughout the world, and a gradual conquest by the gospel will usher in the millennial reign of Christ. This will be a victory for the Christians on the earth, and this period of peace and righteousness of at least a thousand years will precede the advent of Christ, Judgment Day, and the beginning of the eternal kingdom.

This view has suffered greatly since war after war has been fought in this century, since the non-Christian world has been growing in population more rapidly than individuals are being won to Christ, and the role of Christianity in the so-called Christian nations is far short of the expectation of the millennium. In fact, rather than a better picture toward the end, Paul warns of "terrible times in the last days" (2 Timothy 3:1), and "evil men and impostors will go from bad to worse, deceiving and being deceived" (2 Timothy 3:13). The very message of Revelation is one of tribulation before the end.

Premillennial

A popular view in Christendom today is the belief that Christ will return to the earth to set up a kingdom on this earth with headquarters in Jerusalem. This reign will last a literal one thousand years and will end with another coming of the Lord in judgment.

That there must be a third coming of the Lord makes the whole system suspect. Granted, the passage of time between fulfillment of prophecies given in a series is a common difficulty in interpreting prophecy. The first coming of Jesus in the flesh was prophesied and also His coming again on the clouds of heaven. There was no way of knowing these would be separated by at least almost two thousand years, and perhaps considerably more. But despite the possible separation of His second coming from the judgment by another thousand years, there is no intimation that the *parousia* of Christ would be more than one return. In this case, it makes more meaningful the return of Christ, the resurrection, and the judgment as one succession of events rather than a succession of returns separated by a thousand years.

Dispensational

Just as both the amillennial and the postmillennial views present the second coming of Christ as coming after the millennium, so the premillennial and the dispensational views expect the coming of Christ before the millennium. Both the premillennialist and the dispensationalist expect a literal kingdom on this earth. They differ, however, at a number of points. The dispensationalist divides the history of the church into seven dispensations, beginning with the message to the church at Ephesus as representing the first dispensation, and each of the seven churches of Asia representing a successive age until Laodicea as the final dispensation at the Christ's advent.

Another departure from most premillennialists is the insistence upon the early rapture of the Christians, sparing them from the trials of the "Great Tribulation."[11] All interpretations for the dispensationalist are extremely literal and based upon an entirely subjective type of key to the symbolic language of Revelation. At

---

[11]See Loraine Boettner, *The Millennium* (Presbyterian and Reformed Publishing, 1957), p. 6. See also below, p. 95, 111ff.

many points, one sees a possible option, now for the literalist, and then for the spiritualist. But when the dispensationalist makes an attempt to build a case for old Israel's displacing new Israel and the church's being treated as a temporary parenthesis, subjectivism has exceeded its bounds.

End-Millennial

Few interpreters accept all the tenets of the average presentation of any one school of interpretation. Most will only admit to a modified version of the major school to which they are closest in their conclusions. It seems unfair, however, to travel under the guise of one of the big four views when one disagrees at so many points with any one of them, and at the same time sees good points in several of them. On the other hand, it seems presumptuous to define a fifth approach in an area where no one has the knowledge or the right to be dogmatic. Whether this is a fifth or a modification of one of the other views, it is necessary to be positive and not simply take the easy course of objecting to points emphasized in the others without at least suggesting a direction for possible solutions.

This view looks forward to a kingdom not entirely figurative, not entirely literal—not all in Heaven, not all on earth. As to the time, before or after the second coming, because of the period of a thousand years, one is inclined to look for the advent following the special reign, for whether one takes the thousand years to be literal or figurative, it still would denote some period of time. If, then, one associates the end of time with the coming of the Lord—as well he might—it follows that the period of Christ's special reign will still be in the framework of time and before His second coming (see the treatment in chapter 12 under Revelation 20 and also in the Concluding Notes, pp. 333-337). It is not so much "post" or "pre" as its close marks the "end" of time.

The Extremes

Overemphasis or Neglect

Unfortunately, the study of the book of Revelation has drawn two extremes. Some individuals become so enamored with the appeal of the future life and the importance of eternity that they spend all their breathing moments dwelling on the subject without any attention to the needs and corrections called for in this world and this time. They find the attraction of the mysterious and the figurative irresistible. They know that the Son of Man will come when He is not expected (Luke 12:40), and warning is given that He himself did not know the day and the hour He would return (Matthew 24:36). In fact, it is not meant for us to inquire as to the times or dates God has set (Acts 1:7). But some in every generation insist upon interpreting the information about the last times in such a way as to be hearing the final bell right then.

On the other hand, some are so certain we cannot know for sure the meaning of the information about Christ's second coming that they avoid the subject entirely. One congregation had studied through the whole of the Bible from Genesis to Jude in their Wednesday-night Bible study. Only Revelation remained for their reading and lessons. It had taken them years to get to this point. When they searched for an individual in the group to prepare for teaching the book, no one could be found. All admitted an ignorance on the subject and the danger of differences of opinion in conclusions. So they decided to skip the book of Revelation and go back to Genesis again in their assignments. What a tragedy to omit deliberately a vital part of God's Word! We should attempt to maintain the same balance and emphasis that is found in the Scripture itself, but we cannot neglect a study because some claim to know more about it than they do or others perpetuate an ignorance about the basic information God makes available.

Dogmatism or Lack of Concern

Unfortunately, again, two extremes develop. Some who study the book of Revelation diligently become so insistent on another's accepting just the interpretation of Revelation they advocate that division results. This, indeed, is another tragedy. In the time of Christ, there were numerous teachers of the law who knew the prophecies concerning the coming of the Messiah. Yet when He came, they did not recognize Him and they shared in His crucifixion. They were so certain of their understanding of the Scripture that they could not accept Him when He appeared. It would be a travesty to repeat this mistake at His second coming—to attempt to make Jesus fit His time table to one particular current view of interpreting Revelation. Some today may be just as mistaken as were the Jewish scholars of Jesus' time.

But then there is the other extreme that shows a complete lack of concern. Because they are not sure of their understanding of the times and seasons or the interpretation of the figures of Revelation, they give no heed to the messages of the book nor thought to preparation for Jesus' return. Despite the refusal to panic at the sound of final alarm issued by some, the time will come at the very end when indeed the alarmist will be right in time—though, perhaps, wrong in much else—and the unconcerned will indeed be wrong. Do not be caught in either of these camps.

Then or Now

Two more extremes have to do with two different approaches to interpreting Revelation. One says everything in the book of Revelation refers to things that happened in the time of ancient Rome (see above, the preterist), or at the other extreme, the position that everything refers to things to happen at the very end, and that we are in those days right now (see above, the futurist).

One should not allow either of these views to smother the living message to all ages, both to those who first received the message in the first century and those who will witness the second coming—plus all those who live in the vast stretch of time in between.

Historical or Spiritual

In like manner, one wants to avoid making dogmatic application of every figure in Revelation to a literal fulfillment in history. This is especially misleading when one goes through the book and looks for consecutive events that might be distorted into matching the description in Revelation. Equally dangerous, however, is the determined attempt to thwart every prediction, removing it from earthly affairs because of a figurative relation. Once again, the extremes must be avoided and the recognition of both the historical and the spiritual be acknowledged.

The Parameters

Individuals read the book of Revelation because of different motives. Also they read commentaries on the book with various expectations. It is well to specify what one might expect from this book, and to warn about what he should not expect.

What Not to Expect

First, one ought not to expect to receive here a guaranteed, valid interpretation of all figures. God cannot tell us of the future with such a certainty that takes away the freedom of man's will as he lives out his period of probation. God informs us of the future with sufficient clarity that we are assured He knows how all of this existence will turn out, and He gives complete assurance that He will win out. But He has given this revelation to serve as challenge and warning for all the ages. No age or individual will have an answer for all the figures of Revelation, and this author certainly makes no such claims.

Second, one ought not to expect to put the figurative on a literal screen. One afternoon, after a family had procured their first television set, the father was surprised to find his son listening to a radio instead of watching TV. He asked his boy, "Why are you listening to this when you could be watching TV?"

His son replied, "There are some things I can imagine better than they can put them on TV."

He was listening to "The Lone Ranger." This is ten times more true of the figures in the book of Revelation. They are not meant to be drawn out in a literal picture (e.g. a lamb opening a scroll, a sword proceeding out of a mouth). The figures are to be used to start the mind to work, but not to be viewed in a literal way.

Finally, one ought not to expect to find compiled here all the variant interpretations introduced to explain Revelation. This commentary on John's record of his vision does not attempt to be a compendium of interpretations, but only seeks to convey messages from God's revelation to his servant, John.

What to Expect

Briefly stated, there are four things one may expect from this study:
(1) A focus on the main thrust of God's purpose in revealing the truths recorded in Revelation.
(2) Stimulation of thought, concentrating on Heavenly matters in a materialistic world.
(3) Encouragement to be alert to the signs of the time.
(4) Application of the principles urged in the book of Revelation to one's own life.

The Overview

To see the book of Revelation in its full scope from beginning to end is important. This requires drawing back to a distance that allows an overview to fill the screen. And this is not all bad. Then you do not allow the host of figures to overwhelm you and draw your attention away from the essential messages of the writing. If you take a closer look at individual passages as they appear in their larger context, you have a better appreciation for what the figures mean and how they fit in.

Because of the importance of viewing the major themes of Revelation, three outlines are offered to the book. The first is in the language of Revelation itself, but probably the author did not intend for it to be a guiding finger to the major divisions of the book. Although the meaning is far more involved, it still provides a simple starting point for discerning one way to divide the material. The second outline is given because you should have one short enough to keep in mind, but long enough to have the outstanding figures in their places. This way, you can know where you are in the unfolding of the whole while you are reading any one part. Once again the number seven is convenient, but it may not have been the intent of the author. The third outline is the course of thought introduced by the author to unfold his vision.

Outline 1
I. Things That Are   chapters 1-3
II. Things That Are to Come   chapters 4-22

Outline 2
I. Things That Are
   A. Introduction   chapter 1
   B. Letters to Seven Churches   chapters 2 and 3

II. Things That Are to Come
   A. Heaven   chapters 4 and 5
   B. Seven Seals   chapters 8 and 7
   C. Seven Trumpets   chapters 8-11
   D. Woman, Dragon, and Beasts   chapters 12-14
   E. Seven Bowls   chapters 15 and 16
   F. The Judgment   chapters 17-20
   G. New Heaven and New Earth   chapters 21 and 22

Outline 3
I. Things That Are
   A. Introduction   chapter 1
     1. The Letter Begins
     2. The Vision of Christ Appears

CHAPTER ONE

The Dauntless Christ

Revelation 1:1-20

A professor stood at the door and passed out pennies as the college students entered for the first lecture in his course. He was teaching archaeology, and he made his opening assignment. "Take your penny and write down what you can tell about the civilization that struck that coin. Use only the information you can conclude from the coin itself." When each student examined his penny, he began to see things he had forgotten or never even noticed before. The man's face on the coin was sure to represent a figure important to the nation in its past history. Some had to inquire about the stately memorial building on the other side. Others wanted the Latin words translated for them. Some needed the reminder, "In God We Trust." Many had forgotten that "Liberty" was spelled out explicitly. A date was there. The worth of the coin was clearly engraved. Its size and shape, the composition of the metal, and the artistic design—all this must be taken into account. But what if you were a person living two thousand years from now, if the Lord should delay His coming; what could you conclude about the people who made that coin?

If a Christian were given a similar assignment, to read the first chapter of Revelation with this kind of discernment, his appreciation and understanding of the whole book that follows would increase greatly. Each detail has its role in tying together the Old and the New, improving perception of the present and anticipation for the future.

Prelude

Overview

By examining the first chapter of Revelation, the reader is able to tune his ear to the voice he hears speaking to him throughout the book. He finds the name of the author—John. He learns the purpose of the writing—to make known a special revelation from God concerning things present and things to come. The centrality of one figure is apparent—Jesus Christ. Even the details in the description of His appearance are picked up and repeated in continuing glimpses of Christ in the second and third chapters, and still further throughout the book. Although the volume describes a series of visions involving both Heaven and earth, John is careful to record the actual time and place he received this revelation—on the island of Patmos, on the Lord's Day. Even the type of literary genre is made clear—it is an epistle sent to the seven churches of Asia. The use of figurative language is introduced and examples are spelled out. Lampstands represent churches, and stars stand for the messengers.

As a coin with its design, material, pictures, and wording tells something of the nation that produced it, so the opening chapter of Revelation introduces the reader to God and the destiny of man in a climactic unveiling of time and eternity.

Key Message

"Write, therefore, what you have seen, what is now and what will take place later" (Revelation 1:19). In these words, you can see an outline of Revelation. "What you have seen" is the description of the vision (chapter 1); "what is now" is the section telling of the immediate present (the letters to the seven churches of Asia, chapters 2 and 3); and "what will take place later" is the future up to and beyond the second coming of Christ (chapters 4-22).

The focus of the message is fastened on the one who delivered it. This opening picture of Christ is not as a conquering general, riding to conquest. Neither is it a ruling king upon a throne, nor a judge at the bar of justice. Rather, this is the majestic figure of Jesus standing in the midst of His churches, giving necessary and urgent instruction to members of His body. He commended the good, condemned the bad, warned of coming dangers, and gave assurance of ultimate victory. This is the dauntless Christ, who cannot be intimidated, who will not be discouraged, who is without fear. He challenges His church to be dauntless as well.

Glossary

Read through the first chapter of Revelation and as you come to the terms listed below, note the explanation.

Revelation	Apocalypse, uncovering, unveiling, disclosure.
Angel	At times, a supernatural being, a messenger from God (Revelation 1:1). At other times, the same Greek word can indicate a human messenger (possibly Revelation 1:20).
John	The apostle John as maintained from the earliest testimony (See below, pp. 325ff).
Word of God	The revelation given to John in this vision and recorded in his report.
Testimony of Jesus Christ	That which was attested by Jesus Christ himself.
Asia	Not the continent, but a Roman province along the western coast of Asia Minor (present-day Turkey).
Spirits (seven)	Since the context anticipates the presence of the Holy Spirit, the sevenfold spirit could describe the Holy Spirit in His fullness.
Faithful Witness	Jesus Christ is the example *par excellence*. His testimony is always true, His word never changes, His promises never fail.
Firstborn from the dead	Jesus was the first to be raised from the dead and to die no more. (See also Psalm 89:27; Colossians 1:18.)
Kingdom of priests	Not Rome nor any earthly power, but a kingdom of priests (Exodus 19:6). The church is the corporate kingdom and its members are the individual priestly subjects.
Alpha and Omega	The first and last letters of the Greek alphabet. It is equivalent to the "First and the Last" or the "Beginning and the End" (Revelation 22:13; 21:6). Jesus applies it to himself.
Seven golden lampstands	These represent the seven churches of Asia who are the original recipients of this epistle (Revelation 1:17).
So shall it be! Amen	Two words at the conclusion of a solemn pronouncement concerning the second coming of Christ. The one is Greek in

	origin, the other is Hebrew. Each gives special emphasis to the truth of the preceding statement.
Patmos	A desolate island about forty miles off the coast of the province of Asia (See below, p. 37).
Word of God	Not the same as in Revelation 1:2. Here it refers to the preaching of the gospel as the reason for John's being in exile (more likely than his being on the island in order to preach the gospel).
Testimony of Jesus	John's preaching about Jesus.
In the Spirit	The description of a prophet under inspiration. (See Ezekiel 3:12, 14.)
Lord's Day	The Sabbath is Saturday, and the Lord's Day is the first day of the week, Sunday. On that day, Christians observed the breaking of bread in the Lord's Supper (Acts 20:7) and their offerings were given (1 Corinthians 16:1, 2).[12]
Son of Man	The title Jesus most often used of himself; a messianic title.
Seven stars	Angels of the seven churches of Asia, either angelic beings commissioned to deliver the letters, human messengers assigned to the task, or designated evangelists of the congregations.
Double-edged sword	The short Roman sword was tongue-like in shape and came from the mouth like spoken words. See Revelation 19:13, 15; related to the Word of God. (See Isaiah 49:2.)
Keys of Hades and death	The keeper of the keys has authority over death, whether a place or a personification.

---

[12]The Lord's Day is terminology used in early Christian writings as the first day of the week, the day of the Lord's resurrection. Cf. *Didache* 14, Ignatius, *Magn.* 9, Melito of Sardis in Eusebius, *Ecclesiastical History,* 4.26. See Henry B. Swete, *Commentary on Revelation* (Grand Rapids: Kregel, 1977), notes on Revelation 1:10.

Mystery	Something kept secret in the past, but now unveiled.

Content Notes

Foreword and Beatitude (1:1-3)

As Greek plays were introduced by words and choruses of introduction, the book of Revelation begins with a paragraph of explanation.

"The revelation of Jesus Christ" (1) can be taken two ways. It can either mean the unveiling has come *from* Christ (a subjective genitive in the Greek) or it is *about* Christ (an objective genitive). Both of these statements are true, for God gave the apocalypse to Jesus, who was to show it to the Christians through the agency of an angel who, in turn, unfolded it to John; but also Jesus is the main figure in the subject matter of the book. Perhaps it is meant to be taken both ways. Although high authorities take opposite positions, one does not have to declare himself either/or so long as he understands it can be both/and. The ultimate source is God, but He speaks *through* Christ and the subject matter of His Word *is* Christ.

"Blessed is the one. . . ." A beatitude is pronounced upon both the ones who *read* this book and those who *hear* it. Some translate the word as "read aloud," but this is not necessary. In that time and place, they did not read silently, but always aloud. It is assuring, however, that the hearers were included as well. Many of the Christians could not read, and an early Christian writing includes a note asking the Christians who *could* read to come early for the Christian worship so that they could read the Scripture (including, of course, Revelation) aloud for those who could not read as they waited for the service to begin. During the service, the Scripture was read as well. One marvels at how many must have laid claim to this promise of the book of Revelation down through the ages. You also must wonder about the neglect of such a simple, direct injunction.

In all, seven beatitudes are given throughout the book of Revelation: Revelation 1:3; 14:13; 16:15; 19:9; 20:6; 22:7, 14. This beatitude has two sides to the coin. The one side is reading and hearing the words; the other side is "and take to heart what is written in it." This is the same message of Jesus as recorded in Luke 11:28: "Blessed rather are those who hear the word of God

31

and obey it." John uses another Greek word for *obey* (translated, "take to heart" [NIV] or "keep" [KJV]; but this is a favorite word of John). James expresses the same thought: "Do not merely listen to the word, and so deceive yourselves. Do what it says" (James 1:22). This is an extremely important admonition to each who undertakes the study of Revelation. If you approach it seeking to know the times and seasons of Jesus' scheduled return, you have missed its message. When you hear its message, you will not simply have something to wait for, but you must do it, keep it, act in accordance with its truths. Only then is the blessing given.

"The time is near." You cannot escape the note of urgency when you read these words. But what does this mean? After all, almost two thousand years have gone by, and we are still looking for the fulfillment of this book. Granted, the term *near* is relative, and Jesus' life on earth was preceded by thousands of years before that, and an eternity before that. His second coming will be followed by an eternity after that. With such a perspective, the time between even the first century and the millennium of His coming will be short. But what would this have meant to someone at the close of the first century? Certainly, he would not have expected thousands of years to intervene.

One might reply that whether he understood it or not, this is the way it is. Others say that John was just wrong. He thought it was going to be fulfilled right away, but it was not. More is involved than just the way John thought about it, however. In the last chapter (Revelation 22:10), the angel gives John the instruction, "Do not seal up the words of the prophecy of this book because the time is near." This command is made all the more impressive when it is compared with the words given to Daniel at the close of his writing: "But you, Daniel, close up and seal the words of the scroll until the time of the end" (Daniel 12:4). So now are we saying that John was wrong, the angel was wrong, and the source of information was mistaken about the time of fulfillment? One can see that Daniel was warned that all was not to be fulfilled immediately: "Seal up the scroll." But John was told, "Keep the scroll open, the time is near."

Several factors must be taken into account. The Scripture is accustomed to dividing time very simply into the "former days" and the "latter days"—just two stretches of time. The Old Covenant was in the period of the former days, and Daniel was in that period. The latter days began with the coming of the days of the

New Covenant, and Peter could say even at Pentecost that they had entered "the last days" (Acts 2:16, 17). The angel could also tell John the time was near because the fulfillment of prophecies in Revelation were not confined to the countdown just before the advent of Christ. There are warnings and messages pertinent to Christians all through the latter days. The churches of Asia were in desperate need for the help they were to receive. We need the same injunctions and the same warnings today. Every year between now and the Lord's coming must hear the cry that the time is near. The book of Revelation does not inform us of when the Lord will come; but its message is to be faithful and ready in living out your days, for the night comes when no man can work. It is not that John was wrong; it is not that the angel was mistaken; it is the wisdom of God that necessitates that His followers live every day on the edge of eternity. John the Baptist could say, "The ax is already at the root of the trees" (Matthew 3:10). James could warn, "The Judge is standing at the door" (James 5:9). The book of Revelation is not an academic exercise in calculating how much longer the Lord will delay. It is a call for action now. The time is near. Revelation tells of both "what is now and what will take place later."

The Letter Begins (1:4-8)

Revelation is written clearly in the form of a letter: the name of the author—"John"—and its destination—"seven churches of Asia"—are stated clearly. Why seven churches? You can name more churches in Asia than that. Paul wrote to Colosse, he worshiped with the church in Troas, and Trophimus was left at Miletus sick. Before fifteen years have gone by, Ignatius will write letters to the Christians in Tralles and Magnesia, as well as Ephesus, Smyrna, and Philadelphia. All of these cities are in Asia and could have been considered for receiving John's revelation. Why seven?

This number is used so often, and at times in such a way that it could easily have been more or less, that there must be a reason. The most common suggestion is that it stands for completeness. The recipients of the letters to Asia did not stop with the seven specified, but they were representatives of the whole of the churches, the complete church. This does not mean that these particular seven churches did not exist, but they marked the beginning of circulation that was to continue for all posterity. As the epistles of Paul were designated to a specific historical need but then continued their teaching to ever widening circles in all of the church, so John's letters were destined for continued application. Notes in the Muratorian Canon point out that the recognized listing of Scripture included Paul's letters to seven churches just as John wrote to seven churches. In all likelihood, these letters of John were not sent separately, each to one exclusive church, but rather each church received a copy of the collected seven letters along with a copy of the whole of the vision as it is read in the New Testament. So this opening of a letter is the true beginning of the whole book of Revelation.

Greeting (4, 5)

The next normal requirement in an ancient letter is a greeting. John uses Paul's usual words of greeting: "Grace and peace" (for example, 2 Thessalonians 1:2), but then he extends Paul's "God the Father and the Lord Jesus Christ" into a fuller title of God: "who is, who was, and who is to come" (a paraphrase of the divine name in Exodus 3:14 and 15). Next, John includes the third member of the Godhead, the Holy Spirit: "the sevenfold Spirit" (the greeting of Peter includes the Holy Spirit as well, 1 Peter 1:2). But John reserves Jesus, the second person of the Godhead, for this last position because he has more to say about Him. After all, Jesus is the leading figure of this vision: "the faithful witness" (He was the perfect martyr who laid down His life in His earthly ministry), "the firstborn from the dead," (His resurrection was not only His single victory over death but promised victory to all who follow Him). When Jesus comes again, it will not be in the same role as before, for He is "the ruler of the kings of the earth."

Doxology (5-8)

Although Paul did not take time for a thanksgiving at the beginning of the Galatian epistle, apparently because he was so distraught over the false teaching there, he did close his greeting with a doxology. Here in Revelation, John also closes his greeting with a doxology. It could be considered a summation of what Jesus has done for us—even as Paul gave the heart of the gospel as the death, burial, and resurrection of Christ (1 Corinthians 15:3). John sums it up: Jesus "loves us ... has freed us ... and made us a kingdom of priests to serve his God."

"Look, he is coming with the clouds" (7). With this startling exclamation, another doxology begins. Here is the underlying theme of the whole vision, the second coming of the Lord. This montage had to be introduced in the opening thoughts or John would not be faithful to his purpose for the book—the revelation of Jesus Christ.

The Setting (1:9-11)

Since the action that follows involves different times and places, the starting point must be established in no uncertain way. John is on the island of Patmos (see the special subject below) on the Lord's Day. As he stopped to sum up Christ's work in three phrases, now John describes his own situation in three aspects. They are not like a triangle, but more like a coin with suffering on one side and reigning on the other, held in a coin holder of patient endurance. John hears "a loud voice like the sound of a trumpet" telling him to write all that he is about to see and send it to the seven churches he names. This assures the reader he has not sent a small portion of the book to one and another part to another. They all receive the whole.

When John turns to see who is speaking, he sees "seven golden lampstands" (the churches in Asia, Revelation 1:20) surrounding the figure who is speaking, someone "like a son of man." Daniel had written centuries before, "In my vision at night I looked, and there before me was one like a son of man, coming with the clouds of heaven" (Daniel 7:13). This was the title used of the Messiah and chosen by Jesus to identify himself.

The Vision of Christ, the Son of Man (1:12-20)

His Appearance (12-16)

The description that follows has great importance. Each individual could find qualities and lessons in each item that is designated. In the end, this would be subjective and one could not claim this was the original intent of John. On the other hand, the description by John has direct relationship to descriptions in the Old Testament. Since Scripture is the best interpreter of Scripture, to view these together would be helpful to one's grasp of what John was seeing. One must remember that John was not creating this scene in his own head. He was trying to describe what he saw in his vision. If the language he used to describe what he saw is

Comparison of the Vision of Christ in Revelation 1 With the Old Testament	
Description	**Old Testament Parallel**
Robe reaching down to His feet (13)	Priestly dignity, Exodus 28:31, 39f, or the majesty of God, Isaiah 6:1
Golden sash around His chest (13)	Of the priests, Exodus 39:29, or the angels, Daniel 10:5
Head and hair white like wool (14)	A description of God, Daniel 7:9
Eyes like blazing fire (14)	Characteristic of the angel in Daniel's vision, Daniel 10:6
Feet like bronze glowing in a furnace (15)	Like the cherubim of Ezekiel 1:7 as well as the angel of Daniel 10:6
Voice like the sound of rushing waters (15)	Described along with the glory of God, Ezekiel 43:2
Seven stars in His right hand (16)	"Those who lead many to righteousness [will shine] like the stars for ever and ever," Daniel 12:3
Sharp double-edged sword out of His mouth (16)	Prophecy about the Messianic servant of the Lord, Isaiah 49:2
Face like the sun shining in its brilliance (16)	The brilliant light surrounding the glory of God, Ezekiel 1:28. [Note also the brilliance of Jesus' appearance on the Mt. of Transfiguration, Matthew 17:2.]

similar to that found in the Old Testament, it may indicate that John was so familiar with the Scripture that he tended to use its terminology to express his own experience. It might also indicate that what John saw in his vision was the same sight that had been seen before. The language may be similar because the details were the same. In either event, to note the similarity increases the understanding of the scene. Second, all the elements in the description are repeated in the coming two chapters in association with the letters sent to the churches. Any particular lesson from a figurative significance can be seen better in association with the particular character of an individual church. Note the parallels with the Old Testament demonstrated on the chart on page 36.

This description should not be read in an attempt to dissect it and find similarities with possible sources, whether Jewish or Hellenistic. Neither should it be used as a mental photograph to form a physical means of identifying Jesus. Rather, it must leave an indelible impression of the dauntless Christ as He stands in all His majesty and glory in the midst of His churches, holding in His control His messengers and the destiny of His people.

John's Reaction (17, 18)

"When I saw him, I fell at his feet as though dead" (17). This was precisely the reaction of Ezekiel (Ezekiel 1:28), and was similar to the feeling of Isaiah (6:5) and the despair of Peter (Luke 5:8) in comparable scenes; for bright lights throw dark shadows. When one comes into the presence of God, he knows how lost he is on his own. But Jesus, though awesome in appearance, was full of love and mercy. He reached out and touched John. "Do not be afraid. . . . I hold the keys of death and Hades" (Revelation 1:18). Not only has Jesus been victorious over the prison house of death, but He holds the keys to it forevermore.

Jesus' Instruction and Explanation (19, 20)

Inasmuch as Jesus possesses the authority to unlock the gates of the grave itself, He instructs John, "Write therefore what you have seen" (Revelation 1:19). He can bring a message of faith and hope beyond the highest dreams, for Jesus has the power to open and to shut. He will start with the seven churches of Asia and extend to all the world and for all time.

Special Subject #1

The Island of Patmos

You see the figure of a lone man standing on a deserted shore. He is looking out across the sea from a little island about ten miles long and six miles across, hilly and rocky, with sparse vegetation and no trees. This is part of a group of islands called Sporades, and on a clear day, the mainland of the Roman province of Asia can be made out in the distance. It is in the direction of Asia that the man is looking, for he is thinking of his brothers and companions who even then were gathering to worship in the cities of the province.

You wonder why the man is here. The island is generally not inhabited, except for temporary stops. Fishermen land on its shores at times when sudden storms come up and they fear not being able to make the mainland, or night falls so quickly they decide to put in to spend the night. Ships going from Rome to Ephesus sometimes make their last stop on Patmos before finishing their voyage the next day. Likewise it was sometimes the first stop on a trip from Ephesus. But this man on the shore looks at home here. Could it be that he has been assigned to this place in exile? It was common for islands of the Sporades and the Cyclades to be used for the banishment of political offenders.

There were different reasons for exile in antiquity. Since the Roman world had no prisons to house convicted criminals (the prison was only for waiting trial or waiting execution), extended punishment was administered in association with exile, a prison without bars. One kind of exile was accompanied by confiscation of property and loss of civil rights. At times, exile was life in a penal colony sentenced to various degrees of hard labor. Work in the salt mines or stone quarries was among the worst. Life expectancy under such circumstances was but a month or two. Another exile was a probationary type of existence away from one's home area where his influence had been felt most. In any event, the exile lived in the most frugal conditions of both food and shelter.

A main purpose of exile was to keep the individual separated from his former field of activity, and surveillance was kept in varying degrees. Nevertheless, interviews and visits from former friends were frequently enjoyed. As for the duration of an exile, it was for life—or until the authority that imposed the exile should rescind the sentence. Besides the imperial verdict in the name of Caesar, a provincial governor could assign a subject to exile somewhere within his own jurisdiction. The governor had no right, however, to rescind an exile made by the imperial power at Rome.

Nowhere does Scripture affirm that John was in exile when he wrote Revelation. Early Christian writers, however, do make this affirmation, stating the time and place as Patmos in the reign of Domitian (e.g. Irenaeus, Clement of Alexandria, and Eusebius). Victorinus (A.D. 303), alone among the early notices, adds that John, though aged, was forced to labor in the mines at Patmos. This is doubtful because no evidence of mining has been found on

Patmos and the Southern Coast of Roman Asia

- Chios
- Smyrna
- **Province of Asia**
- Ephesus
- Samos
- Miletus
- Patmos
- **Southern Sporades**
- Cos
- Cnidus
- **Dodecanese**
- Rhodes

Patmos. Possible quarries may even be volcanic formations, and this type of exile does not seem to be indicated.[13]

Perhaps some labor was required, but this is not certain. Whether there were others on the island is not known; but it is noteworthy that he was sent to an island just fifty miles from his home and not to the other end of the empire. Tertullian mentions John's exile with a word that usually means an exile imposed by the provincial governor. This would account for John's being located close to home. Reports are uniform, however, in relating John's return to Ephesus after the death of Domitian (Roman emperor from A.D. 81 to 96). When the new ruler (Nerva, in this instance) came into power, ordinary practice indicated that all exiles not a threat to the state would be allowed to return home. Such was probably John's case. This, however, may point toward imperial involvement, not just provincial. Eusebius indicates that John was in exile for eighteen months.

Evidence from other exiles indicates that Christians may have been able to visit John during his exile. Musonius Rufus was a well-known Stoic who may have preached in the streets of Rome in the very time when Paul was there (61-63). He was sent into exile on at least two occasions, once in the reign of Nero and again in the time of Vespasian. Philostratus illustrated the fondness of the Hellenes for Musonius in that while he was living in that bleak, desolate island of the Cyclades,

> they were all making voyages by ship to visit him, as they now do to visit the spring; for until Musonius went there, there was no water in the island, but he discovered a spring, which the Greeks celebrate as loudly as they do the horse's spring at Helicon.[14]

If this is true of Musonius, it might also be true that elders from the churches of Asia gathered to meet with John on different occasions as the elders of Ephesus met with Paul at Miletus when he was passing through (Acts 20:17).

---

[13]William M. Ramsay, *The Letters to the Seven Churches* (Grand Rapids: Baker, reprint, 1979) pp. 85ff. Cf. C. B. Caird, *A Commentary on the Revelation of St. John the Divine* (New York: Harper & Row, 1966), pp. 21ff.

[14]Philostratus, *Apollonius of Tyana,* 7, 16.

Although another story about Musonius is highly doubtful, one account in Philostratus puts Musonius in the role of the common laborer. Demetrius the Cynic happened upon Musonius in chains being forced to dig at the Isthmus. Demetrius gave him what hope and encouragement he could (which is unlikely), but Musonius only thrust his spade in the ground more resolutely and proudly said, "You are troubled to see me digging through the Isthmus for Greece, but if you saw me playing the harp like Nero, how would you feel then?" Musonius, as a true Stoic, preferred the rugged role of hard labor to the luxury role of Nero. That John suffered an exile including hard labor has not been established.

Domitian's behavior toward the end of his life fits a time of persecution for the Christians. Although Nero had instigated a dreadful period of persecution following the burning of Rome (A.D. 64), and Peter had written his first epistle including the very province of Asia when he warned the Christians of coming trials and suffering, no persecution had come as yet comparable to Nero's. Now, thirty years later, at the close of Domitian's reign, he had executed his own cousin, Titus Flavius Clemens, and exiled Clemens's wife, Domitilla, and put to death other eminent Romans on charges later used to convict Christians. In addition to this, Domitian introduced the demand that all subjects worship him as "Lord and God."[15] Thus, it is quite possible that the emperor himself imposed the exile on John.

The fact that John cites the death of Antipas as a martyr in the church at Pergamum (Revelation 2:13) is evidence of persecution, but it also indicates that the deaths had not been numerous because of the single example. But John was in exile, a true "brother and companion in the suffering and kingdom and patient endurance" (Revelation 1:9) with the Christians in the churches of Asia.

Remains show that the Dorians and Ionians were original settlers on the island of Patmos. But in the early Roman period, few notices are preserved except to let it be known it existed. In the later Roman and Byzantine times, however, it became venerated because of its association with the Revelation of John, despite its being attacked and depopulated by pirates. In 1088, a new period began when a monk, Christodulos, built St. John's Cloister where an old temple of Artemis had stood. Through the centuries, an

---

[15]Dio Cassius lxvii.13; Suetonius, *Dom.* 13; Martial V.8.

outstanding library has been assembled with a celebrated collection of manuscripts and printed books. The Muslims took over with the advance of the Turks, and in 1832, Patmos was put under Turkish dominion. After 1912, it became a part of the Italian Dodecanese, and in 1947, the island was ceded to Greece. Its population with the port of Skala was 2,534 in 1981.

Today, a cave is pointed out along the ascent to the monastery as the place where John received his vision, but little credence can be put in the local traditions about the exact location. But the island as a whole lends impressive, authentic setting to the study of Revelation. The sound of the waters and the sight of the sea fill the description of the vision. One does not know whether all the scenes of the book were viewed in one day or whether the angel's instruction to write (some ten different occasions) indicates that the vision was on a series of days.

It helps to visualize the lone figure along the shore. (A variant reading at the close of chapter 12 and the beginning of 13 reads: "As I stood on the shore of the sea, I saw a beast coming out of the sea.") You can follow the figure of John on the shores of Patmos, and as you read through the book of Revelation, he leads you through the corridors of time to the very gates of eternity.

CHAPTER TWO

A Call to Be Faithful

Revelation 2:1—3:22

In Cairo, Egypt, an interpreter sat down with an American lecturer just before his speech. This was to be a meeting of Christians, and at a time not long after an aborted uprising of the Shiite Muslims. The Egyptian translator wanted to know ahead of time what the talk was going to be about. Included in the lecture, the speaker wanted to point out that the words of Revelation 2:10b, commonly translated as in the King James, "be ... faithful unto death," meant not only that one should remain true to Jesus until the time he died, but that he should be dedicated to the point that he was willing to die for his faith in Christ throughout his life as a believer. The translators of the New International Version had tried to bring out this thought from the Greek by rendering the verse, "Be faithful, even to the point of death, and I will give you the crown of life." After the speaker had gone over his outline with the interpreter, and just before the two went to the speaker's platform, the interpreter said to the lecturer, "Don't forget that part about a Christian must be ready to die at any time for his faith in Jesus." This Christian in Egypt could identify in a special way with the plight of Christians in ancient Smyrna, who were among the first to receive this book of Revelation with its challenge and assurance.

Some places in the world are safer than others for the Christian. When a person lives in a land that is predominately Christian, he has difficulty in appreciating what it means to bear up under the constant pressure of jeopardy to his physical life. Until the occasion actually rises, no one really knows what he would do if faced with the proposition of renouncing Christ or suffering immediate death. Still worse, what if the lives of loved ones are at stake, too?

But there are other pressures that plague the lives of Christians. Two students took an important oral exam before a battery of professors who no longer accepted the trustworthiness of the Scriptures. The views of these teachers differed vastly from the Biblical position on a number of subjects. One of the students went along with the professors. Their lines of questioning made clear their views, and the one student agreed every step of the way. He passed the exam with flying colors. The other student, however, felt compelled to bring up evidence in the opposite direction. He defended the Scriptures, and refused to support the conclusions advocated by his professors. He failed the exam and did not receive the advanced degree he was working for. The next day, however, the student who was failed happened to meet one of the examining professors on a street corner. After an embarrassing period of silence, the professor made a declaration. Referring to the other student who had taken the exam, he said, "He didn't believe *anything* enough to stake his life on it." The inference was a high compliment to the student who, in this instance, had suffered loss in academic credits, but had left the realization that his faith in Christ was more important than life itself to him.

The Christian feels other pressures increasing today in a society where immorality is becoming more blatant day by day. The toll of broken lives from alcoholism, drugs, sexual immorality, homosexual relations, and other hedonistic idols is on the increase, not only in the world, but drawing its victims from the church as well. Nomenclature is changed, and perverted attempts are made to escape the explicit condemnations of Scripture. Under very similar conditions, the letters were sent to the churches in Asia to help steel taut nerves against the wiles of Satan. Their message goes on generation after generation.

Prelude

Overview

If a composite picture is drawn of all seven letters to the churches recorded in chapters 2 and 3, four main subjects stand out: commendation for the good, condemnation for the evil, a warning about indifference, and a plea for faithfulness. Two of the churches receive nothing in condemnation: Smyrna and Philadelphia. One of the churches receives nothing in commendation: Laodicea. All the rest are given some of both.

Key Message

"Be faithful even to the point of death, and I will give you the crown of life" (Revelation 2:10b). Be faithful. Be a witness. Be ready.

Glossary

Read through chapters 2 and 3 of Revelation. As you come to the terms listed below, note the explanation.

Chapter 2

Ephesus   The most important seaport in the province of Asia; the fourth city of the Roman Empire, after Rome, Alexandria, and Antioch.

False apostles   Traveling teachers who claimed higher authority than the elders in the places they went, but were deceiving in their claims and instruction.

Forsaken your first love The fervor of their initial dedication was waning.

Nicolaitans   From two Greek words meaning "to conquer the people" (the word Balaam means the same thing from two Hebrew words, see Revelation 2:14, 15). They practiced immorality and ate food offered to idols.[16]

To him who overcomes To all those who remain faithful in doing the will of God despite whatever trials (Revelation 2:26), whether by martyrdom or not.

Tree of life   Introduced in Eden (Genesis 2:9). Adam and Eve were denied access to it after the fall (Genesis 3:22). It is reintroduced in Heaven (Revelation 22:2, 14, 19). To eat of its fruit is to enjoy eternal life with God.

Paradise of God   Used in the Greek translation of the Hebrew (Genesis 2:8) to mean Eden. Then used of a spiritual region for the blessed dead (see Luke 23:43; 2 Corinthians 12:4).

---

[16]Irenaeus reports of them, "They lived lives of unrestrained indulgence" (*Against Heresies* 1.26.3).

Smyrna	Known as the "Ornament of Asia." Modern Izmir, second busiest seaport of Turkey (second to Istanbul).
Synagogue of Satan	Synagogue used especially to denote a gathering of the Jews, perhaps renegade Jews, who sought to gain favor with the Gentiles and Roman authorities in persecution of the Christians.
Persecution ten days	Probably indicates a brief period of time rather than a literal ten days. Either imprisonment leading to possible death or beating, or a concerted effort to find the Christians and arrest them.
Crown of life	There were the two kinds of crowns: royal *diadema* for rulers and victorious *stephanos* for the winner in a contest. This is the crown of joy and victory (*stephanos)* in the contest of life.
Second death	Hell. Even if a Christian loses his physical life as a martyr, he will be a winner in Heaven beyond the reach of the eternal, second death in Hell. (See Revelation 20:6, 14; 21:8; Luke 12:4f.)
Pergamum	An important city serving in some periods as the capital of Asia, situated on an imposing height. Ramsay called it "a Royal City."
Satan's throne	Three alternatives: a center for the worship of Asklepios (worshiped in other places as serpent); the great altar of Zeus Soter, celebrating the victory of Attalus over the Gauls; the Satanic spirit of persecution against the Christians, particularly strong in Pergamum.
Days of Antipas	Identity of this individual is unknown, except for this reference to his martyrdom. Later legend describes him as the bishop of Pergamum. Probably of Jewish background because of name, Antipas, a shortened form of Antipater, and associated with the house of Herod.

Teaching of Balaam	An international pagan prophet associated with immoral behavior and participation in idolatrous feasts. The account in Numbers 25:1 does not have reference to his seduction of Israel, but in Numbers 31:16, the enticement into union with Moabite women and the worship of Baal-peor is attributed to the advice of Balaam. (See also 2 Peter 2:15 and Jude 11.)
Balak	King of Moab who engaged the services of Balaam to thwart the advances of Israel (Numbers 22). His own plans were unsuccessful then, but the continued deceits of the Moabites and the Midianites are associated with Balaam and Balak (Numbers 25; 31).
Hidden manna	Pot of manna kept in tabernacle (Exodus 16:34) commemorating the manna supplied by God in the wilderness. There had been no ark in the temple, no golden pot of manna in it for centuries now, but the Christian as he conquered would again be fed from above from the Heavenly archetype (Hebrews 8:5; 9:4, 23ff), supplied in Jesus.
White stone	Four general alternatives: token of acquittal given by the judge in a court case; token used to gain entrance to a marriage supper or some formal occasion where authority for admission must be given; token (*tessera*) granted as a special privilege of honor to public heroes with purchase power in the market place; token given for protection in contrast to charms—this was genuine.
New name	Associated with the stone and giving power and authority to its possessor. However, the name was known only to the chosen. In all likelihood, this refers to the name of Jesus Christ. (See Revelation 3:12.)
Thyatira	Not of highest importance in Asia, but a city of considerable wealth. Many trade

	guilds were there. It was located midway between Pergamum and Sardis (forty miles).
Jezebel	Named for the daughter of Ethbaal, king of the Sidonians, wife of Ahab, merciless enemy of the prophets of God and supporter of the prophets of Baal and Asherah. Jehu said of her, to her son, "How can there be peace as long as all the idolatry and witchcraft of your mother Jezebel abound?" (2 Kings 9:22). Three alternatives for the Jezebel at Thyatira: the wife of a leader in the congregation; a woman of great influence in the congregation and the community; a name to designate a group similar to the Nicolaitans.
Satan's secrets	The false teachers, like the Gnostics of the next century, may be claiming secret, deep knowledge, and these secrets are now designated as having Satan for their author, not God as was claimed.
Iron scepter	Symbolic of a rule of power and strength inasmuch as worldly nations will be broken like bowls of clay.
Morning star	A reference to Jesus himself (see Revelation 22:16). Not that He is the star, but He will be clothed with the glory of the brightest star, and it is a sign that the dawning of a new day is at hand.

Chapter 3

Sardis	A high citadel, a gateway from the East into the West, a center for trade and industry, an ancient capital with a long history and deep tradition.
Seven spirits	This represents the sevenfold Spirit, who was introduced in Revelation 1:4 and soon will be seen again in the throne room of God (Revelation 4:5). The Holy Spirit, especially associated with life, a serious need of this church.

Dressed in white	A figure often used in Revelation to denote purity and victory; unspotted by the world (James 1:27; Revelation 3:4). The clothes of the redeemed (Revelation 6:11; 7:9, 13).
Book of life	The register of the citizens of Heaven, the saved. A person cannot earn his place in the book, but by grace and obedient faith, his name is written there; then as he is faithful and he overcomes, his name will not be blotted out.
Philadelphia	Built where the Hellenistic territories of Mysia, Lydia, and Phrygia met—for the purpose of preserving and spreading Greek language and culture.
Key of David	Reference in the Old Testament to Eliakim, who received "the key to the house of David" (Isaiah 22:22), giving him the authority to admit or prohibit one's entrance to Hezekiah's court. Here Christ, the Son of David, has the key to the kingdom of God.
Open door	Christ opens the door of opportunity to Philadelphia or the door of entrance to the kingdom. No one can shut it. They can enter, but they must choose to move.
Hour of trial	Period of testing. Jesus' promise to "keep you from the hour of trial" is a promise either to prevent their having to undergo a period of testing or to assure them they will be kept safe through the trial.
Pillar in the temple	Supported by all those who win out, not just the leaders of the congregation.
Laodicea	One of three towns along the Lycus river within six to ten miles of one another. Colosse and Hierapolis are the others.
Amen	A guarantee for the truth of a testimony. Used by Jesus in John's Gospel to demand special attention, to assert unmistakable authority, or to declare a truth contrary to popular understanding.

Gold refined	Just as gold is freed from its impurities by the heat of the fire, so a spiritual refinement results from the trials of suffering.
White clothes	See "Dressed in white," above.
Salve for the eyes	Smarted after the first application, but enabled a person to see more clearly afterward.

Content Notes

The meaning of these seven letters can be best understood in the context of the time and situation in which they were written and received. They were designated to real congregations made up of living, believing people. You can go to the sites of these cities still today, sit on stone remains, and look out over the same countryside. But the understanding of these letters does not stop with the first-century setting. There is never an age when Christians no longer need encouragement—encouragement to remain faithful, to grow in Christ, to act with urgency, not to be discouraged, to bear witness of Christ, to be wholly committed, and to be single-minded. Understanding the meaning of the letters begins with the setting, but the continuing value of the letters has come with the realization of the application to the lives of Christians throughout the ages in every generation including our own. These congregations may not represent dispensations in the history of the church, but they certainly are representative of churches in their strengths and weaknesses, in their dangers and security in every time and place.

Good News and Bad News—
The Message to the Church in Ephesus (2:1-7)

The Good News (1-3)

This is a hardworking congregation. The Christians have persevered. They have refused false teachers, and have not grown weary. This indeed is good news. What more could one ask?

But there is more. Jesus is walking in their midst. Each letter is introduced with a description of Jesus, and each description is drawn from a part of the details given in the preview-vision John had given in the first chapter. This links the whole narration together. Jesus "holds the seven stars" (the messengers going to the churches, the leaders in the churches, or the angels commissioned to these churches) and "walks among the seven golden lamp-stands"—the seven churches of Asia (Revelation 2:1). He sees things in the Ephesian church they are not aware of. He knows the bad news as well as the good news.

The Bad News (4, 5)

They are losing ground in their love. They need to rekindle the flame and return to their "first love." To begin with, they need to realize certain things: "Remember the height from which you have fallen!" Then, "Repent!" (Revelation 2:5).

In Australia, they are more explicit with their road signs than in most lands. Most countries are satisfied with indicating simply "wrong way" to stop a person from continuing in the wrong direction on a one-way ramp. But in Australia, they have three lines on the sign: "Wrong Way," "Turn Around," "Go Back." This is what Jesus is telling the church at Ephesus.

Warning and Promise (6, 7)

What will be the consequences if they do not give heed? "I will come to you and remove your lampstand from its place" (Revelation 2:5). Jesus will no longer be walking in their midst. His presence will be missing. Without the light, darkness will take over, and all hope will be gone. They do hate sin and falsehood and "the practices of the Nicolaitans" (Revelation 2:6), but they need proper love as well. They must heed, they must win out, and they will receive everlasting reward in paradise. This way, it will end with good news.

Yet You Are Rich—
The Message to the Church at Smyrna (2:8-11)

Poverty and Affliction (8-10a)

To this congregation, Jesus introduces himself as "the First and Last, who died and came to life again" (Revelation 2:8). He is the Son who "learned obedience from what he suffered and, once made perfect, he became the source of eternal salvation for all who obey him" (Hebrews 5:8, 9). He had to die that He might conquer death. Through His suffering, He has brought salvation. This is an especially appropriate reminder to a church that has "affliction." It lives in "poverty." And the Christians are told that they will "suffer persecution" in the future (Revelation 2:9, 10).

Not a very encouraging outlook. So why does Jesus tell them, "Yet you are rich"?

Wealth and Victory (10b, 11)

As Jesus walks among His churches, He can see beyond the present. The persecution will be of a limited duration ("ten days"). If they are faithful to the extent they are willing to die for their testimony for Jesus, they will receive the "crown of life." Furthermore, they will not be hurt by the "second death" (Revelation 2:11), the eternal punishment of Hell. They are indeed rich.

A little girl was saying her prayers one night as her father and she kneeled beside her bed. As she was giving thanks for one thing after another, she included the words, "Thank you for letting me live in a rich family. . . ." The father almost reached out his hand to stop his daughter. He did not consider his family rich. They could not buy the things for the children they wanted to buy. They could not do the things they would like to do if they had the money. But then the little girl finished her sentence: "because we know Jesus as Savior." The father was ashamed he had let the idea of material wealth crowd out his appreciation for the true riches in Jesus Christ. Still the little girl went on. "And I pray for all those poor people who do not know You."

The church at Smyrna was indeed rich. Only two congregations out of the seven addressed received nothing but commendation. Smyrna was one of them.

Tried and True . . . But—
The Message to the Church in Pergamum (2:12-17)

Resistance (12, 13)

This church was located at a hub of pagan activities. People came from all over the Roman world to seek physical healing from Asklepios there. A famous temple to Zeus was built on its heights. It was a provincial capital. Yet with all its trials situated alongside Satan's throne, it has remained true. The Christians have not renounced their faith in Jesus, not even when Antipas was martyred. They are tried and true.

Compromise (14-17)

But there are some faults that Jesus must make known. Some have compromised by accepting immorality and associating with pagan worship. Jesus is introduced in this letter with the sharp double-edged sword. If they do not repent, He will come to use the sword in His fight—not against the pagans, but against the compromisers in the church. But to the ones who overcome, He will give spiritual sustenance from the "hidden manna" and special provisions through the tessera ("white stone") with the "new name" written on it.

Hold On—
The Message to the Church in Thyatira (2:18-29)

Good Deeds (18, 19)

As with Pergamum, Jesus tells the commendable part first. Their good "deeds" are evident. "Love and faith" are seen as the groundwork of everything they do. Their "service" speaks well for their motives, and "perseverance" proves a depth to their dedication. In fact, unlike the Ephesian church, they are "doing more" than they had done at the first (Revelation 2:19).

Evil Deeds (20-23)

Jesus is introduced in this letter as having "eyes like blazing fire" and "feet like burnished bronze" (Revelation 2:18). One may expect from Jesus' analysis of Thyatira a penetrating look at her condition and a solemn call to take a solid stance, remaining immovable in the face of all influences. He does find fault with this church. They have compromised with an insistent false prophetess with grave consequences to come. Since she has been unwilling to repent of her "Jezebel" ways, she is going to suffer in a bed of sickness, and all her collaborators, if they do not repent, will "suffer intensely" also. Her "children" (those committed to following her?) will be struck dead. Jesus warns, "I will repay each of you according to your deeds" (Revelation 2:23). Although we are saved by grace, our judgment cannot be entirely separated from our deeds. A judgment based on works is taught by Jesus (Matthew 16:27), by Paul (Romans 2:6), and by John (Revelation 18:6; 20:12, 13; 22:12).

"No Other Burden" (24-29)

But to "the rest" in Thyatira who have not succumbed to the wiles of the false individual, He promises the real authority and telling power of the "iron scepter" (Revelation 2:27). No further teaching or demands are placed upon them. They must remain faithful to what they have, and to the work they have been doing. Let them continue to hold on.

Wake Up—
The Message to the Church in Sardis (3:1-6)

"You Are Dead!" (1-3)

The two most adverse reports are sent to Sardis and to Laodicea. In this letter to Sardis, Jesus passes over any estimate of their "deeds" and their "reputation" to give the bottom line: "You are dead" (Revelation 3:1). Their only hope is to "Wake up!" How do they do this? They must complete the deeds they began at a former time, "Remember, therefore, what you have received and heard; obey it, and repent" (Revelation 3:3). What will the consequences be if this is not done? Certainly it will be no less than His warning to the Ephesians, "I will come to you and remove your lampstand from its place" (Revelation 2:5). Or to Pergamum, "Otherwise, I will soon come to you and will fight against them with the sword of my mouth" (Revelation 2:16). But to Sardis, Jesus simply warns, "I will come like a thief, and you will not know at what time I will come to you" (Revelation 3:3).

A Few Still Live (4-6)

Even in a congregation judged as dead, a few individuals have managed to stay alive and refused to be entangled in either the sin of the world or the apathy of a dying congregation. They "have not soiled their clothes." Jesus promises, "They will walk with me, dressed in white" (Revelation 3:4). He promises the one who overcomes, "I will never blot out his name from the book of life" (Revelation 3:5). By inference, Jesus is saying unless a person remains faithful, his name will be blotted out.

As Jesus introduces himself to this church, He is described as holding the sevenfold Spirit (the Holy Spirit) in one hand and the seven stars (angels or messengers) in the other. This is appropriate to the deepest need of the congregation. They need life, and the Spirit is associated with giving life: "The Spirit of God has made me; the breath of the Almighty gives me life" (Job 33:4).

An Open Door—
The Message to the Church in Philadelphia (3:7-13)

"The Key of David" (7, 8)

This is the second letter to receive all commendation and no condemnation. The introductory description of Jesus uses language related to Old Testament passages. "The Holy One" is a title of God (Habakkuk 3:3; Isaiah 40:25). "Holy and true" is used to describe Jesus, not only here, but in Revelation 6:10 as well. In Isaiah 22:22, one reads of the role of Eliakim in the same language as that used to describe Jesus' use of the key of David, which has far greater significance.

Before such a congregation as the one in Philadelphia, Jesus places an open door. He himself has the key to open the door, and no one can close it once He has opened it. Perhaps this is a door of further service, further preaching of the gospel and winning souls to Christ. This primarily sees opportunity for missionary effort and has clear Pauline parallels (1 Corinthians 16:9; 2 Corinthians 2:12; Colossians 4:3).[17]

Another interpretation favors its reference to the eschatological kingdom, assuring the Christians who are being persecuted and shut out now, that it will be different in the final days. In the future, Jesus will be opening the door to believers and closing it to those who rejected Him. Perhaps this had particular reference to unbelieving Jews who had closed the doors of the synagogue and their messianic kingdom against those who accepted Jesus as the Messiah; but Jesus would close the doors of New Israel to them and open it for Jews *and* Gentiles who believed on Him.[18] This latter view fits well the situation in Philadelphia as the scene unfolds in the letter. However, the former view (evangelizing opportunity) fits well the meaning of this figure in other places in Scripture, and it is corroborated by the history of this congregation in its future record.[19] Actually, it is not

---

[17]H. B. Swete, *Commentary on Revelation,* p. 54.

[18]Isbon T. Beckwith, *The Apocalypse of John* (Grand Rapids: Baker, 1979), pp. 479f.

[19]See below, p. 65.

necessary that one of these alternatives must be exclusive of the other.[20]

The assessment of the church at Philadelphia continues. "I know that you have little strength" (Revelation 3:8). From the rest of the report, it is obvious that this is no reflection on the condition of the church. This is the outward appearance and a realistic look at the setting. It is a small town. It does not rate highly in the annals of history. This is a small congregation, and they have been plagued with abuses. Furthermore, when one realizes his lack of strength to cope with all that life brings, he at that very time becomes strong as he looks to the Lord for help (2 Corinthians 12:9, 10). In the matters that count most, the church at Philadelphia shows great strength: "Yet you have kept my word and have not denied my name" (Revelation 3:8).

"The Synagogue of Satan" (9, 10)

The greatest source of the trouble seems to have come from "the synagogue of Satan" (Revelation 3:9), a name given to a hostile Jewish (not genuinely Jewish, but falsely claiming to be) block who denied the Christ and sought to destroy the Christians. Christ's answer raises a string of questions.

1. When will the enemies of Christ "come and fall down at [the Christians'] feet and acknowledge" that Christ has loved the Christians all along (Revelation 3:9)? Will this come to pass near the time of writing, or is this something that will come to pass in the eschatological closing? If this was fulfilled locally and in that contemporary generation, it is not known. It could be relevant, however, in the same way that all the other letters are representative of congregations down through the centuries and their promises are likewise promises to each generation. Since, however, Philippians 2:11 does declare that the exaltation of Christ will eventually include a worship by all, this may be a time when Philadelphia and the Christians may be included with the glorified Christ. Nothing is said of the Jews' conversion or nonconversion at that time, only acknowledgement.

---

[20]Colin J. Hemer, *The Letters to the Seven Churches of Asia in Their Local Setting* (Sheffield, England: Journal for the Study of the New Testament, Supplement Series 11, 1986), p. 162.

2. What is this "hour of trial that is going to come upon the whole world" (Revelation 3:10), and when will this be, contemporary to the time of writing, in the distant future, or the closing eschatological period? The same must be said here as in the previous question. If fulfillment is found immediately in the subsequent history of Philadelphia,[21] the significance to each succeeding generation is that similar promises can be claimed through the years; and if it pertains to the last times, this gives that final generation the same hope and strength it gave to Philadelphia in the beginning, and in like manner throughout the intervening ages. But the trial is not specified and the "whole world" must allow the probability of the known Roman world (Luke 2:1). This still does not clarify whether it would be overt persecution, subtle attack, physical sickness, natural calamity, or catastrophe of some other nature.

3. Another question is the extent of the promise. *To test those who live on the earth* is an expression regularly used to denote the enemies of Christ.[22] But what of the faithful; will they be tested, too? Jesus assures them, "Since you have kept my command to endure patiently, I will also keep you from the hour of trial . . ." (Revelation 3:10). One difficulty in understanding this is that the meaning for *keep you* could either be "delivered from" or "brought safely through" the trial. (See John 17:15; James 1:27). How this is interpreted will depend greatly upon what is understood about tribulation and rapture in the chapters to come.[23]

"Hold On to What You Have" (11-13)

As in every letter, Jesus closes by addressing the individual. "I am coming soon." (See the note on Revelation 1:3.) "Hold on" (Revelation 3:11). Remain faithful, patiently endure, enter the door Jesus holds open. Do not forfeit your crown and have someone come to take your place in the kingdom. You will be a solid supporting pillar in the house of God. You will bear the name of

---

[21]See below, p. 65.

[22]Revelation 6:10; 8:13; 11:10; 13:8, 14; 17:8.

[23]See the Special Subjects 4 and 12, below; pp. 111 and 294.

God, the name of His city, and the name of His Christ. This is promised to the one who overcomes, who remains faithful.

Blind Self-satisfaction—
The Message to the Church in Laodicea (3:14-22)

Their Blindness (14-17)

The letter of highest commendation (Philadelphia) is immediately followed by the letter of severest condemnation. Laodicea felt she was in a superior position. She said, "I am rich; I have acquired wealth and do not need a thing" (Revelation 3:17). To such an attitude Jesus replies bluntly with the true picture: "You are wretched, pitiful, poor, blind and naked." Jesus is introduced in this letter as the "Amen" (Revelation 3:14), a title used in the Old Testament for God (Isaiah 65:16, God of "truth" is, in the Hebrew, God of "Amen"). He is the "faithful and true witness." *Faithful* can be used in two distinct meanings. Man can be faithful in his belief in God, but God is faithful in His trustworthy action in all His ways. He is trustworthy in His assessment of Laodicea, but they have failed to ascertain their own plight. He knows their work. They are self-satisfied and lack seeing their condition as it really is.

Perhaps the figure involving drinking water may have been introduced because of the location of Laodicea between the towns of Colosse and Hierapolis. Colosse was known for its cold, pure water, and Hierapolis, in antiquity as well as today, was noted for its hot springs, which provided water used for medicinal purposes as well as for a hot drink. But the Laodiceans did not have an adequate water supply and had to resort to aqueducts to convey water to their city, either from Hierapolis with its hot water and medicinal qualities or from Colosse with its cold water. By the time the water arrived at Laodicea, much of it was tepid and unpalatable, but they continued to use it. They were independent and self-satisfied. They would not admit any lack. This would have made this figure much more telling to those who were living in the time it was written and at the place of destination where a real water problem existed.[24] But Jesus was informing them of a still more serious situation.

---

[24]Hemer, *Letters to the Seven Churches,* pp. 186-191.

The problem in Laodicea does not seem to be so much one of indifferent negligence as of a self-satisfied blindness. If "hot" is taken as an all out acceptance of Christ—a high measure of spiritual intensity—then "cold" is an all out rejection of Christ or, at least, a frigid indifference tantamount to rejection. The "lukewarm," then, becomes an indifferent lethargy in between the two. But such an interpretation reads into the text a twentieth-century idiom and ignores the historical context in which the words were written. In addition, how can Jesus give equal approval to His acceptance or rejection, as this interpretation implies, just to make a point about the in-between? Furthermore, Jesus does not level His criticism at this type of half-hearted support when He specifies their fault.

Jesus does not tell them to rekindle their spiritual fervor as at Ephesus, nor even to "wake up" as at Sardis. It is not a matter of compromise with a Jezebel in their midst as at Thyatira, or compromise with the teaching of Balaam as at Pergamum. Rather, Laodicea is just the counterpart of Smyrna, who is poor but spiritually rich. Laodicea is rich in a materialistic way but spiritually poor—and blind about it. They cannot work out their problem by their own smartness and resources any more than they had solved their water problem. They claim to have it all, but they are not looking at things realistically. Especially their spiritual depravity is being ignored in their typical self-satisfied blindness.

The Cure (18-22)

They need to receive "gold refined in the fire" (Revelation 3:18), not from the famed banks in their city, but from Jesus himself. They need to put on Christ (Galatians 3:27) as their "white clothes," not depending on the well-known black wool of the sheep in their fields. Their "eyes" must be enlightened by the Spirit (John 16:8), for their renowned eyesalve had only left them blind. Jesus tells them, "Be earnest [zealous], and repent" (Revelation 3:19).

Still, Jesus uses the tender, personal word for *love (phileo)* when He issues His "rebuke and discipline." He stands at the door of each individual heart and asks invitation to enter. To the one who overcomes, He promises a place with Him on His throne, the same way that God exalted Jesus when He had overcome.

Special Subject #2

The Cities of Asia

Ephesus

On the cutting edge where East meets West, Ephesus provided a gateway between the two. Located at the mouth of the Cayster River, its once busy harbor has long since been filled with the silt of centuries. The city reached its height of wealth and influence in the Hellenistic and Roman periods. In the first century A.D., it had a population of 250,000. The important province of Asia had been added to the Roman holdings in 133 B.C. upon the death of Attulus II, and Ephesus was one of its leading cities from the beginning. Pergamum and Smyrna were its constant rivals, but whether Pergamum was the capital at the time or not, Ephesus was the hub. It was proud to be the warden of the temple of Artemis, one of the seven wonders of the ancient world. She was warden of three of the temples dedicated to the worship of the Roman emperors (Claudius or Nero, Hadrian, and Severus). Domitian, probably the emperor who exiled John to Patmos, had an altar and temple erected on Curetes Street. The head and forearm of a colossal statue of Domitian (four times life-size) have been recovered and are on display in the Izmir (Smyrna) Museum. In 1970, a colossal head of Mark Antony was found in the upper civic agora.[25] Ephesus was also headquarters for popular magical arts practiced throughout Asia Minor. (See Acts 19:19.)

Paul founded the church at Ephesus about A.D. 54, when Nero was just coming to power. He spent over two years there (Acts 19:8, 10), longer than at any other of his missionary points that are known. Timothy was in this city when Paul wrote both of his epistles to him. The apostle John is supposed to have come to Ephesus some time after the fall of Jerusalem in A.D. 70. The rest of his years may have been spent in the area. It was only about sixty miles away from the island of Patmos, where John was in exile as he wrote this first epistle of the seven to churches of Asia.

---

[25]Edwin Yamauchi, *New Testament Cities: In Western Asia Minor,* (Grand Rapids: Baker, 1988), pp. 83-85.

Smyrna

Another port on the coast of the province of Asia was the city of Smyrna. It was about thirty-five miles north of Ephesus and had a population of over 100,000 in this period. This city was the first in Asia Minor to build a temple dedicated to the cult of the city of Rome—in 195 B.C. Later, in the early years of Rome as an empire, Tiberius chose Smyrna as temple warden of the imperial cult in that area.

Some well-known Greek sources assist in adding to the background material concerning Smyrna. A speech of Aelius Aristides delivered on the occasion of the city's restoration after an earthquake in A.D. 178 is helpful. It tells of historical traditions of the past and of present fortunes and benefactors involving the city. Philostratus wrote a popular *Life of Apollonius of Tyana.* Although the writing was not done before 200, the fictitious story concerns Smyrna in the probable decade of John's writing the letter to the city. Early Christian writings involve Smyrna, also. Within twenty years of John's life, Ignatius from Antioch of Syria came through Asia on his way to die in Rome. He wrote a letter to the Smyrnaeans and also one to Poycarp, who was bishop of Smyrna at the time. Polycarp himself was killed in 156, and an account of his martyrdom tells still more about Smyrna and persecution in that period.

Pergamum

About forty miles further north from Smyrna along the coast, and then fifteen miles inland to the northeast is the ancient site of Pergamum (modern Bergama). This is two miles north of the Caicus River. The view, both of the city's remains and from the city out over the whole countryside, is so imposing that Ramsay called it, "A royal city."[26] Included on the upper acropolis was the library, second only to the library in Alexandria. On a lower level stood the Altar of Zeus, 120 by 112 feet. The podium was nearly 18 feet high. The term *altar* is used of more than the surface on which sacrifice is given. This is a tremendous structure of stone surrounded by a magnificent frieze of dramatic artwork portraying battles of the gods. It was moved to Germany and is displayed in the Berlin Pergamum Museum of East Germany today.

---

[26]W.M. Ramsay, *Letters to the Seven Churches,* p. 295.

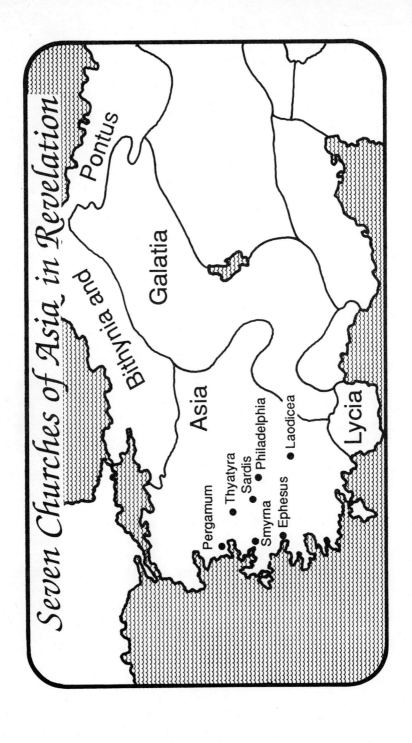

Seven Churches of Asia in Revelation

Another famous center at Pergamum is the complex of buildings complete with a small theater that was erected by the cult of Asklepios. Healing claims drew people from all over the empire. The cult was brought to this place from Epidaurus in Greece and reached its height in glory by the second century A.D.

The first Asian temple built for Augustus as divine was here at Pergamum. For forty years, it was the one center of the imperial religion for the whole province.[27] Although the capital of the province of Asia was moved from Pergamum to Ephesus, the center of the worship of the Roman emperors seem to have remained at Pergamum.

Any one of these three centers would be candidates for the epithet *where Satan's throne is*—that is, the altar of Zeus, the precincts of Asklepios, or the temples of the imperial religion insisting on the worship of the Roman emperor.

Thyatira

Some forty miles southeast of Pergamum was this Lydian city close to the borders of Mysia. Pliny the Elder considered it less than a first-class city. However, it was noted for its thriving commerce and high number of trade guilds. The city had been founded by Seleucus I as an outpost to guard one of the western approaches to his Syrian empire. But the site had no military strength, and when it was absorbed into the Roman empire, it depended upon its trade for existence. Among the guilds were both textile workers and dyers. This was the hometown of the business woman Lydia, and she may well have been associated with one of the guilds there (Acts 16:14). It had no temple dedicated to the emperors until later in the reign of Severus Alexander.

Among the guilds listed at Thyatira was one for coppersmiths (or bronzesmiths). At Revelation 1:15 and 2:18, the Greek word *chalkolibanos* is used, translated "burnished bronze" (describing the feet of Jesus). This is the only known use of this word in all of Greek literature. Suggestion is made that since it is used in the letter to Thyatira, the metal workers may have been knowledgeable of its technical meaning.[28]

---

[27]See W.M. Ramsay, *Letters to the Seven Churches,* p. 294.

[28]C.B. Caird, *Commentary on the Revelation,* p. 43. See also Hemer, *Letters to the Seven Churches,* pp. 111ff.

By the end of the second century, the Alogi report no church was found in the city.[29] On the other hand, Epiphanius maintained that it later became a nest for Montanism. The modern Turkish town of Akhisar occupies its site today with a population of about fifty thousand.

Sardis

This ancient capital of Lydia was situated thirty miles southeast of Thyatira and forty-five miles east of Smyrna at the foot of Mount Tmolus. It was in a strategic position in the Valley of the Hermus at a converging point of roads from Thyatira, Smyrna, and Laodicea (the Lycus Valley). Both its famous traditions and its difficult terrain contribute to an understanding of this letter sent to Sardis (modern Sart).

Croesus was the most renowned of her kings. Tales associate him with fabulous gold possessions, and the evidences of gold panning in the Pactolus stream provide a starting ground for the exaggerations that followed. His interpretation of a Delphic oracle led to a foolish attack against Cyrus of Persia. Croesus was defeated, and retreated to his stronghold at Sardis. Much to his surprise, Cyrus and his army pursued him to the ascent to his acropolis defense. But here Croesus thought he was safe. He was wrong. Soldiers, supposedly under the cover of night, scaled a side of the 1,500-foot precipice thought to be unscalable and took the guards unawares. In that day, Sardis became a part of the holdings of Persia (546 B.C.). The same thing happened again in 214 B.C. when Antiochus III took it to use as a defense in his struggle with Rome. This time, it was a skillful Cretan, Lagoras, who managed the ascent and arrived from an unguarded direction. In recounting the experiences of Sardis, one finds this impregnable fortress changed hands no less than half a dozen times. How then was it considered so impossible to take Sardis? The greatest fault she had in the actual defeats in battle was a lack of vigilance.[30] Can such a city fail to hear the words, "But if you do not wake up, I will come like a thief, and you will not know at what time I will come to you" (Revelation 3:3).

---

[29]See H.B. Swete, *Commentary on Revelation,* p. 41.

[30]Hemer, *Letters to the Seven Churches,* p. 133.

In the year A.D. 17, a large area including Sardis suffered a severe earthquake. Twelve cities of Asia were affected, but Sardis and Magnesia were the hardest hit. Rome responded with providing help because the consequences of this disaster had been so devastating.

In 1962, the unearthing of a large building was begun to the north of the highway going through the area of Sart. It turned out to be the remains of the largest synagogue found so far. This has been restored in a magnificent way.

In A.D. 26, Sardis was in competition with Pergamum, Smyrna, and Ephesus for the privilege of erecting a temple to Augustus. Sardis has not figured in a significant way in the history of the church except for the name of Melito. He was bishop there and was the first to refer to the Scriptures as divided between the Old Testament and, by inference, the New Testament (180). And among his works is listed the earliest note we have of a commentary on the Apocalypse.[31]

Philadelphia

Attalus Philadelphus, king of Pergamum, who died in 138 B.C., built this city, and it was named after him by his brother Eumenes. This was the youngest of the cities addressed in the seven letters. The door of opportunity referred to in the letter fits the basis for its founding, but with important differences. It was meant originally to serve as a missionary center for Hellenism in order to spread the Greek language and culture especially to the backward people in the mountains of Lydia and Phrygia. It was on what became the greatest trade route for the whole country. While its military value could not be ignored, it was not on a frontier and the enemy should be stopped before he ever penetrated that far. Its Christian challenge saw this city as a missionary site also, but for evangelistic efforts for Christ. No condemnation was included in this letter, but a challenge for patient endurance and good use of the door opened for them.

This whole city had needed patient endurance for a good many years. No city had suffered as much through the years from earthquakes. Strabo describes the city as depopulated in several periods because people were so terrified by recurring quakes that they

---

[31]Eusebius, *Ecclesiastical History,* 4.13, 26; 5.24.

lived out in the countryside rather than be caught in the city in another quake.

Ignatius passed through here on his way to martyrdom in Rome, and wrote an epistle to Philadelphia before going much further. Montanus preached in the vicinity. At least the controversy over Montanism raged along the route from Philadelphia into Phrygia.[32] A prophetess, Ammia, was supposed to have flourished in Philadelphia between A.D. 100 and 160.[33]

The modern town of Alashehir has covered over the ancient city's theater and stadium.

Laodicea

Forty miles southeast of Philadelphia, the road that came from Sardis reached Laodicea. This town originally bore the name of Diospolis, then Rhoas. Antiochus II rebuilt the city between 261 and 253 B.C. and named it after Laodice, his wife, who later poisoned her husband. The rulers received little military advantage from the site, but in the period of peace under Rome, the city thrived because of commerce.

From the letters of Cicero, one learns of the banking importance of the center. On his way to his province of Cilicia, he stopped to cash his money supply at Laodicea before going any farther. The city was also famous for its textile industry. Buyers liked to get manufactured cloth from the glossy-black wool of the particular sheep they grew. Two more specialties were ear ointment and eyesalve. People came from far and wide to buy Phrygian Powder for the treatment of eyes.

A number of cities in Asia were helped by Rome again in an earthquake disaster of A.D. 60. This instance was most noteworthy, however, in that Laodicea refused Rome's offer to provide aid. They were affluent enough and independent enough that they financed their own rebuilding program.

The trouble was that their self-dependence was accompanied by a self-satisfaction. The lukewarmness in the church was not one of indifference, but a self-centered failure to recognize their own essential needs.

---

[32]Hemer, *Letters to the Seven Churches,* pp. 170ff.

[33]Eusebius, *Ecclesiastical History,* p. 399.

Laodicea was associated with Colosse, ten miles east, and with Hierapolis (modern Pamukkale), six miles north on the other side of the Lycus valley. The modern city of Denizli is five miles away.

A rewarding exercise is to take a map of your own area and to find a horse-shoe shaped series of towns around you that are spaced comparably to the seven churches of Asia. Then apply the messages to the churches in your own setting. Do not be too specific in judging your neighbor's condition, for we have neither the insight nor the wisdom of Jesus. Then, too, these messages must be taken personally for the individual as well as for the congregations. The basic thrust, both then and now, is a call to faithfulness. Finally, remember that in the midst of every circle of churches stands the figure of the dauntless Jesus.

CHAPTER THREE

Glimpses of Glory

Revelation 4:1-5:14

Did you ever make a move from one house to another? Were you interested in seeing the new place before you moved there? Would you like to see now where you hope to be living for eternity? Can you imagine the apostle John's surprise when he saw a door standing ajar? A voice invited him to come in, and he was given a glimpse of our final move—to Heaven!

But that's not all! Would you like to see God himself? Follow John and see what you can for yourself. Promise not to ask questions. Just stand quietly and see what's happening. The place is so different, it's hard to begin to understand it all.

Everyone has wanted an opportunity to see God. Moses was particularly anxious. He boldly requested of God:

> "Now show me your glory."
> And the Lord said, "I will cause all my goodness to pass in front of you, and I will proclaim my name, the Lord, in your presence. . . ."
> Then the Lord said, "There is a place near me where you may stand on a rock. When my glory passes by, I will put you in a cleft in the rock and cover you with my hand until I have passed by. Then I will remove my hand and you will see my back; but my face must not be seen."

> . . . .

> Then the Lord came down in the cloud and stood there with him and proclaimed his name, the Lord. And he passed in front of Moses, proclaiming, "The Lord, the Lord, the compassionate and gracious God, slow to anger, abounding in love and faithfulness, maintaining love to thousands, and forgiving wickedness, rebellion

69

and sin. Yet he does not leave the guilty unpunished; he punishes the children and their children for the sin of the fathers to the third and fourth generation."

Moses bowed to the ground at once and worshiped (Exodus 33:18-23; 34:5-8).

Note what Moses sees of God is not described in any physical features, but in the qualities of His nature—love and faithfulness, forgiving but punishing the guilty.

Ezekiel is another example of one who experienced glimpses of glory while he was in exile in Babylon along the Kebar River.

> Then there came a voice from above the expanse over their [the creatures'] heads as they stood with lowered wings. Above the expanse over their heads was what looked like a throne of sapphire, and high above on the throne was a figure like that of a man. I saw that from what appeared to be his waist up he looked like glowing metal, as if full of fire, and that from there down he looked like fire; and brilliant light surrounded him. Like the appearance of a rainbow in the clouds on a rainy day, so was the radiance around him.
>
> This was the appearance of the likeness of the glory of the Lord. When I saw it, I fell facedown, and I heard the voice of one speaking (Ezekiel 1:25-28).

Although Ezekiel does liken God's appearance vaguely to a man, he can only describe his features as surrounded by the impression of a precious stone, burning fire, and the presence of a rainbow. He, like Moses, was constrained to bow down in worship as the glory of God overshadowed him.

Still another Jew in exile to whom God appeared was Daniel.

> As I looked, thrones were set in place, and the Ancient of Days took his seat. His clothing was as white as snow; the hair of his head was white like wool. His throne was flaming with fire, and its wheels were all ablaze. A river of fire was flowing, coming out from before him. Thousands upon thousands attended him; ten thousand times ten thousand stood before him. The court was seated, and the books were opened (Daniel 7:9, 10).

The figure seen by Daniel is described in still more anthropomorphic terms. Characteristics are white hair, white clothes, and flaming fire. Still other revelations in the Old Testament tell of scenes in God's presence (Isaiah 6:1; 1 Kings 22:19), but none give it in more physical features, only impressions of grandeur and power. One finds both similarities and differences in comparing each of the accounts with the others. The similarities can be expected because the subject matter is the same, a description of the appearance of the one, true, living God. He cannot be seen with the physical eye, for God is spirit; still the impressions viewed in a vision can be recorded in terms conveying as close an impression to persons limited to earthly experience as can be rendered. But then differences can be expected also. The accounts are independent; they involve different times and circumstances. They may not be consciously related, but their source is the same: Almighty God.

Prelude

Overview

The first sight that greeted the eyes of John as he entered Heaven was that of God seated on His throne. His appearance could only be described as the blending of colors from precious stones encircled by a rainbow. In a still larger circle were twenty-four more thrones and twenty-four elders seated on them. The Holy Spirit was there also in the appearance of seven torches in front of God's throne. And all this rested on a sea of glass. Four living beings, each in a different form, constantly gave utterances of adoration to God. This was accompanied by the worship of the twenty-four elders as they presented their crowns before the throne.

God held a scroll in His hand, but it was tightly sealed with seven seals. A mighty angel asked whether anyone was worthy to open the seals. When no one was found, John's eyes filled with tears. But one of the elders comforted him because the Messiah had won out, and He was able to open the scroll.

Then John saw another figure on God's throne with Him. He was described as a Lamb with a scar on its throat showing He had been slaughtered. The throne was large enough to hold many people, but only the Lamb stood in the center of the throne beside God. He had seven horns and seven eyes. After He went to God,

He took the scroll from His hand. Then the four living beings and the twenty-four elders worshiped the Lamb. They played harps, held bowls of incense, and sang a new song.

After this, John saw that the circle of elders was surrounded by thousands upon thousands of angels. They, too, sang the praises of the Lamb. Then Heaven and the whole universe joined in the worship of God and the Lamb.

Key Message

"Come up here, and I will show you what must take place after this" (Revelation 4:1b). "Show me your glory" (Exodus 33:18).

Glossary

Read through chapters 4 and 5 of Revelation. As you come to the terms listed below, note the explanation.

Chapter 4

Door in Heaven	Not the door of opportunity (Revelation 3:8) or the door of an individual's heart (Revelation 3:20), but the door to visions symbolic of Heaven and the future.
Voice like a trumpet	The voice first heard in Revelation 1:10 to give instruction speaks again to give invitation.
In the Spirit	Not only able to hear and see a vision in the prophet's state of exaltation (Revelation 1:10), but also transported from Patmos into the Heavenly places.
Throne in Heaven	Not confined to a single seat, but a magnificent stage, perhaps square, semicircular, or round. The center of rule and authority for the whole of the universe, physical and spiritual.
One who sat there	Not described or named here, but clearly God the Father because the Spirit (Revelation 4:5) is distinguished from Him, and the Lamb to come (Revelation 5:6) is the Messiah, the Son. The Lord God Almighty is on the throne (Revelation 4:8).
Jasper	Instead of describing His person, the magnificence of His presence is likened to

flashing colorful light rays from a precious stone. Some identify this with the diamond, some the opal, or green chalcedony, but not our jasper today, for it is too opaque, whether red, green, or yellow. The same word is used at Revelation 21:11 and seems to demand something sparkling and transparent.

Carnelian (Greek: sardius) A stone, translucent and fiery red. The word *sardius* is related to the name of the city of Sardis.

Rainbow The rainbow is a reminder of the mercy of God in making a promise in Noah's time (Genesis 9:13). In coming to the tribulations foretold in this book, the rainbow gives both beauty and comfort. From the Greek, it seems to surround the throne in a complete circle rather than arch above it in a half circle (but compare Ezekiel 1:27, 28).

Emerald Green in color. Whether the rainbow was all green or had a greenish hue, it had an emerald effect.

Twenty-four thrones Another circle was formed around the throne of God by lesser thrones.

Twenty-four elders Some maintain these are the twelve apostles (see Revelation 21:12-14; Matthew 19:28) and twelve patriarchs representing the tribes of Israel. Some maintain they are representatives of the redeemed. Others maintain they are angels or some representatives of supernatural beings.

Dressed in white White regularly is associated with holiness and the apparel of the redeemed in Revelation.

Crowns of gold These are the victory crowns, not the ruling ones; but they are golden rather than made of garlands that wither away.

Seven lamps Torches representing the seven spirits (sevenfold Spirit)—the Holy Spirit. (See Revelation 1:4; 3:1.)

Sea of glass	In front of Solomon's temple was a brazen "sea" (1 Kings 7:23). In front of the tabernacle was a bronze basin of water between the Tent of Meeting and the altar (Exodus 30:18). In front of the Heavenly abode of God was a glassy sea, calm and transparent, probably solid. (See Revelation 15:2.)
Four living creatures	Not beasts,* not wild creatures, but probably best translated, "Living beings." Distinguished from the angels (Revelation 5:11) and of a higher order who are close to God's throne to perform His will. They resemble the seraphim of Isaiah (Isaiah 6:2, 3) and the cherubim of Ezekiel (chapters 1 and 10). But each has differences from the other.
Lion	Living beings are not like these animals in looks but in the best qualities characteristic of each. The lion is king of the animals. He represents majesty and power.
Ox (calf*)	The most useful of the domestic animals, representing patience, strength, and continuous labor.
Face like a man	Man is the highest of God's creation, representing intelligence and rational power.
Flying eagle	Excels among the birds and portrays swiftness and supremacy.

Chapter 5

Scroll (written on both sides)	A roll of papyrus so filled with writing that the verso side was used as well as the recto. (See Ezekiel 2:9.)
Seven seals	A seal was used (1) to designate ownership, (2) to assure genuineness of authorship, (3) to protect against change or abuse of contents, or (4) to conceal until an official opening by the proper authorities. In the case of a will, seven seals were required

---

*Translation in the King James Version.

74

	with the presence of designated individuals for the solemn opening.
Mighty angel	An important angel (Gabriel? see Daniel 8:16; 9:21; 12:4) designated to make a solemn announcement. The term appears twice more—Revelation 10:1; 18:21.
One of the elders	Role of one of the twenty-four elders included encouraging and informing this prophet, John.
The Lion of the tribe of Judah	Reference to Judah as a lion's cub and the ruler's coming from this tribe (Messianic). Genesis 49:9, 10.
Root of David	A branch from the root of David (a descendant from his family), the Messiah, will come from the stump of David (Isaiah 11:1).
A lamb	Instead of a lion, in the center of the scene, a lamb appeared, one that had been sacrificed. From here on this is the word most often used to designate the risen Christ. "Look, the Lamb of God, who takes away the sin of the world!" (John 1:29, 36).
Seven horns	Horns, the symbol of power (1 Samuel 2:10); seven, the symbol of completeness. In contrast with the natural qualities associated with the lamb, this makes this lamb all powerful—omnipotent.
Seven eyes	Eyes, the symbol of keen observation, understanding; seven, the symbol of completeness. Omniscient (see Zechariah 4:10). These were the same as the seven spirits (the Holy Spirit).
Harp	Not the large instrument so designated today, but a lyre or zither, a stringed instrument accompanying the singing of the Psalms in the Old Testament. This speaks of praise in the worship of God.
Golden bowls of incense	More like saucers than what are called bowls today. This speaks of the prayers coming from the Christians.

New song	Common phrase in the Psalms (e.g. 98:1; 144:9, 149:1). But now a new message above all others because of God's grace in Jesus Christ.
Angels	An innumerable multitude of supernatural beings who inhabit Heaven encircle the throne and beings of higher order, but their presence is important in the role of praise and worship.

Content Notes

The fourth chapter of Revelation introduces a third major section of the book. At first we were with John on the island of Patmos, and we saw the figure of Jesus, striking and awesome in His power and dauntless demeanor. The next two chapters do more than acquaint us with seven churches of Asia, for they orient us for the trials of the church through the ages. They prepare us for the tribulations that recur in the church both in John's age and in the passage of time through the centuries. Then when we include Heaven in the picture, we are not surprised to find a conflict between good and evil there, between the forces of God and the agents of the devil. But the minute we cross the threshold into Heaven, we have a new difficulty. It becomes still more difficult to interpret figurative, symbolic language when it describes a place we have never been and an order of existence we have never experienced. We are not there long before we know that all things in the descriptions cannot be taken literally. How can a lamb step forward and take a scroll to open it? How does a figure like a lion or like an ox never stop saying, "Holy, holy, holy is the Lord God Almighty . . ."? We take warning from this opening scene that we ruin the meaning if we try to put this down in a line drawing on a paper. It is intended for our mind's eye and the impression on our whole being. The truths of this book penetrate so far they leave impoverished the extent that language can take us. But we must be willing to soar in our thoughts to the realms John was taken. We do not even know whether this is an ordinary day we see as we enter Heaven with him, or whether it is a composite of many days, whether it is in John's time or closer to our time or some other time. These questions are only asked at the outset in order that we may deliberately set them aside for now. We only want to see what

God intended John to see and to receive the message He wanted John to convey to us. In this opening scene, we cannot miss the glory and sovereignty of God and the power and sacrificial role of the Lamb, who alone was worthy to open the scroll.

Invitation to Heaven (4:1-11)

The Door (1)

After John has received the messages to the seven churches of Asia, the next vision is introduced. He finds himself before a door. It does not say this door was in the sky. In fact, those who insist that the theology of the Bible reflects a three-story religion are only reflecting their own failure to allow to antiquity the latitude that they insist they themselves must be allowed in their language. John uses *heaven (ouranos)* in different ways. He does use it to mean the sky as a part of the physical, created universe (for example, Revelation 6:13: *ouranos* is translated "sky"), but he also uses it to denote where God dwells in the spiritual realms that cannot be located in a geographical direction related to the material world. Solomon built a temple for God. He felt His presence there, nevertheless he also expressed, "But will God really dwell on earth? The heavens even the highest heaven, cannot contain you." Yet in the same prayer, Solomon could pray: "Hear from heaven, your dwelling place, and when you hear, forgive" (1 Kings 8:27, 30). It was not higher still where God dwelt; it was a spiritual Heaven that was different from any physical heaven (sky) that could be seen.

John could have seen the door from his place on the shores of Patmos, and the same voice that told him to write to the churches of Asia now told him to come up (not necessarily into the sky) where he was. This leads to another question. Could it be that John, in the Spirit, had already crossed over into Heaven and the door he saw was a door standing ajar *in* Heaven instead of *into* Heaven. It could be either case. But what followed is clear. John accepted the invitation and entered.

The One on the Throne (2, 3)

The first object noted as John entered spacious Heaven was the throne. This in no way exceeded the importance of the one who was sitting on it, but the particular attention to the throne is in keeping with the whole book's emphasis on the sovereignty of

God. Since no specific feature of God's form is to be given, this quality of His being is given implied recognition in this manner. The magnificent display of light and color is breathtaking, but the only other quality that is subtly suggested comes in the additional detail of the rainbow. Besides supplying still more color in an emerald hue, it couples the element of rule on the throne with the promise of mercies with the rainbow. That the crystal brilliance of the jasper stands for purity or the fiery red of the sardius (getting its name from the city of Sardis) refers to wrath (judgment) is less sure. The same is true of any connection between the stones and the fact that they are the first and last stones in the ephod of the high priest. It is enough that the feeling of magnificent grandeur is conveyed through the comparison with these precious stones.

Surrounding the Throne (4-8)

"Twenty-four elders" (4). Beyond the halo of the rainbow, another circle was formed by the thrones and figures of twenty-four elders seated on them. Their description is briefly given. What they did can be easily reviewed. Their importance is clearly felt. But who they are remains uncertain.

They occupy thrones of rulers, not just seats. On the other hand, they have the crowns of victors (*stephanos*), not the crowns of kings (*diadema*). The apostles were promised thrones in the coming kingdom from which they would judge. But all Christians are promised a reign if they endure with Jesus (2 Timothy 2:12). Paul was not one of the twelve, but he expected a crown (2 Timothy 4:8). To the faithful Christians at Smyrna, Jesus promises the crown of life (Revelation 2:10b), and to the Philadelphian Christians, He warns of the danger that someone might take their crowns away if they did not hold on (Revelation 3:11). These twenty-four elders are clothed in white robes. So also the faithful in Sardis are promised they will be dressed in white as they walk with Jesus (Revelation 3:4, 5). In fact, we read later how all those under the altar have been given white robes (Revelation 6:9, 11), and the multitude of redeemed who had come out of the great tribulation are wearing white robes. Angels also are consistently described as wearing white.

But what do the elders do? They lead in worship and giving homage to God throughout the book of Revelation. They convey the prayers of Christians to God (Revelation 5:8) and give John encouragement and help (Revelation 5:5; 7:13-15).

Now who are these elders? Have we met them before? Do we meet them again with any other identification? Similarities are seen between the living creatures and description of the seraphim and cherubim, but what about the elders in Old Testament descriptions? Some would see a likeness to the council described in 1 Kings 22:19, but this seems to be the whole host of Heaven "standing around him on his right and on his left," and does not fit the role of this august body of twenty-four in Heaven. Nor is it convincing to point to the Jewish gerousia or its possible early vestiges in Exodus 24:9-11 or Isaiah 24:23 and its prediction. In all of this, the number twenty-four is puzzling. If there is symbolism to the number, it is only found in the book of Revelation and then only of the number of the elders. The number was used in the Old Testament of the number of courses established for the orders of the priests because their numbers had increased so that it was necessary to platoon their service at the temple in Jerusalem. Here the number is the same, but the similarities stop at that point. The Heavenly body does not have a priestly function unless the association with the prayers of the saints could be interpreted in that way. As for the number twenty-four, the early suggestion made by Victorinus and followed by other early interpreters of Revelation makes good sense.[34] He maintained the number twenty-four is the combination of the twelve patriarchs and the twelve apostles, thus having a representation of those from the Old Covenant and from the New. Some have objected to this, saying that would perpetuate a separation of faithful from Old Israel and the faithful of New Israel. On the contrary, this would show the complete unity of the saved, and it is noteworthy it is not labeled as half one and half the other. When the foundations and the gates of New Jerusalem are named, however, they are named after the twelve apostles and the twelve tribes of Israel (Revelation 21:12, 14). There are difficulties with this view, however. If twelve of these are the apostles, does this mean that John recognized himself as already present there when he is now making a preliminary visit to Heaven? Even if this is so, could he refrain from greeting his friends among them or at least make some mention of seeing them? Innumerable questions of this nature could be raised, and they only betray our own ignorance. But it also may be indicative

---

[34]H.B. Swete, *Commentary on Revelation,* p. 69.

of John's failure to know all the answers to individual identity in Heaven. Since they are not designated as patriarchs and apostles, however, it may be safer to regard them as representatives of the saved from all of the old and the new dispensations. Some, moreover, would deny they are the human redeemed at all, but rather representatives from the angelic hosts.[35] The key verse used to sustain the view is not sufficient, however. Just because the elders are listed along with the angels on one hand and the living creatures on the other (Revelation 5:11) does not necessitate the elders' being supernatural beings, also. If representatives of the redeemed are positioned in a circle close to God's throne, the order of the groups may depend upon the position in the concentric circles. There is no established rule that would exclude the human redeemed from such a position. Perhaps, however, they are not the apostles and patriarchs but are representatives from the old dispensation and from the new, twelve and twelve; but the twenty-four is a complete number representing the whole of the redeemed, Jew and Gentile.[36] Perhaps also these elders rotated on the thrones as the priests did in their twenty-four courses of service.

Four Living Creatures (6). When you speak of beasts, you usually mean wild beasts. The King James Version uses the word *beast* to translate the word for the four figures that have positions around the throne of God. But this word does not leave the ultimate impression we are meant to have in order to understand this scene in Heaven. So other translators have tried to tone down the word in order to avoid a term that leads off with a wrong impression. They came up with the word *creatures* instead of *beasts*. But what do you think of when you hear this word? It seems to indicate something abnormal or alien, something grotesque, perhaps crawling or inferior. This, too, is terrifying and misleading. Actually, the first meaning of *creature* is "something created." This is helpful, but in most minds, it probably becomes mingled with the unpleasant. For this reason, some have insisted that simply "living beings" would be a better translation. This is more

---

[35]N.B. Stonehouse, *Paul Before the Areopagus* (Grand Rapids: Eerdmans, 1957), pp. 197ff.

[36]H.B. Swete, *Commentary on Revelation,* p. 69.

faithful to the Greek, but is so neutral in its phrase that the image in our mind is left blank. When we are informed that the first living being is like a lion, our mind sees a lion and we immediately conclude that the King James was not so wrong after all, for a lion is a wild beast. But we are on the wrong track if we *end* with a mental picture of a lion to be the first living being close to the one on the throne. He is *like* a lion, but not a lion.

One of the important early lessons for computer users is the concept of directories. Without this, one cannot follow the proper path to get on the screen the file that he wants to use. The operator must enter through the main directory, then choose the proper route from the options given there. Likewise, choices must be made from sub-directories, if they are involved, until he comes to the menu that actually has the file he wants to use on the screen. There is no short cut. He must use the prescribed path to get to the file he wants to use. But he cannot stop along the way. To remain in the directory is of no value to him until he reaches his destination, the file on the screen.

God seems to use directories for John to record the truths He wants conveyed. When John follows the path of the four living beings, he finds a sub-directory of lion, ox, man, and eagle. But this is not the end. We are not ready to flash these physical figures on the screen and feel we have an accurate picture of God's throne room. We are still in the directories. The next choice is to see how they are *like* these figures, but not identical with them. In other words, what are the attributes of these figures that accompany each of them and make them the individuals they represent? These are the files we want to put on the screen. These are the truths we want to work with. This will be the true picture of Heaven and enhance a glimpse of the glory of God.

The lion is the king of the jungle, endowed with a royal strength and authority, moving with a confident, dauntless stride toward the achievement of his goals. The ox has tremendous strength also, but it is applied in a plodding, steady gait that is relentless in its service and labor. But man has intelligence, leadership, and understanding. And what of the eagle? Who can fly higher than the eagle, soar longer, keep on course, and dart more swiftly for its goal? These are the types of things that should flood our minds as we strive to feel the atmosphere of God's home. Some would maintain that these have also a fierce attitude foreshadowing the coming judgment of God. This seems to go beyond what is seen in this particular spectacle and the way that God is introduced here at the outset.

Objections will be raised. How can we put these attributes on a screen or even in our mind's eye? Besides, these animals, this man, and this bird all have bad points as well as good points. Doesn't this mar the picture? What about all the things we thought would be there? Where's Gabriel? Where's Michael? Where are the seraphim and the cherubim?

To begin with, we must recognize that John is trying to describe Heaven, and we have known nothing but earth. We have learned some things from other parts of the Scripture about this Heaven, but other times and occasions may make differences and should not detract from the details John sees in his own vision. Everything cannot be included in this first scene, but it may be that more is included than we realize. These four living beings may be the main directory for sub-directories to follow. This is Heaven, and those around the throne are not typified with bad qualities, but good. We may have difficulty in viewing them in the abstract, but they are there. Just as God is described by color and light and precious stones, a throne and a rainbow, so that which surrounds him is described in the language of four living beings, twenty-four elders on thrones, the sevenfold Spirit, and a multitude of angels. The magnificence is more felt in our spirit than seen in our mind's eye. This is to be expected.

Glory to God (8-11)

What the living creatures do is important to understanding who they are. Their function here is to lead the worship of Heaven. Day and night, meaning constantly, even as we are admonished to pray without ceasing, the four are proclaiming the holiness and power of the eternal God. Whenever they do this, the elders follow suit with witness of their own. In their tribute, they emphasize God's work of creation.

The Lamb Takes the Scroll (5:1-14)

The Scroll With Seven Seals (1-5)

Attention is now directed to a scroll held in the right hand of the Sovereign. That the scroll is full of writing is evident from writing seen on the outside of the roll, and one would assume the inside is also filled. Usually a roll was only transcribed on the inside.

"No one . . . could open the scroll" (3). Since no one could open it, John's remorse is understandable. Perhaps he felt that he was not going to learn what he had come to be shown. Perhaps he felt this was associated with the book of life or the names of those who would be saved. Perhaps it was not so much that he would not know what was coming in the future as that the plans of God could not be put into effect. At any rate, he knew that matters could not progress until one worthy could be found.

The Lamb and His Praise (6-14)

The Messiah was the answer. (See the description of the Lamb below under Special Subject #3.) When the Lamb took the scroll, all Heaven broke out in rejoicing.

"Worthy is the Lamb" (9-12). A new song was sung about the sacrifice of the Lamb. It was a song of praise that Jesus had purchased the salvation of persons from all the peoples of the earth and made them a special kingdom of priests and rulers. Then a song was sung by hundreds of thousands of angels as though they were singing antiphonally back and forth with the inner circles of living creatures and elders around the throne.

"Praise and honor" to God and to Christ (13, 14). Finally, in the finale, all the universe both in Heaven and on earth join in the praise and worship of both God on the throne and the Lamb standing beside Him. Some maintain that the Lamb was located between the circle of elders and the living creatures, but it is more likely that Jesus is in the throne area in the center with God. The time of this concluding scene may traverse all of time to the scene depicted by Paul in Philippians 2:9-11.

> Therefore God exalted him to the highest place
> and gave him the name that is above every name,
> that at the name of Jesus every knee should bow,
> in heaven and on earth and under the earth,
> and every tongue confess that Jesus Christ is Lord,
> to the glory of God the Father.

Special Subject #3

The Lamb

"Look, the Lamb of God, who takes away the sin of the world!" With these words, John the Baptist introduced Jesus the day after His baptism (John 1:29). The lamb was a familiar animal to those who heard John on that day. They could be seen grazing in the fields nearby. The shepherds knew them especially well, but everyone knew about sheep. They were particularly docile, but playful. They were prone to wander, but innocent and submissive. They were so helpless when they got into trouble. They did not have a tremendous roar, but only a plaintive bleat. A translator has a real problem as he tries to make an equivalent translation for a people who are unacquainted with sheep and have no word for such an animal in their own language. Does the translator follow ordinary procedure by substituting some term they are familiar with? For example, a hog was well known to them. Could hog be substituted for lamb? Or a donkey—could that serve as a substitute? Or a calf? You will probably agree, nothing would be satisfactory for a lamb, especially when taken in the context of the Bible.

The lamb played an important role in the Old Testament. When Abraham was preparing to take the final step in following the instructions of God to sacrifice his own son, Isaac, they had arrived alone on the mountain for the sacrifice. Isaac said to his father, "The fire and wood are here, . . . but where is the lamb for the burnt offering?"(Genesis 22:7). The son knew the lamb was the usual animal that filled this need. The hand of Abraham was stayed from sacrificing his son, and God provided a goat instead in this instance. When Moses recorded God's commandments in the Old Covenant, the lamb had a constant role in the requirements of sacrifice (for example, the sin sacrifices in Exodus 29:38-42). Especially important was the keeping of the Passover. The Israelites were commanded to slaughter a lamb, cook it, and eat it that evening to commemorate the time when God delivered them from Egypt. Not only was this essential to the keeping of the Old Covenant, but when the New Covenant was established, it became clear that the whole of the Old Testament system was a foreshadowing of the fulfillment in Jesus Christ. Paul expressed it: "For Christ, our Passover lamb, has been sacrificed" (1 Corinthians 5:7).

The predictions of Isaiah bear this out from a time seven centuries before their fulfillment.

> We all, like sheep, have gone astray,
>   each of us has turned to his own way;

and the Lord has laid on him
   the iniquity of us all.
He was oppressed and afflicted,
   yet he did not open his mouth;
he was led like a lamb to the slaughter,
   and as a sheep before her shearers is silent,
   so he did not open his mouth. . . .
Therefore I will give him a portion among the great,
   and he will divide the spoils with the strong,
because he poured out his life unto death,
   and was numbered with the transgressors.
For he bore the sin of many,
   and made intercession for the transgressors (Isaiah 53:6, 7, 12).

But what of the use of the lamb in the New Testament? This is surprising. Up to the book of Revelation, *lamb* is designated but six times, and three different Greek words are used in those six times. One Greek word (*amnos*) is used four times and each of these makes reference to Jesus as the sacrificial lamb that has taken away the sin of man. Two of these references have been quoted above from John (1:29, 36). One is a quotation from the Isaiah passage quoted above (the Ethiopian eunuch and Philip, Acts 8:32). The fourth is in 1 Peter 1:18, 19:

For you know that it was not with perishable things such as silver or gold that you were redeemed from the empty way of life handed down to you from your forefathers, but with the precious blood of Christ, a lamb without blemish or defect.

Of the two other uses, another Greek word is used in Luke 10:3 (*aren*): "Go! I am sending you out like lambs among wolves." And the third Greek word (*arnion*) is used in John's Gospel as Jesus admonishes Peter, "Feed my lambs" (John 21:15).

After noting how seldom the word has been used in most New Testament writings, its use in the book of Revelation is even more startling. It appears in Revelation twenty-nine times. This is the favorite title used to denote Jesus Christ. Just as Jesus used the phrase Son of Man to refer to himself during His ministry as recorded in the Gospel narratives, so the book of Revelation uses the title Lamb. No more striking passage is found than this opening scene under study now. God is on His throne. He is enveloped in a crystal clear translucent light of brilliant white and fiery red with a rainbow of greenish hue around the base of His dias. He is surrounded by seven flaming torches, representing the Spirit of God, and the four living beings represented by the lion, the ox, the body with the face of a man, and the eagle. Each of these figures has six wings and eyes observing all things in all directions. They move with effortless grace and give constant praise and thanks to the Holy God. Beyond these is the circle of the twenty-four elders on their thrones. The elders rise from their thrones one by one and come over the vast expanse of the sea of glass with its bright crystal sheen to the foot of the throne. As they remove their crowns of gold, bow low and present them before His ineffable person, they add their adoration for the God of creation. All of this action is punctuated by "flashes of lightning, rumblings and peals of thunder" (Revelation 4:5).

A problem has developed. John is in tears. No one is able to open the scroll held in God's hand. One of the elders comes from his throne to comfort John. "Don't be sad. Look over there! The Lion of Judah, the Root of David has won out, He can open it." John hopefully lifts his eyes to look for the lion that has been promised. And then the unexpected—he does not see a lion, but a Lamb. When the Lamb approaches God and receives the scroll from His right hand, this is a signal for a new round of praise and worship, including a new song—this time for the worthiness of the Lamb. Now for the first time, another circle around the throne is acknowledged. For gathered around and beyond the elders are the thousand upon thousands of Heavenly angels singing and giving honor and glory and praise to the Lamb. One characteristic stands out above all else concerning the Lamb. They sing to Him who is worthy "because you were slain, and with your blood you purchased men for God . . ." (Revelation 5:9).

Now another unexpected has come into view. Of the three Greek words used in the New Testament for lamb, one means the sacrificial lamb offered for sin. Of course, this must be the one John will use to describe the person and work of Jesus in Revelation. Right? Wrong! He uses another word—one that appears only one other time outside the book of Revelation in the whole of the New Testament. It is not the sacrificial lamb, but the word used by Jesus speaking to Peter instructing him to care for the Christians as they are nurtured in God's kingdom (John 21:15). As they grow, however, they are among the victorious, not destined for future sacrifice. But why did not John use the word with the sacrificial-lamb meaning? The answer seems obvious. The Lamb on the throne showed clearly a death wound on the throat, for this was how all lambs were slaughtered for sacrifice. But the lamb was not lying there lifeless as a slain victim. He was standing, very much alive and triumphant. The scar showed the sacrifice, but the word chosen to designate the lamb was a living, triumphant one, ready for action, and worthy of the praise and honor given Him.

Not all of the characteristics of a lamb are pertinent here. Try not to stop in your mind's eye with the image of a lamb. This is simply a part of the directory, the path that leads us to the file of vital truths. When there, the file is opened. Now two sides stand out clearly in this scene of the lamb. On one side of the coin is written "sacrifice," and on the other side appears "victory." Another important pair in this glimpse of glory is God on one side and the Lamb on the other. These two are represented respectively by "creation" and "redemption." The whole of the throne room of Heaven breathes with the sovereignty of the one on the throne. "The four living creatures said, 'Amen,' and the elders fell down and worshiped" (Revelation 5:14). Moreover, they are encircled by the rainbow, the promise of God's mercy.

The air is charged with the qualities of God and the person and worthiness of the Lamb. They are alive and ruling, sustaining and loving. The scene leaves no doubt, we would like to live there—for eternity.

CHAPTER FOUR

Steeped in Tribulation

Revelation 6:1—7:17

A young woman stood before a predominately Christian audience in a rented auditorium in Tokyo. She was there to sing a special solo before the message of the evening. Before she sang, she explained that she was blind, but that she was blind for the glory of God, and to Him only she would be singing. Then with her face lifted to Heaven, she sang with all her heart, "I sing because I'm happy, I sing because I'm free. For His eye is on the sparrow, and I know He watches me."

Later, after the service was over and the people had gone, she described to the evening speaker an experience she recently had on the subway. A woman had sat down beside her and asked whether she was blind. When she said she was, the woman urged her to come to her religious cult and made promises to help her, perhaps even to make her see again. The woman had replied that she was a Christian. At this, the other woman began a tirade against Christianity and against Christ. The young Christian defended Jesus, and declined continued invitations to come to the religious cult for help. Finally, the young woman who was physically blind said to the insistent woman, "I am sorry for you because *you* are blind. I am not blind because I can see Jesus."

Despite the tribulations and judgments of Revelation 6 and 7, if you face toward God and belong to Him, you will see the Lamb, the victorious Jesus by God's side, and you will have nothing to fear.

Prelude

Overview

The opening scene in Heaven had been filled with stunning grandeur and awesome worship. The absolute authority of the one on the throne and the homage to the Lamb were manifest. No unpleasant note or hint of suffering had been sounded throughout the first view of Heaven, except for the death wound on the throat of the Lamb. Suspense had been built up as Heaven prepared for the opening of the scroll.

Now the Lamb opens the first of the seven seals. One of the four living creatures in a thundering voice gives the command, "Come." (Not "Come and see," as some manuscripts, which would be an invitation to John to step forward and look into the scroll; the command is issued to the horseman out of sight in the folds of the scroll.) The instruction is answered, not by an attempt to unroll the scroll or to read its contents, but with exciting action. A white horse carrying a rider dashes forth to speed on his way. His destination is the earth, and his marks of identification are a bow and a crown. He is determined to conquer. As he fades in the distance, the Lamb breaks the second seal, and a red horse and rider spring forth. Evidently, the first rider has left peace in his wake, for now the rider of the red horse takes peace from the earth. He leads to men slaying each other, as he is given a sword. This is war. Close on his hooves, famine follows in his path. This is the black horse. And finally, the pale horse brings up the rear with pestilence (death) and Hades. They are given power over as much as one fourth of the earth.

When the fifth seal is opened, the scenario changes. The setting of this vision is another corner in Heaven, a vision within a vision. An altar is there; souls of the slain are there. Perhaps this episode is related to the four horsemen in that these are some of the victims from the trials just described. This is a picture of the redeemed, in their white robes, and they are concerned about the justice among those who were still on earth. The scene closes with word they must wait a little longer. Then the sixth seal follows with a flash of the terror of the lost as the Judgment Day arrives.

Key Message

"These are they who have come out of the great tribulation; they have washed their robes and made them white in the blood of the Lamb" (Revelation 7:14).

Glossary

Read through chapters 6 and 7 of Revelation. As you come to the terms listed below, note the explanation.

Chapter 6

First seal	The scroll has seven seals probably made by tying the roll with seven strings and sealing each knot with a waxed, stamped seal. The scroll could not be unrolled and read until all seven seals were broken. This would be the ordinary procedure with a legal will. Nothing is said here about reading the document, but the breaking of each seal introduces an action.
Living creatures	See the glossary under Revelation 4 (p. 74, above).
Voice like thunder	A voice like a trumpet had spoken before (Revelation 1:10; 4:1), now one of the living creatures sounds forth like thunder.
White horse	Variant suggestions (see p. 96): (1) Righteous, because white is associated with the white robes of the redeemed. (2) Victorious, because it is a matter of conquest whatever the cause. (3) Some say deceitfully bad, because the other three horses represent evils.
Rider with a bow	Variant positions (see p. 98): (1) Jesus Christ, because identified in Revelation 19:11. (2) Parthian (because of bow?). (3) The gospel because of the Word of God. (4) Spirit of conquest. (5) Antichrist.
Given a crown	The victor's crown, not the king's. The same as the elders' and the redeemed's crowns (Revelation 2:10; 4:10).
Conqueror	The rider represents conquest. It only remains to specify what kind of conquest. Odd that conquest precedes war unless the conquest is of a different kind than the war that comes afterward. (See Mark 13:11ff, where the preaching of the gospel precedes war and pestilence.)

Second seal	The second living creature was the ox and gave the command "Come" when the Lamb opened the second seal.
Fiery red horse	Red is the appropriate color for war and bloodshed. It fits the results: he removed peace, men slay each other, given a large sword.
Third seal	Third living creature had the face of a man and said "Come" when this seal was opened.
Black horse	Black is a color accompanying gloom, mourning, and pathos. The added details confirm this mood as the results of famine are clearly indicated.
Pair of scales	Reference to scales and the high price of grain point to famine as the basis of the mourning.
Quart of wheat	The cost of this measure of wheat was a denarius (about one day's wage for the ordinary laborer). In Cicero's day, one could ordinarily get twelve measures for a day's wage.
Three quarts of barley	Wheat was thus three times more expensive than barley (the ratio of two to one was ordinary).
Oil and wine	Do not waste the oil and wine either. They may not be so quickly affected as the grain, but they will run out, too.
Fourth seal	The last of the living creatures called, "Come," as the fourth seal was opened.
Pale horse	More accurately a sickly green color to denote the pallor of death as a result of pestilence following in the wake of war.
Rider (death) and Hades	These two are riding double. Death is personified as a rider who exacts his toll from the results of war, famine, and pestilence. The grave (Hades) follows after to engulf those who suffer death.
Power over one fourth of the earth	Why the limit is one fourth is not indicated, but a limitation is definitely given. It is not total loss of life, but it is considerable.

Fifth seal	A new section begins. No longer a series of riders, headed for earth, but a scene in Heaven.
Altar	A place where burnt offerings have been made and the blood of the victims poured out at the base (Leviticus 4:7). Possibly a Heavenly counterpart of the altar in Jerusalem where honored individuals had been buried beneath the altar.
Souls slain	This is not a general view of Heaven, but a side vision representing a scene taking place in Heaven. The altar is, no doubt, much larger than its earthly counterpart, and no blood, but the souls of the saints are there because their lives have been laid down in martyrdom for their loyalty to Christ.
White robe	Representing righteousness, holiness, and celebration of salvation. They are both innocent and conquerors. But judgment has not yet arrived. The number of the martyrs has not yet been filled.
Sixth seal	Another visionary scene, this time on earth. Parallels judgment scene as described by Jesus (Matthew 24:29). Introduces signs of the coming final judgment. Variant views, see below.
Great earthquake	Not a local quake as Sardis, Philadelphia, and Laodicea had in the first century, but one of cosmic scope described in the details that followed.
Sun turned black	Earth has known numerous eclipses before, but this seems to be something more, not scheduled.
Moon turned blood red	Not that the moon will be blood, but will be the color of blood.
Stars fallen to earth	Showers of stars, meteorites, objects from the sky will mark the dissolution of the universe.
Sky Receded	Whole sky will roll up just the way you roll up a window shade or they rolled a book-scroll to completion in antiquity.

Mountain and island removed To move mountains remained beyond human power and John was on an island and did not anticipate its sudden dropping out of sight.

Great day of wrath The final Judgment Day.

Chapter 7

Four angels Evidently in charge of the winds, as one was in charge of fire (Revelation 14:18) and another over waters (Revelation 16:5).

Four winds Instead of a continuation to the Judgment Day, this interlude may take us back to a time prior to the release of the four horsemen.[37] They may hold missions comparable to the four seals.

Another angel from the East An angel of the same order as the four, yet distinct from them. From the East—probably good because of the light from the rising sun.

Seal of the Living God Seal—for protection, for declaration of ownership, for guarantee of genuineness.

Seal on the forehead How is not known (2 Timothy 2:19, Ezekiel 9:1-8).

144,000 The number is intended to denote completeness. Twelve tribes of Israel times twelve for New Israel times 1000 for completeness = 144,000, representing not the Jewish Christians alone, but Gentile Christians as well. Probably representing the redeemed who were still alive on earth.

Great multitude The 144,000 were introduced as a representative number of the redeemed, but now the view is extended to include a multitude beyond numbering of all the redeemed.

White robes These robes assure those who wear them of purity from sin and its guilt, of a salvation in perfect joy and peace for eternity, of a dwelling place in the presence of God.

---

[37]C. B. Caird, *Commentary on the Revelation,* p. 94.

Great tribulation	Variously interpreted.
	(1) General tribulations through the ages.
	(2) A specific severe period of suffering at the very end.
	(3) A number of tribulations along the way, but a most severe suffering at the end.
	see Special Subject #4, pp. 111ff.

Content Notes

Six Seals Opened (6:1-17)

The First Seal (1, 2)

Identification of the first horseman of the Apocalypse is one of the most disputed points in the book of Revelation. At the same time, this passage provides an excellent example showing how the variant approaches to the overall interpretation of the book influences how differently a person can look at an individual scene. Then again, this section provides an illustration of how differently one figure can be interpreted and still have much common agreement as to the main message of Revelation. Since this is the case, more space will be given to stating a preference and giving the pros and cons to the various positions than is usual. This does not mean the conclusions maintained on this point are dogmatically certain or absolutely necessary to an understanding of the rest of Revelation, but to present a preference in as clear a way as possible is best.

The preference supported here is that the rider on the white horse represents the gospel of Jesus Christ (the Word of God). As was stated above, the variant schools of interpretation gravitate towards different views here, each selecting the possibility that best fits one's overall pattern.

Since the Preterist maintains that all of the action took place in or around the very days the book of Revelation was being written, he finds a likely candidate in the Parthians. They were feared enemies of Rome, they brought about wars, and they used bows. The height of the Parthian invasion occurred under Vologses' leadership in A.D. 62.

On the other extreme, the Dispensationalist assigns all of the action from chapter four on as occurring in the period just before the return of Christ in the countdown years seen to be designated by Daniel. Thus, they tend to assign the first horseman to the role of the world "ruler" (Daniel 9:26) and the same individual as the beast out of the sea in Revelation 13. Some believe this period follows the "rapture" of the church and includes the "Great Tribulation" designated by the pictures of all four of the horsemen.[38]

Others who see in Revelation a backdrop that extends from the first century to whatever century it takes for the Lord's return, tend to find the work of this first horseman covering the whole panorama throughout the history of the church. This is the emphasis of the cyclical interpretation, and is the one preferred here. But those seeing the extended fulfillment of the mission of the white horse are divided in their view of the significance. Some look in the direction of war for introducing slaughter and famine and death, while others see the white horse as a bearer of light in contrast with the darkness of the remaining three. The interpretation favored here is the white horse as the bearer of good tidings.

In the first place, the color of this horse is white. In the book of Revelation, white is the color regularly employed to denote purity, righteousness, and victory. It would be indeed strange if this pattern is broken and depicts something as bloodthirsty as war, seen in the breaking of the second seal. In fact, this is a weighty objection to the first seal's being considered war when the second seal is admittedly viewed as war. Why repeat the same significance in both? It is a strain on a position when it is necessary to draw a line between civil strife and a deadly, internecine war to get out of a difficulty that is not really there.

More indications surface that point the service of the first horseman toward the good rather than the evil. The rider is given a crown, the same crown the redeemed were promised; he is called the conqueror, the same conqueror the redeemed were promised to be. He left peace in his wake for the arrival of the next horseman (Revelation 6:3, 4). It might be possible to slough off the white as being acceptable even though it violates the otherwise consistent use of it in Revelation, or to point to other uses of crowns in Revelation, good or bad, or other conquests of the evil of a temporary nature, but the accumulating number of signs pointing to the good and denying evil in turn becomes too much.

---

[38]John F. Walvoord, *The Revelation of Jesus Christ* (Chicago: Moody, 1966), p. 127.

The single most severe objection to interpreting the first rider as Christ or the gospel is that the next three horsemen are omens of coming trials; so it seems necessary that the first must also be something of the same nature or else the symmetry of mounting tribulation will be ruined. It is ironic that some are more concerned about adjusting individual scenes to a symmetry superimposed on Revelation rather than yield to the indications of the passage so as not to violate a larger symmetry of the book and ruin another part of the picture. What is so wrong with having one good herald followed by three bad ones? Does it have to be two and two or four and none? As good a case can be made for the mounting tribulations in the last three horsemen with or without the first one's corroborating them. In fact, this is a serious fault in taking the first to indicate internecine war and make it a near duplication of the second. Rather, the contrast of the proclamation of the gospel going out to conquer the world as was commissioned to be done makes all the more striking the tribulations in the world. The contrast is continued in opening the fifth and sixth seals, a comparison of the saved though martyred and the terror of the unsaved at the coming of judgment. This is an expected progression: preaching the gospel, persecution, trials, wars, suffering, judgment. It is not a ruination of the symmetry.

The words of Jesus concerning the last times have been appealed to, showing the similarity between them and what one reads in this section of Revelation. His eschatological discourse is recorded in all three Synoptic accounts.[39] Among the signs of the coming tribulations, Mark records: "And the gospel must first be preached to all nations" (Mark 13:10). Lining up the material found in Mark and the material found in Revelation for this section, no words could better express the mission of the rider on the white horse than the preaching of the gospel to all nations.[40]

---

[39]Matthew 24:6, 7, 9a, 29; Mark 13:7-9a, 24-25; Luke 21:9-12a, 25, 26. Although the source theories of R. H. Charles are not acceptable, he has put this material in convenient form. *A Critical and Exegetical Commentary on the Revelation of St. John,* I (New York: Charles Scribner's Sons, 1920), p. 159.

[40]See William Hendriksen, *More Than Conquerors* (Grand Rapids: Baker, 1939), pp. 118, 119. Homer Hailey, *Revelation: An Introduction and Commentary* (Grand Rapids: Baker, 1979), pp. 188, 189.

Whether this indicates a mission just before the end or whether this is an accurate picture of many cycles that will have transpired throughout the ages and reached a climax in the final consummation, one cannot say. Certainly wars continue to be followed by famine and pestilence and death. The gospel continues to be preached and persecution continues to add its numbers to those beneath the altar.

But what about the figure of the "bow" in the emergence of the first horseman? Doesn't this indicate war? A preliminary observation is in order. Compare the first and second riders. A sword was given to the rider on the red horse. His ride was associated with slaughter. He took away the peace that had preceded him. But the rider on the white horse had a bow. Could this be a reference to the Parthians? They were noted for their use of the bow in warfare. It is also true that Rome had difficulty in conquering these people. They were a threat to the borders of the empire. They even lost some individual battles to them. But the Parthians never conquered Rome. One could not look upon this series of visions and say that it referred to Parthia and was right in the outcome. If it has already failed in its outcome, this is good indication that the interpretation is at fault. In looking for sources associated with the bow in Revelation, the Old Testament is a more likely spring to draw from than the Parthians. If God is the guiding Spirit behind the authorship of Scripture and God is the Mind behind the visions given to John, one may help explain the other. Psalm 45 is considered a Messianic Psalm describing the deeds of God's anointed (verses 6, 7 are ascribed to Christ in Hebrews 1:8, 9).

> In your majesty ride forth victoriously
>> in behalf of truth, humility and righteousness;
>> let your right hand display awesome deeds.
> Let your sharp arrows pierce the hearts of the king's enemies;
>> let the nations fall beneath your feet.
> Your throne, O God, will last for ever and ever;
>> a scepter of justice will be the scepter of your kingdom
>>> (Psalm 45:4-6).

In the prayer of Habakkuk, one can read:

> Were you angry with the rivers, O Lord?
> Was your wrath against the streams?

Did you rage against the sea
   when you rode with your horses
   and your victorious chariots?
You uncovered your bow,
   you called for many arrows.
You split the earth with rivers;
   the mountains saw you; and writhed....
Sun and moon stood still in the heavens
   at the glint of your flying arrows,
   at the lightning of your flashing spear.
In wrath you strode through the earth
   and in anger you threshed the nations.
You came out to deliver your people
   to save your anointed one (Habakkuk 3:8-13).

Some object to identifying the first rider as the Christ or the gospel because this section of the seals is so filled with judgment. To have the good news of the gospel would at this point break the continuity of the section. To the contrary, the gospel is good news to those who accept it, but is judgment upon those who reject it. In the message of the first seal, the crown is the mark of victory, but the bow is the sign of judgment, divine judgment, not international war, as is seen from these Old Testament references to God, or the Messiah, and the bow.

My shield is God Most High,
   who saves the upright in heart.
God is a righteous judge,
   a God who expresses his wrath every day.
If he does not relent,
   he will sharpen his sword;
   he will bend and string his bow.
He has prepared his deadly weapons;
   he makes ready his flaming arrows (Psalm 7:10-13).

Resistance to identifying the first rider as Christ reaches a low ebb when the claim is made the rider could not be Christ because the Lamb is opening the seals, and Jesus is the Lamb; therefore, He could not be the rider at the same time. But who has not attended a slide presentation when the operator of the projector has shown pictures of himself in the program? How much more are things like this to be expected in the apocalyptic, where one is dealing with symbols another step removed from physical reality?

Jesus Christ has been identified as the rider on the white horse from the earliest of extant interpreters. All through the ages, association has been made between this horse and rider and the identification of the white horse and rider described in Revelation 19:11. Practical unanimity agrees in specifying the victorious Jesus as the individual in Revelation 19.

One more objection to allowing this identification to be applied to the opening of the first seal is that all the other seals are connected with a thing, not a person (war, famine, pestilence, and death). If this criticism is valid, it would be preferable then to identify the person by the message He delivered, the gospel with Jesus at its center, the very Word of God. And the name of the rider in chapter 19 is actually given: "His name is the Word of God." This fits best for the rider introduced at the opening of the first seal as well.

The Second Seal (3, 4)

The opening of the second seal is the signal for the fiery red horse to come forth. There is no dispute among the interpreters that this rider represents war. But the question still remains, which war? There were many conflicts in the Roman period contemporary with the writing of Revelation. Much slaughter has been seen through the ages. Or is this strife still to come? Is this a particular period of bloodshed as the final act of man's history is getting underway? Some feel this is particular warfare that rises as a reaction against the spread of the gospel. This is a form of persecution, and will result in the martyrdom of many Christians. Could the souls seen under the altar in Heaven after the opening of the sixth seal be victims of this warfare? It may be. But the plain message to each generation is a warning that the tribulation and horrors of war will take its toll in our own times as well as before us and after us.

The Third Seal (5, 6)

Likewise, considerable unanimity is shown in interpretations of the third horseman. The rider on the black steed must represent famine. When you must weigh out the wheat you buy for your daily bread, and it costs a whole day's wage to buy enough just to keep you alive, the wheat must be scarce, and the cost too high to feed your family, too. That's when you decide to buy barley instead because it is cheaper, and you might be able to keep your family alive, too. The reference to the oil and wine is taken differently by different interpreters. Some feel they are luxuries and available only to the rich, others look upon them as staples and necessary to normal fare. At any rate, they should be treated with care and not wasted. The roots of the vine and the olive trees are deeper and might endure a single drought better than a grain field would. Famine is another tribulation that follows time and again as an aftermath of war.

The Fourth Seal (7, 8)

The word for death can also be translated pestilence in this context. The sickly green color used to designate this fourth horse (pale) presents the picture of the hue of death, paler as one comes to the last hours of his life. *Hades* (in the Greek) and *Sheol* (in the Hebrew) both can be translated "grave." To have Death and the Grave riding together is fitting. Different suggestions have been made for the way this should be pictured. Were there two horses, one after the other? Or was Hades walking behind collecting the bodies as Pestilence rode on ahead delivering the death stroke? What is most likely is that Hades was riding double behind Death.

Their work had a restriction. They could not strike down more than a fourth of the people on earth. The list of means they would use to fulfill their purpose gives assurance for the interpretations of the passage above: "They were given power over a fourth of the earth to kill by sword [second rider], famine [third rider] and plague [fourth rider—pestilence] . . ." (Revelation 6:8). The addition of "the wild beasts of the earth" may have reference to persecution of the Christians as took place in the Roman treatment in the early centuries of Christianity.

The Fifth Seal (9-11)

Now the setting changes. In the first four seals, we have stood alongside John as he witnessed the Lamb break the seals on the scroll, and one by one four horses have galloped forth from the roll and dashed off earthward into the distance. But when the fifth seal is opened, a new vision flashes into view showing a room in Heaven where the souls of those who had died as martyrs were gathered. If this scene is related to the former scenes, then these must be some who have died in the tribulations depicted there.

This may be a surprising thought to some, who presumed that these were godless people suffering the judgment of God, and He is in control. Were there Christians who suffered in these ways too—from sword, from wild animals, from death? Evidently so, and this is the reason the martyrs are asking, "How long will it be before you avenge our death? How long will our brothers go on dying in this unjust way?" And this is the reason this scene is included. This is the reason this revelation is given and this book has been written—to alert the Christian to expect trials in life even to the point of dying, despite the fact of victory in Christ, and despite the fact that God is in control at all times, and despite the truth that God is faithful and just. This question of the martyrs, "How long?" is important both to them and to us. It has been important down through the ages, and will remain vital until the end of time.

The spirit of the question should not be considered a request for revenge, a selfish and malicious desire to see others suffer because they had brought suffering on a Christian. Rather, the request comes from hearts filled with faith and trust in a God who is just and faithful; and these martyrs are anxious for their God to prove himself and to settle the accounts fairly and put a stop to the continued suffering of the saints. But the Lord God Almighty will not be hurried along by the impatience of nearsighted humans. The answer was given in three ways:

1. "Wait a little longer" (Revelation 6:11). The plans are not yet completed, more numbers are yet to follow you.
2. Receive now the "white robe" given to you. This robe stands for victory in Christ. It means a pure, righteous life with Jesus for eternity. It means all the blessings of Heaven come with it. In the next chapter, the elder describes those in the white robes:

> These are they who have come out of the great tribulation; they have washed their robes and made them white in the blood of the Lamb. Therefore,
>
> "they are before the throne of God
>   and serve him day and night in his temple;
> and he who sits on the throne will spread his tent over them.
> Never again will they hunger;
>   never again will they thirst.

The sun will not beat upon them,
        nor any scorching heat.
For the Lamb at the center of the throne will be their shepherd;
        he will lead them to springs of living water.
And God will wipe away every tear from their eyes"

(Revelation 7:14-17).

3. The opening of the sixth seal is part of the answer given to the
    question that is raised in the message of the fifth seal. One
    might object that the martyrs under the altar did not have the
    opportunity to hear the message that we can read in Revelation
    6:12ff. This may be true, but neither does the one living on
    earth have the opportunity to fill in from further information
    experienced in the next world. But from the sixth seal, al-
    though the action remains in this life on earth, one can com-
    pare the terror of the lost as he is confronted with the final
    judgment with the victory and joy of the saved in Heaven. The
    settling of the accounts is underway.

The Sixth Seal (12-17)

This is one of the crucial passages in the book of Revelation.
Not only does it appear as the climax to the opening of the seals,
but its interpretation will be a deciding factor in one's choice
among the five general approaches to the understanding of Revelation (see pp. 14-17 of the Introduction) or, on the other hand, a
person's predetermined choice of an approach will govern what
interpretation he will take for this passage. Questions that must be
decided include the following:
1. Does this refer to the immediate coming of the final judgment?
2. Does this refer to the beginning of the Tribulation, but more
    remote than the immediate coming of the end?
3. Does this refer to some major change in political, social order,
    but not the final end times—such as the fall of Jerusalem or
    the fall of Rome?
4. Does this refer to every great calamity in history as the sinful
    world is overtaken each time?
5. Does the passage have significance to successive judgments
    throughout time, but with the final judgment as the ultimate
    application?
Details that first impress the reader associate the passage with
the end time. Earthquake, darkened sun, bloodlike moon, falling

stars, recoiling sky, moving hills and covered islands—all these point to the end time.

Some, however, deny this. They maintain that the language is symbolic and a literal, catastrophic happening should not be expected. Rather, it refers to the fall of an important political power anywhere along the line, and why not Rome, in the time of the writing of the book? This sounds like the preterist interpretation, and so it is. One trouble here is that Rome did not fall in the time of the writing of the book, not for hundreds of years.

Others say that's right, but it refers to the fall of Jerusalem in A.D. 70. But that's too early, even before the writing of the book. Besides, they say, it is a reminder of other Old Testament passages, and they were not referring to the end of time, but some more immediate local situation. This is something that happens all along the way, before and after Christ. This sounds like the spiritualist interpretation. And so it is. This is the interpretation one expects from his approach.

But others say you must be more literal, and it sounds like the conditions are so extreme that the universe could not continue to exist as described. It must be the end time, but not the immediate end. Since this appears in the sixth chapter, this must be the entering of the last days, say the time of the Great Tribulation, but the end of time and the final judgment does not come for another thousand years. Now this begins to sound like the Premillennialist or the Dispensationalist view, and so it is.

Finally, one concludes that each commentator interprets this passage just the way his approach demands he interprets it—and so it is!

The embarrassing question comes, "And what makes you different from all the rest?" The admission must be frankly made, "And so it is." The same type of influence is here, also. This passage is crucial, not only because it is the climax of the seven seals, but because it is a clear example of how a person is influenced by his general approach when he interprets a particular passage. On the other hand, one passage might be so significant that its interpretation may tip the scales toward his choice of approach to the overall book. If this passage becomes that important to a person, then it is doubly crucial in his understanding of Revelation. More space is given in noting these verses because of this reason. Furthermore, constant reminder must be made that each passage should be interpreted on the basis of the immediate context and not because of a forced fitting into one theory of approach.[41] This necessitates listing the reasons that favor the correctness of saying this passage refers to the coming of the final judgment.

First, the description of conditions leave the first, natural impression that the end has been reached and final judgment is pending. The terror of the wicked is final in its desperation. No escape is sought, no plea for relief is made, only destruction is preferred to certain condemnation. "Let the rocks fall on us."

But, after all, they could be wrong. Maybe this still is not the end. But this is combined with the complete dismantling of the universe—sun, moon, stars, sky, mountains, and islands. Whether this is literal collapse or symbolic of something else, what could it more naturally symbolize than the end? Wherever additional reasons may lead us, the first and simplest indication is that the end has come.

Second, the possible significance of Old Testament references and words of Jesus point toward the judgment at the end of time. Each figure used to describe the action in this scene of the sixth seal can be paralleled by references from the prophets of the Old Testament and the words of Jesus concerning judgment (except the phrase "the wrath of the Lamb"). For example, Nahum describes the Lord's taking vengeance on Nineveh:

> The Lord is slow to anger and great in power;
>> the Lord will not leave the guilty unpunished. . . .
> The mountains quake before him
>> and the hills melt away.
> The earth trembles at his presence,
>> the world and all who live in it.
> Who can withstand his indignation?
>> Who can endure his fierce anger?
> His wrath is poured out like fire;
>> the rocks are shattered before him (Nahum 1:3, 5, 6).

Hosea used language similar to John's concerning the destruction of Samaria:

---

[41]"Each passage must be taken in light of its own context and not forced into an over-all scheme." Leon Morris, *The Revelation of St. John* (Grand Rapids: Eerdmans, 1969), p. 18, footnote.

> Then they will say to the mountains, "Cover us!"
>   and to the hills, "Fall on us!" (Hosea 10:8).

Isaiah used some of the same symbols as John did in this passage but concerning ancient Babylon:

> The stars of heaven and their constellations
>   will not show their light.
> The rising sun will be darkened
>   and the moon will not give its light (Isaiah 13:10).

Jesus, however, quotes this passage and makes another application of it. He says such signs will follow days of distress and

> at that time the sign of the Son of Man will appear in the sky, and all the nations of the earth will mourn. They will see the Son of Man coming on the clouds of the sky, with power and great glory. And he will send his angels with a loud trumpet call, and they will gather his elect from the four winds, from one end of the heavens to the other (Matthew 24:29-31).

From this, one sees that these passages from the Old Testament can be applied in a different way from that in which their first application was made. Thus it is possible to apply a passage, as Jesus did, to His second coming and the judgment. Some, however, maintain that Jesus was applying this to the fall of Jerusalem and not to the second coming (for example, Luke 21:20-24). The problem here is that Jesus was asked three questions by His disciples (in a parallel passage, Matthew 24:3):
1. When will the temple (Jerusalem) be destroyed?
2. What will be the sign of Jesus' coming again?
3. What will be the sign of the end of the age?
Jesus answered all these questions, but the answers are intermingled. His instruction to flee from the city to the country follows the sign, "When you see Jerusalem being surrounded by armies" (Luke 21:20). This has reference to the destruction of Jerusalem and the temple. But the time when they will see the Son of Man coming in a cloud immediately follows the statement: "There will be signs in the sun, moon and stars" (Luke 21:25). So these are signs of His coming again and of the end of time.

Third, we must note John's own context, for the way a passage is used in its Old Testament context or the way Jesus used a figure in His own context is not the final word on how John used it in his. One needs to remind himself constantly that John was reporting on a genuine revelation. He had first-hand scenes and experience to describe. He was not quoting from Old Testament books or lifting material from alleged apocalypses. If there are similarities, it is because God is the true source, and truth will be consistent with truth. John may well be influenced by what he is familiar with, but he uses it as he chooses, and the context raises questions of its own. One is not sure how independent the seals are of one another, but it is noteworthy that the signs enumerated by Jesus in His discourse on the end times (Mark 13, parallel Matthew 24) go through six steps similar to the six seals here in the sixth chapter of John's Revelation.[42] The fifth step in Jesus' discourse and the fifth seal have to do with persecution (the souls who have been martyred and were beneath the altar, then supplied with white robes).

The question left from the fifth seal was when would the vengeance of the Lord bring justice upon those who had brought death to the innocent? There were two parts to the answer. It could not be immediately because the number of the martyrs was not yet complete, but it would be a little later. How long must they wait for the judgment? Then the sixth seal seems to show the other side of the coin. The martyrs were safely in Heaven, but on earth, the wicked were terrified at the sudden prospects of judgment. Some suggest this means it must be in the time of John's writing—from the same generation as the martyrs newly arrived from Roman persecution—but that does not necessarily follow. Little assurance can be gained in the times, seasons, and chronology in Revelation, but the context is set by the one figure that is new to all the parallel passages that have been suggested, "the wrath of the lamb." *Wrath* is a surprising description for a lamb. But we must remember that Jesus is no ordinary lamb. The "Lamb" is a figure representing Jesus, not only in His sacrificial role but His position on the throne with God. Now we are reminded of His role as judge. *Wrath* is a word that is consistently

---

[42]See G. R. Beasley-Murray, *The Book of Revelation* (Grand Rapids: Eerdmans, 1974), pp. 129ff.

used in the New Testament of God in the role as judge. The wrath of the Lamb is another way of referring to Jesus as judge. "For the great day of their wrath has come" (Revelation 6:17). This is the context of the sixth seal. "Their" is the preferred reading here although one might expect "His." But the great day of *their* wrath means the judgment of God and the Lamb. "Who can stand?" No one dares stand before God and Christ in an attempt at self-justification either in this scene or in the case of Nineveh in the time of Nahum when he asked the same question (Nahum 1:6).

Thus far in the three points considered, arrival at the brink of the final judgment has been favored for the setting of the sixth seal: (1) the natural meaning of the first impression, (2) the possible meaning from Jesus and the Old Testament, and (3) the probable meaning from the context. Finally, the question is asked, "How does this fit into the different approaches to interpreting Revelation?" Not well at all, for most of them. To arrive at the brink of the final judgment so early in the book makes impossible major tenets of some approaches. On the other hand, this view of this passage supplies a clue that provides grounds for the cyclical approach to understanding the structure of the book. Three series of seven figures are going to follow one after the other in rapid succession. "Each of the three cycles cover the whole period from the writer's own to 'the end'; and the sixth seal, like the sixth trumpet and the seventh bowl, is concerned with things which immediately precede the end."[43] "This threefold attainment of the brink of the last day, without the day itself being described, is John's way of letting us know that his representations of the messianic judgments depict the last times from different vantage points."[44] Of the suggested interpretations listed above, either #1 (the final judgment) or #4 (a series of judgments ending with the final judgment)[45] suggests the cyclical type of approach and is supported by such an interpretation.

---

[43]C. Anderson Scott, *The New Century Bible: Revelation* (New York: Henry Frowde, n.d.), p. 185.

[44]G. R. Beasley-Murray, *Revelation,* p. 138.

[45]"But in the providence of God, the signs of His approach, and events more or less resembling those immediately preceding it, have occurred repeatedly: and this Book accordingly intimates, that they will occur repeatedly." W. H. Simcox, *The Revelation,* p. lvi.

Despite the numerous interpretations of this passage, the message is clear. While the martyrs are safe in Heaven, clothed in white and enjoying all the blessings in the presence of God, the terrified lost on earth in their final plight are not seeking to be saved, but plead for destruction to escape the coming judgment of the wicked.

A Comforting Interlude (7:1-17)

The Sealed Servants of God (1-8)

"Four angels" (1). Something unexpected occurs here. Instead of continuing with the opening of the seventh seal, the vision interjects an interlude describing two related scenes in Heaven. They give relief from judgment and encouragement to those still bound on earth by giving them this glimpse of life in Heaven. Four angels, situated so they can control all the winds of the earth, are not allowing a blow of destruction "on the land or on the sea or on any tree" (Revelation 7:1).

"Another angel" (2) comes from the east with instruction for the four angels to continue their restraint until he has put a mark on the forehead of those who are God's rather than the world's. They are "sealed" (Revelation 7:2) as belonging to Him, His slaves. Thus, they are protected by Him; no harm will come to them without God's knowledge and care. Even if death should come, they have their place in Heaven. They are marked as genuinely God's.

> Nevertheless, God's solid foundation stands firm, sealed with this inscription: "The Lord knows those who are his," and, "Everyone who confesses the name of the Lord must turn away from wickedness" (2 Timothy 2:19).

"Those who were sealed" (4). John does not count the number who were sealed; he does not even report he saw them at this time, but he did hear their number: 144,000. They were from the tribes of Israel. Does this mean old, literal Israel? Does this mean a new division of Jews to be perpetuated in Heaven with a group specially marked and set apart? Or does this mean new Israel, spiritual Israel, including both Jews and Gentiles who were faithful believers in Christ. Certainly this last would seem most likely. But why called Israel, and why 144,000? Just as you have twenty-four

elders, which is twelve and twelve, just as you have twelve gates and twelve foundations, which are the apostles and the patriarchs, now you have a number that is twelve times twelve—and then to show it is vastly more than that, and in fact representing the total, no matter how many—multiply 144 by a thousand.[46] This could be the number to represent the whole of the redeemed. The suggestion is made that it may well represent the Christians who are living on earth at any given time. This seems to be the best explanation. This group of 144,000 in Heaven is representing all the redeemed still alive on earth. After all, what value would come from sealing those who are already in Heaven unless there was some significant connection between them and those who were on earth living through the tribulations? They are the "redeemed from the earth" (Revelation 14:3) in a special sense.

A Great Multitude (9-17)

"Wearing white robes" (9). John looks up and sees a crowd so large that it would be difficult even to estimate its size. There are people in that number from every nation, race, and language. "Who are these in the white robes?" we wonder. An elder asks John this very question (Revelation 7:13). John replies, in essence, "You tell me; you're the one that knows." And the elder's answer is, "These are they who have come out of the great tribulation" (Revelation 7:14). The problem here is whether these have come out of one "Great Tribulation" or whether he is speaking of tribulation in general. Has this tribulation already transpired, or is it still in the future? Will it be at the very end just before the Lord's return? Tribulation is treated more fully as a special subject at the end of this chapter. Suffice it to say at this point that the very presence of tribulation all along makes the book of Revelation more meaningful through the ages, but the message indicates that tribulation will increase in intensity especially as the end draws near. But these redeemed in front of John have washed their robes in the blood of the Lamb. The blood Jesus shed in dying on the cross cleanses us from all sin (1 John 1:7; see Romans 3:25; Ephesians 1:7; 1 Peter 1:18, 19).

---

[46]No solution satisfactory to a majority, let alone to all, has been suggested for the order and the selection of the tribes named in the line-up of Israel at this point.

"Around the throne" (11) we find "all the angels" and the twenty-four elders and the four living beings. They are continuing to worship and praise God, much as they did in chapters 4 and 5. But attention is drawn back to the multitude in white robes (Revelation 7:13). They are "before the throne," and because "they have washed their robes . . . in the blood of the Lamb" (Revelation 7:14), special blessings are promised to them.

The interlude closes with a comforting list of blessings Christians have in Heaven (Revelation 7:15-17). First, God is there, and they have the privilege of giving worship-service to Him continually. The glory of His presence settles over them. Then follows a list of physical wants they will never be troubled with again. No hunger, no thirst, no scorching heat. And the Lamb who has been their sacrifice but is alive and victorious, the Lamb who has the wrath of a judge bent on meting out justice to the wicked, this same Lamb will be a shepherd for the redeemed. He will lead them to springs of living water. This is no picture of mass operation in Heaven. It comes down to being as personal as you can get. God will wipe away every tear from the eyes of both great and small.

Special Subject #4

Tribulation

Tribulation and the Problem of Suffering

Why do people suffer? This is a universal question asked at all times and in every place. Sometimes suffering comes from natural calamities, sometimes from deliberate acts of cruelty and aggression. At times it hits the just as well as the unjust. It may come in physical sickness, economic poverty, or purely mental anguish. This must be expected by all. The Christian must accept it with patience and even cheerfulness. Paul urges the Roman Christians to maintain such an attitude, "rejoicing in hope, persevering in tribulation, devoted to prayer" (Romans 12:12, New American Standard Bible).

Tribulation for wrong. Not all tribulation is a part of the ordinary lot of man. At times, it comes because of wrongdoing. It is impossible for man always to identify the tribulation directly resulting from his sin, but God has assured us that the consequences are there. The Psalmist tells about the worker of iniquity:

He has made a pit and dug it deep,
and he himself shall fall into the hole that he has made.
His mischief shall recoil upon himself,
and his violence fall on his own head (Psalm 7:15, 16, NEB).

Paul makes plain the punishment for sin.

There will be trouble and distress for every human being who does evil: first for the Jew, then for the Gentile; but glory, honor and peace for everyone who does good: first for the Jew, then for the Gentile. For God does not show favoritism (Romans 2:9).

Tribulation for the people of God. Tribulation has more meaning than simply the punishment of the wicked. Job insisted this when his friends tried to mark him as a particularly bad sinner because he was experiencing such severe suffering. Job denied that his suffering was great simply because his sin was great. Paul would agree. He was anxious to point out that the people of God must expect tribulation, not for the same reason as the wrongdoer, but suffering nevertheless. He quoted the Psalms (44:22): "For your sake we face death all day long; we are considered as sheep to be slaughtered" (Romans 8:36). He reminded the very community where he had been stoned: "Through many tribulations we must enter the kingdom of God" (Acts 14:22, NASB). Jesus had warned that the depth of a person's commitment would be seen in how he stood up under the hardships of life.

The seed sown on rocky ground stands for the man who, on hearing the word, accepts it at once with joy but as it strikes no root in him he has no staying-power, and when there is trouble or persecution on account of the word, he falls away at once (Matthew 13:21, NEB).

The example for Paul's suffering and our own is none other than Christ himself. A remarkable phrase about Christ is found in Hebrews, "son though he was, he learned obedience in the school of suffering" (Hebrews 5:8, NEB).

Therefore we do not lose heart. Though outwardly we are wasting away, yet inwardly we are being renewed day by day. For our

light and momentary troubles are achieving for us an eternal glory
that far outweighs them all. So we fix our eyes not on what is seen,
but on what is unseen. For what is seen is temporary, but what is
unseen is eternal (2 Corinthians 4:16-18).

Tribulation and the book of Revelation. Tribulation plays an
important role in the book of Revelation. All the way from the
tribulations among the churches of Asia to the battle of Armageddon, there are trials and tribulations in this apocalyptic book.
Sometimes it comes as persecution on the Christians. Sometimes
it is punishment on the world. Sometimes it takes the form of war
and its consequences, Sometimes it follows in the wake of calamities of nature. In much of this, it would seem that both the Christians and the world would be involved. Jesus has warned us not to
pull out the tares from the grainfield before the harvest for fear of
losing some of the wheat along with the weeds (Matthew 13:24-
30). Always it seems to bear to the world a call for repentance
before it is too late. Although suffering even to the point of dying
comes to the Christian, the cause of justice will be served in
the end.

The Great Tribulation

Interpreting the book of Revelation is like putting together a
jigsaw puzzle. The central, important piece of the puzzle is the
second coming of Christ. Other important pieces are the judgment and the end of time. Still other pieces that must be put into
place in order to complete the eschatological picture are the millennium, the resurrection, and the great tribulation. How long
must we face tribulation? It will continue to the end of this earthly
existence. In fact, it would seem that the most severe trials of all
can be expected toward the end of time. One passage of Revelation uses the precise expression *great tribulation* and has become a
center of attention to some in their reconstruction of the end
times.

Pertinent passages. Three passages are grouped together in the
conventional treatment of the great tribulation: one is in the
prophecy of Daniel, another in a discourse of Jesus, and the third
involves the last times of John's Revelation.

At that time Michael, the great prince who protects your people,
will arise. There will be a time of distress such as has not happened

from the beginning of nations until then. But at that time your people—everyone whose name is found written in the book—will be delivered. Multitudes who sleep in the dust of the earth will awake: some to everlasting life, others to shame and everlasting contempt (Daniel 12:1, 2).

For then there will be a great tribulation, such as has not occurred since the beginning of the world until now, nor ever shall. And unless those days had been cut short, no life would have been saved; but for the sake of the elect those days shall be cut short (Matthew 24:21, 22, NASB; see also Mark 13:19, 20).

Then one of the elders asked me, "These in white robes—who are they, and where did they come from?"
I answered, "Sir, you know."
And he said, "These are they who have come out of the great tribulation; they have washed their robes and made them white in the blood of the Lamb" (Revelation 7:13, 14).

Schools of Interpretation. The time of this great tribulation and the individuals involved remain grounds for ceaseless debates among interpreters of Revelation. It becomes obvious that one's view of the tribulation is greatly dependent upon his overall interpretation of the whole book. This provides a clear illustration how the interpretation of particular details is influenced by each of the five approaches already noted in the study of Revelation.

The Spiritualist, who interprets the action of Revelation as a figurative presentation of the conflict of good and evil through the ages, sees the great tribulation as the whole gamut from the passion of Christ—or the stoning of Stephen—to the consummation at the end of time (one even extends the period of tribulation back to the time of Adam).

The Preterist, who identifies the action of Revelation with the time of the author and its message as observation rather than predictive prophecy, sees the tribulation as simply the Roman persecutions of his time.

The Continuous-historical school, being locked in to a chronological arrangement of the action in Revelation, must make an early place for the great tribulation since its reference appears in the seventh chapter of Revelation.

The Historical-cycle interpretation has no trouble fitting a tribulation period at the end, but this would also include the possibility of recurring fulfillments along the way to the end. Thus the abomination of desolation (that is, the desecration of God's holy altar by, for example, sacrificing a sow to Zeus on the altar of God, thus resulting in the spiritual desolation of the site [Daniel 11:31]) in the time of Antiochus Epiphanes (168 B.C.) does not disallow the abomination of desolation (the destruction of the temple) in the Roman conquest of Jerusalem (A.D.70; see Matthew 24:15), and these do not disallow still another type of fulfillment in the final climax (2 Thessalonians 2:8-12). A number of exegetes suggest that eschatological events described in Revelation at the end have already been foreshadowed in earlier historical events.

The Futurist interpretation, which views the whole of Revelation beginning with the fourth chapter as describing the final period before Christ's coming and a reign of a thousand years on earth, looks at the great tribulation as a seven-year period indicated in the book of Daniel.

Another piece to the puzzle, related to the tribulation and the futurist approach is the rapture, or "catching away" of the believers from the earth at the coming of the Lord. If one holds to the doctrine of the rapture, there are three ways of coupling the tribulation to it:

1. The ones who believe the rapture takes place before the time of the great tribulation on earth are called *pre-tribulationists.* This position pictures Jesus as coming to receive His saints before the years of suffering on the earth, and then coming again with His saints for another coming after the tribulation. But who is left of the people of God to suffer in the tribulation then? Under this view, the Jews, the nation of Israel, remain and are particularly involved in the suffering of the great tribulation.

2. Others, however, believe that the church begins to suffer the tribulation on earth and that the rapture occurs midway through the tribulation. Instead of locating the rapture in chapter 4 of Revelation, as the pretribulationists, they place it between the second and third woes. The last trumpet of Paul, the seventh trumpet of Revelation, a resurrection, and the last half of the seventieth week of Daniel figure in this reconstruction. This is called the *mid-tribulation theory.*

3. Still others, however, maintain that the church will not be raptured until the manifestation of Christ occurs at the end of the tribulation period. The second coming of Christ, the day of judgment for the beast and the false prophet, the glory for the church and repentant Israel, and the end of the tribulation period, all are a part of the same "day of the Lord." This is called the *post-tribulation view*.

Long lists of Scripture passages are given in support of each of these views, but each use is wholly dependent on one's prior commitment to the placing of other pieces in the puzzle, such as the millennium, the judgment, the resurrection, and, finally, one's overall interpretation approach. The danger is evident that so much effort be given to determine the time and sequence that the basic meaning is lost in the controversy. Perhaps the reason for the lack of further identification is to keep us from placing the tribulation period in a remote time that has no connection with us. The coming of Christ is meant to be imminent—so also the presence of tribulation. This is to be a time of judgment upon the nations for sin and rejection of Christ. It is a period of such suffering never known in the world before. A great multitude is saved from all nations and kindred and people and tongues—but only after martyrdom is experienced. The Christians will draw relentless hostility in consequence of their testimony and activity; but in the face of it all they are urged to endure, to prove themselves, and to be patient.

The real message of tribulation is not how it fits into a theory of interpretation, but how it fits into one's own life. The Christian does not glorify suffering as the Hindu. He does not heroize it as the Stoic did. But the Christian uses tribulation to come closer to Christ. In some degree, suffering comes to all men—expect it and look to the Lord. Tribulation comes in a particular way to the wicked. The message to him is, "Repent and look to the Lord." Tribulation comes to the righteous also. His word is, "Be faithful, the Lord is coming again." It has been said, "Tribulations are but the rounds of the ladder set up on earth, whereby the soul goes upward to God, and God comes down to us."

> Who shall separate us from the love of Christ? Shall trouble or hardship or persecution or famine or nakedness or danger or sword.... No in all these things we are more than conquerors through him who loved us (Romans 8:35, 37).

CHAPTER FIVE

Woes Again

Revelation 8:1—9:21

When a person grows up in the downtown of a city, he becomes conscious of the noises that mingle to identify the metropolis. Every morning, the giant begins to throb with activity as it comes alive. The constant drone of heavy equipment, the swish of mounting traffic in the street, the approaching siren of a lone emergency vehicle—all cut through the still air of a new day.

The noises of the woods at night are entirely different. A moving animal on the prowl, leaves rustling in the breeze, a single call from the wild breaks out, loud and clear—all this is natural to that habitat. Even a corn field at midnight has noises of its own. Then, too, a person gets accustomed to noises. He can live within a few hundred feet of the Florida Turnpike and yet become oblivious to the constant roar of passing cars and trucks.

But what are the sounds associated with Heaven? A voice speaks forth like a trumpet, and you know an announcement is coming. Another voice is heard, as pleasant as rippling water. Loud voices are heard, like the roar of a lion. Some moments are accentuated with the thunder of a storm. But the sound that seems to characterize Heaven best is its music, reverberating through its corridors but reaching its crescendo around the throne of God. The songs of praise and worship, sung by countless choirs, are heard from one end of Heaven to the other.

After drawing attention to the importance of sound, it should be obvious that the lack of any sound would make silence itself appear deafening. To "hear" silence would be striking in Heaven as well as on earth. In worlds filled with sounds, no one sound would be as remarkable as silence itself. This is what marks the opening of the seventh seal and the reading of the eighth and ninth chapters of Revelation—a period of silence of about half an hour in Heaven. But why did it come? What was its purpose?

To note the long period of silence between the Old Testament and the New Testament may prove helpful. A four-hundred-year period of silence, when God did not speak through His prophets or in other special ways that we know about, separated the close of the Old Testament period and the establishment of the New Covenant. The closing of the old period and the beginning of the new cannot be mistaken. Nor can the importance of the new be unnoticed.

Could it be something like this was intended to separate the series of the seven seals from the coming series of the seven trumpets? On the other hand, they may not be entirely separated because the last seal introduces the first trumpet. In the cyclic approach to understanding the book of Revelation, the period of silence provides a mark of punctuation closing the series of the seals and making ready for the sounding of the first trumpet. If the cyclic theory is correct, it provides a moment for a return in thought back to the beginning of the former series in order to travel another track through time once more. But why traverse the same span of time again? For one thing, this pattern occurred frequently as God made himself known in visions and dreams. Jacob's son, Joseph, had two dreams. In one, Joseph's sheaf of grain stood upright while the sheaves of his brothers gathered around it and bowed down to it (Genesis 37:7). In the other, the sun and moon and eleven stars were bowing down to him (Genesis 37:9). Both of these dreams had the same prediction that Joseph would reach a position of superiority over his brothers, and the second included his position above his father and his mother as well. This was the same message using different figures.

The same repetition was true of Pharaoh's dreams. He saw seven ugly and gaunt cows come up out of the Nile and eat seven sleek, fat cows. In another dream, he saw seven healthy and good heads of grain swallowed up by seven thin and scorched heads of grain (Genesis 41:1-7). The import of the dreams was the same. God was predicting the seven years of plenty and the seven years of famine that Egypt was going to have. "The reason the dream was given to Pharaoh in two forms is that the matter has been firmly decided by God, and God will do it soon" (Genesis 41:32).

Likewise Daniel is a good example of one who interpreted several different visions with different figures but covering the same span of time and having similar messages. Daniel was able through God's help to tell Nebuchadnezzar both his dream about the huge statue and its being smashed by a rock (Daniel 2:31ff) as well as the interpretation of the rise and fall of kingdoms. But Daniel also had a vision of four beasts, and these beasts seemingly turned out to represent much the same kingdoms as had already been represented in the statue he had interpreted before (Daniel 7:1-28). Then, in the next chapter (Daniel 8), Daniel tells of another vision in which he saw a ram with two horns and a goat with one large horn, and after them the rise of still more kingdoms. This, too, covers some of the same period. These are cycles that cover the same span with different figures and different details.

Since, in the book of Revelation, the sixth seal has taken us to the final signs of the Day of Judgment, one expects to go on to the judgment itself in the next frame. This we do not find. Instead, there is the definite break signified by the period of silence and the introduction of another series of seven. The most reasonable expectation is that we are returning to view again the period from John to the judgment, and within the cycle, we will expect the second coming of Christ to be included. We can only follow where the text leads us.

Prelude

Overview

After the sixth seal with its final signs before the judgment, one expects the conclusion immediately. Instead of the opening of the seventh seal, however, a delay is made for the sealing of the 144,000. After this is done, then the seventh seal is opened. Another surprise results. No new action follows, in fact, no sound is heard for half an hour. Then the stage is set for a new scene. Seven important angels are given seven trumpets ready to sound a call. But more preparation is necessary. Another angel goes up before God with the smoke of incense together with the prayers from the saints. Then he combines this with fire from the altar and throws them to the earth. It is as though this combination of prayers from Christians on earth and the fire of God inaugurates the action. Thunder, lightning, and an earthquake result.

The message of the trumpets is one of continued hardship and suffering. The first four have to do with catastrophes of nature: the land, the sea, the inland waters, and the celestial bodies. Everything is controlled in the destruction. No more than one third is allowed to be taken away. Although some human life is

119

lost along the way, no direct assault is made to take life. Still, in the fifth trial—by locusts—the command is to bring torture but not death. The sixth trumpet leads to the release of four angels at the borders along the Euphrates. The advancing hordes of horsemen result in the slaughter of one third of humanity. But the remaining of the wicked do not repent.

Whereas the plight of the sufferers in the seals after the first seem to include both the believers and the nonbelievers, the second set of seven seems particularly to be aimed at the rejecters of Christ. Still it is clear that the Christians are there because they have to be distinguished from the non-Christians by the seal of God on their foreheads. It must be observed that the trials of the trumpets are a continued enumeration of tribulation between the time of John and the coming judgment; but it is not what you can call a parallel course, but one that is concurrent. The fifth and sixth seals have scenes in Heaven and on earth, but the fifth and sixth trumpets dip into the demonic realms.

Key Message

"The rest of mankind that were not killed by these plagues still did not repent of the work of their hands" (Revelation 9:20a).

Glossary

Read through chapters 8 and 9 of Revelation. As you come to the terms listed below, note the explanation.

Chapter 8

Silence in Heaven	A half-hour interlude between the opening of the seals and the sounding of the trumpets, marking a separation between and the importance of that which had ended and that which was about to begin. Perhaps it was a warning against taking what was to follow as a continuation of the last series and an indication the new series was another beginning.
Seven angels	A special group of angels, superior in rank—"who stand before God." This may include Gabriel (Luke 1:19).
Another angel	Certainly not Christ, for there is no indication He is intended, and He is not so

	designated. This is not one of the seven angels above, but is perhaps of the same rank (see also Revelation 7:2).
Golden censer	The dish or tray where coals from the fire of the altar were placed and the incense put on top of it (Leviticus 10:1; 16:12).
Altar (incense)	Not the altar of burnt offering referred to in Revelation 6:9, but the altar of incense. In the earthly tabernacle, this was in the Holy Place just outside the curtain separating it from the Holy of Holies. It was the place where the Presence of God met man as the priest represented the people (Exodus 30:6; Hebrews 9:3-6). This golden altar in Heaven was situated in front of God's throne.
Thunder, lightning, earthquake	An evidence of the power, majesty and glory of God (see Revelation 4:5), and the earthquake adds the element of judgment (see Revelation 6:12).
First trumpet	Used for assembly (Numbers 10:7), for warning of danger (Ezekiel 33:3f), and for judgment. Also a note of the last times (1 Corinthians 15:52; 1 Thessalonians 4:16).
Hail and fire mixed with blood	Destruction brought by hail storm and fire (lightning?). The results included bloodshed and mark it as more than natural.
One third of the earth burned*	In the first four trumpets, the destruction comes for the most part upon the world of nature, not man. The consequences are limited to one third in this instance, limited but considerable.
One third of the trees burned	No plausible explanation of the one third has been given. Perhaps both the percentage and the destruction are symbolic warnings of great losses to the evil among men.

---

*missing in the King James

All the grass burned No explanation is given for the total destruction of the grass in comparison with the limitation in the earlier plagues. The presence of grass is assumed again in Revelation 9:4.

Second trumpet Whereas the first trumpet dealt with catastrophes on the land, the second involved the sea.

Mountain thrown into the sea See Jeremiah 51:25; Psalm 46:2. A scene of terror to the godless, but to be viewed without fear by God's people. Could refer to the downfall of a great heathen power.

One third of the seas turned into blood This is a reminder of the plague in Egypt (Exodus 7:17), but it could be symbolic of still worse conditions.

One third of the sea-creatures died As a result of this calamity, one third of the marine life died.

One third of the ships destroyed This is not simply a matter of the pollution of water because a considerable part of the ships were destroyed. It is not a natural occurrence, but once again it could be the symbolic representation of losses suffered by those who dwell on the earth.

Third trumpet Inland waters and springs affected now.

Star fell from the sky A shooting star or a meteor is indicated. The name Wormwood is given, associating it again with Old Testament passages (for example, Jeremiah 9:15).

One third of the water turned bitter This is the reverse of the helpful miracle for the Israelites at Mara (Exodus 15:25). Later occasions are associated with the bitter fruits of idolatry (Deuteronomy 29:17).

Many people died Although the term *wormwood* denotes something noxious, in this case it works as poison. It brought trouble, sorrow, and death.

Fourth trumpet Now even the lights in the sky are affected.

One third of the sun struck The sun is the most dependable member of nature, but it lost one third of its power. The ninth plague in Egypt had to do with darkness (Exodus 10:21ff).

One third of the moon The failure of light is a serious judgment coming from God whether it is the direct radiance of the sun or the reflected light from the moon.

One third of the stars In the Old Testament, light is associated with salvation, joy, wisdom, and truth. Any diminishing of light would symbolically signify losing its figurative attributes.

Eagle (angel**) The seven-trumpet series is divided into two groups of four and three just as the seals were. This division is marked by the announcement of the eagle (this reading better attested in the manuscripts than angel), denoting the extreme severity of the coming trumpets. *Eagle* can also be translated "vulture," making the announcement all the more ominous.

Woe! Woe! Woe! The three woes denote three catastrophes that are coming. They are synonymous with the fifth, sixth, and seventh trumpets.

Chapter 9

Fifth trumpet (first woe) The remaining trumpets are directed to the "inhabitants of the earth," the term regularly used of the unbelieving world. Whereas the former trumpets involve primarily the world of nature and only indirectly the fate of men, now the catastrophes are aimed directly at human beings.

Star A fallen angel, probably the devil, an evil agent that is permitted to introduce trials toward his own destruction.

Key The evil agent is given the key. Only by the permission of God can he use it.

Abyss (bottomless pit**) Place where the demons in the Gadarene did not want to be sent (Luke 8:31) and

---

**King James translation

Paul refers to it as the place of the dead (Romans 10:7). All other uses are in Revelation. A narrow shaft at the top that broadens farther on, but can be locked securely from above. Inhabited by evil spirits but under God's control. This is the intermediate place of confinement for the fallen angels.

Locusts Reminiscent of the eighth plague in Egypt (Exodus 10:1-20) and the plague of Joel's day, warning of judgment and urging repentance (chapters 1 and 2). An invasion of ordinary locusts is devastating enough, but these demonic locusts have the sting of scorpions and harm only human beings not having the seal of God on their foreheads.

Abaddon (Apollyon) *Abaddon* is the Hebrew word for destruction and is often used with death and with Hell (Job 26:6, Psalm 88:11, Proverbs 15:11). *Apollyon* is the Greek present participle for the verb "to destroy." The substantive would be "Destroyer." This is the name given to the king of the demonic locusts.

Sixth trumpet (second woe) Tribulation is intensified. At the fifth trumpet, they were severely hurt; now some are killed.

Four angels at Euphrates Probably not the same angels as at Revelation 7:1 restraining the winds from harming land and sea. This has now happened (Revelation 8:6-11). These angels were at the four corners of the earth, not the Euphrates. Why the Euphrates? Is it indicative of the Parthians? Or the boundaries of the Roman Empire? Rather it is probably because that was the ancient promised boundary of Israel (Genesis 15:18).

One third of mankind killed In the destruction brought from the sounding of the trumpets until now, some deaths had been involved, but only in the

	sixth does it reach the proportion of one third of mankind.
Mounted troops	The number of the cavalry was heard to be 200,000,000. The heads of the horses looked like lions, and from their mouths and by their tails, they inflicted injury.
Three plagues	The horses spewed from their mouths three deadly plagues of fire, smoke, and sulfur.

Content Notes

Seventh Seal (8:1-5)

Silence in Heaven (1)

The immediate result of opening the seventh seal was a period of silence for half an hour. What was this for? It could be done to draw more attention, both from the seer (John himself) and from the occupants of Heaven, as well as from the countless readers down through the ages who have read and studied the record of this revelation. Whatever follows this impressive silence must be of the utmost importance.

Some have suggested the silence could be to mark unmistakably the separation of the series of the seals from that of the trumpets. If this is the whole of the answer, the seventh seal could have been opened before the interlude of the sealing of the 144,000 (chapter 7) and the seventh seal kept with the other six more clearly.

Perhaps the reason is not simply importance or separation, but also anticipation. This gives us time to think about what is coming. Will we arrive at the eternal rest in the seventh seal, or will it be the actual judgment? Instead of either of these, John witnesses the setting of the stage for a new series of visions.

The Stage Is Set (2-5)

Seven angels stand forward and each is given a trumpet. Another angel stands by the golden altar of incense before the throne of God. He performs two duties. He delivers up both the smoke of the incense and the prayers of the saints on earth in the presence of God. What were the saints praying about? Could it be for relief from the trials of life? From the injustices the souls under the altar had been praying about? The angel then heaps coals from the altar on top of the incense on the censer and throws it earthward. The immediate result is thunder and lightning, but we have seen those before in the majesty and power of the one upon the throne (Revelation 4:5). To these, however, is now added an earthquake, an indication of coming judgment (Revelation 6:12). The combination of the prayers of the saints from earth and the fire of God from Heaven has been sufficient to open the action in a new series of visions. The stage is set.

The Trumpets Are Sounded (8:6-13)

The First Trumpet (6, 7)

As the first trumpet is sounded, destruction comes upon certain areas of nature. The calamities that follow are related to the plagues suffered in Egypt when Pharaoh refused to let the people of God go forth:

> So the Lord rained hail on the land of Egypt; hail fell and light-ning flashed back and forth. It was the worst storm in all the land of Egypt since it had become a nation. Throughout Egypt hail struck everything in the fields—both men and animals (Exodus 9:23-25).

Perhaps the *mixed with blood* (Revelation 8:7) may have refer-ence to the bloodshed associated with the figure. But the conse-quences specifies nothing about the loss of life—only the destruc-tion of land and trees and grass. And the blood seems to be already mingled with the hail and fire before it falls, so perhaps it indicates the blood from former sins returned upon the heads of the sinful (cf. Genesis 9:6). But the ruin is not complete except in the case of the green grass. This is not the final step. The loss is limited to one third—a substantial percentage, but not the major part. The whole of this series of trumpets seems to hold a limita-tion on the destruction that there might be reconsideration, true repentance that includes reformation. This is aimed at the "inhab-itants of the earth," the unbelievers of the world.

The Second Trumpet (8, 9)

The moving of mountains is posed as one of the impossibilities for man, but undertaken today by either tremendous blasts or scoop by scoop with the earth movers. But the prospect of a huge mountain, volcanic or not, cast in its totality into the sea is awesome, reserved for God, and therefore terrorizing to the godless. But when it brings destruction upon one third of the sea life, panic strikes the soul. It is not simply a matter of polluted water as in an oil spill or waste disposal. One third of the ships are also destroyed. Whereas the seals had brought one kind of tribulation, this is another type of suffering entirely.

The Third Trumpet (10, 11)

The first two trumpets have devastated the land and the sea. Now the third poisons the inland waters, the rivers, and the springs that are vital to the drinking supplies of the living beings. A star identified with Wormwood falls like a flaming meteor to bring this bitterness to the waters. This Wormwood is encountered frequently in the Old Testament, a bitter wood used in connection with the consequences of idolatry. (See, for example, Deuteronomy 29:18; Jeremiah 9:15; 23:15.) Calamity, sorrow, and bitterness result.

The Fourth Trumpet (12, 13)

Light has always been the sign of God's wisdom (1 Corinthians 2:6-13), His understanding (Psalm 119:130), and His Word (Psalm 119:105). The darkening of the sun, moon, and stars is an indication that man is living in a diminished light, foreshadowing utter darkness and loss of the presence of God that may be ahead. These first four trumpets are grouped in a series of four like the four seals. These first four are minor judgments designed to serve as trumpets of warning, giving opportunity to repent and turn again in reformation.

The last three trumpets are more severe in nature. They are preceded by a screaming cry of an eagle as he flies across the sky giving special warning of the woes to follow.

Trumpets of Woe! (9:1-21)

The Fifth Trumpet and the First Woe (1-12)

Isaiah made reference to a fallen morning star (commonly referred to as Lucifer, from the Latin translation of the Hebrew), perhaps a figure for the king of Babylon (Isaiah 14:12). Upon the return of the seventy from their evangelistic tour, Jesus said He had seen Satan fall like lightning from Heaven (Luke 10:18). Now John tells of seeing a fallen star who was given a key to the Abyss

(Revelation 9:1). Probably the occasions are all different, but there may be a common involvement of Satan.[47]

The agent using the key here and his purpose for using it are quite different from the scene in Revelation 20:1ff. Here in chapter 9, the agent is a fallen star, and he is unlocking the Abyss and loosing the loathsome plague of locusts. In chapter 20, an angel from Heaven binds Satan and locks the Abyss. Although God is allowing demonic powers to have their way for a time in this instance, it is only toward their own ultimate destruction and brought on by the unrepentant inhabitants of the earth. All through the Old Testament, one finds examples of the judgments given in the form of locust plagues. In Egypt, the eighth plague was the locusts, and in Joel 1 and 2, a description is given of a dreadful attack from the locusts. But here in the onslaught begun at the sounding of the fifth trumpet, the locusts have a demonic dimension added to the already volatile destructive power of the locusts. They have stings like scorpions in their tails. Their appearance is gruesome in its particulars: like human faces, crowns (something like the victor's crown) of gold, women's hair, lions' teeth, something like breastplates of iron, and thunder-sounding wings. Another feature differing from normal locusts is their assignment. They are not to attack vegetation, but only human beings—and of these only the ones who do not have the seal of God on their foreheads. Their torture is worse than death to the human beings, but still they live on. The plague lasts for five months, which is the ordinary life span of the locust. The king of the Abyss is one named Destroyer. This is the first woe.

Sixth Trumpet and the Second Woe (13-21)

The next woe is still more severe. Men suffered severely in the last catastrophe, but they were not killed. Now one third of mankind tastes death. This death is meted out, not by plagues of nature, not by attacks from animals or insects, but by hordes of mounted troops. They come from the boundaries of the west, the Euphrates. They are fearsome in appearance. Once again, as in

---

[47]A great variety of identifications are suggested for the star, all the way from Nero, Satan, or a fallen angel; or on the other hand, the preaching of the gospel, a good angel, or even Jesus himself. See Leon Morris, *The Revelation,* p. 127.

the last trumpet, they seem to loose demonic forces. It seems without point to attempt certain identification through the descriptive details. For example, those determined to show connections with first-century fulfillment call attention to the deadly power in the horses' mouths and their tails. Of course, this fits the Parthians, they insist. The Parthians are supposed to be the only warriors of antiquity whose cavalry rode and shot volleys of arrows at the same time. Even as they retreated, they were known to twist around and shoot a volley over the horses' tails. Thus, their power was both to the front over the horses' mouths or to the rear over their tails. Is this the true interpretation? One is prone to withhold judgment, however, after he listens to an explanation equally difficult to accept coming from the futurist, who insists that it represents the modern bomber planes that have gunners at the mouth of the planes spewing fire and smoke, while the rear gunners are doing the same from the tail of the plane. The particulars are unfathomable, but the message is plain. Mankind will suffer to the point that a significant percent of mankind will be killed.

Once again, as in the first series of seven, the last in the series does not follow the sixth immediately. Instead, at this point, a summary is given. Those of humanity who have not died in the trials and woes thus far still do not repent. This indicates that the basis of the tribulations is not simply vengeance for sin and injustice, but that it is not too late for some. There is still time to repent. Even their basic sins are enumerated:

> They did not stop worshiping demons, and idols of gold, silver, bronze, stone and wood—idols that cannot see or hear or walk. Nor did they repent of their murders, their magic arts, their sexual immorality or their thefts (Revelation 9:20, 21).

Special Subject #5

Judgment

Everyone knows deep in his heart that judgment is inevitable. Somehow, as a part of his built-in equipment, every person has a conscience. This is innate, he was born with it. Every person, no matter how remote the time of his records in antiquity or how remote the place he lives today, reflects a conviction there is a line beyond which he cannot go without doing wrong, even in his own sight. This moral imperative that urges him to do right is one of the strong marks that separate man from the beast of the field.

Coupled with this feeling of right and wrong is also a sense of consequences for violating the dictates of his conscience. A person may choke off the pleading of his or her conscience to such an extent that its voice becomes a whisper and then may cease to be heard altogether. Even in such an extreme case of depravity, he still can remember the day he feared the coming judgment. He may try to deny this as an individual case, but it is clearly seen as a testimony of the whole of experience that nature suggests a judgment. Paul's words, "A man reaps what he sows," have become axiomatic to the world as well as the Christian. But what is usually presumed for the context is the sowing of wild oats and reaping evil for the evil that has been planted. Paul goes on to use the statement positively as well as negatively. Those who sow to gratify their fleshly desires will reap destruction, but those who sow to please the Spirit will reap eternal life (Galatians 6:7-10).

Not only does nature suggest a judgment, but justice demands a time of judgment. In the name of justice, the accounts left unfair in life need balancing. Insofar as the cries of justice will be heard, certain conditions must be met. Someone in control must be just. He must have all knowledge and be able to weigh all of the factors involved. He must be able to pursue the demands both of righteousness and justice, but also adding love, grace, and mercy, and come to a final decision worthy of the one true God. Experience and observation, however, have brought the conclusion that, on this earth, the wicked have sometimes prospered, and the good have suffered more than their share of hardship. If life is to close with a settling of accounts, justice demands a reckoning day sometime ahead.

More important to the final answer, as well as to the study of Revelation, one looks for a Judgment Day because God declares it. We can well expect a final Judgment Day ahead, not only because nature suggests it and justice demands it, but assuredly God has declared it.

Judgment in the Old Testament

Adam and Eve were under judgment as they were driven from the Garden of Eden. All of mankind has suffered physical death as consequences of their sin. In the time of Noah, the whole world perished in the flood except Noah and his family. This judgment took almost all of mankind. After the call of Abraham, and the later exodus from Egypt, God made a covenant with His people in the time of Moses. They finally entered into the promised land. Time after time, however, Israel departed from the ways God had commanded of them. As a result, they were oppressed by the hostile neighboring people. Time after time, God raised up a deliverer. But there were continued judgments throughout the Old Testament period. "He comes to judge the earth. He will judge the world in righteousness and the peoples in his truth" (Psalm 96:13).

God brought judgment upon the heathen nations who persecuted His people and worshiped idols. Amos listed six nations and their judgments in the first two chapters of his writing. He continued with judgment on Israel and Judah themselves. Through Amos, God said to Israel:

> "I overthrew some of you as I overthrew Sodom and Gomorrah. You were like a burning stick snatched from the fire, yet you have not returned to me," declares the Lord. "Therefore this is what I will do to you, Israel, and because I will do this to you, prepare to meet your God, O Israel" (Amos 4:11, 12).

Finally, Jeremiah had the sad task of delivering a whole series of judgments on the kingdom of Judah, doomed for destruction and exile. He used eloquent language and often times repeated striking phrases to deliver his truths. An example of such a phrase included "sword, famine, and plague" (notice the order and symbols of the second, third, and fourth seals in Revelation 6:8). This phrase was used in Jeremiah fifteen times, as in Jeremiah 14:12:

> Although they fast, I will not listen to their cry; though they offer burnt offerings and grain offerings, I will not accept them. Instead, I will destroy them with the sword, famine and plague.

Some judgments were given as punishment: "I will punish you as your deeds deserve" (Jeremiah 21:14). Some were given as discipline, seeking repentance and reformation:

131

Therefore as surely as I live, declares the Sovereign Lord, because you have defiled my sanctuary with all your vile images and detestable practices, I myself will withdraw my favor; I will not look on you with pity or spare you. A third of your people will die of the plague or perish by famine inside you; a third will fall by the sword outside your walls; and a third I will scatter to the winds and pursue with drawn sword (Ezekiel 5:11, 12).

And some were given as purification: "Then will I purify the lips of the peoples . . ." (Zephaniah 3:9-20).

Judgment in the New Testament

Just as man is destined to die once, and after that to face judgment, so Christ was sacrificed once to take away the sins of many people; and he will appear a second time, not to bear sin, but to bring salvation to those who are waiting for him (Hebrews 9:27, 28).

For he has set a day when he will judge the world with justice by the man he has appointed. He has given proof of this to all men by raising him from the dead (Acts 17:31).

He commanded us to preach to the people and to testify that he is the one whom God appointed as judge of the living and the dead (Acts 10:42).

Judgment in Teaching of Jesus

When the Son of Man comes in his glory, and all the angels with him, he will sit on his throne in heavenly glory. All the nations will be gathered before him, and he will separate the people one from another as a shepherd separates the sheep from the goats (Matthew 25:31, 32).

Judgment in Paul

But because of your stubbornness and your unrepentant heart, you are storing up wrath against yourself for the day of God's wrath, when his righteous judgment will be revealed. God "will give to each person according to what he has done." To those who by persistence in doing good seek glory, honor and immortality, he will give eternal life. But for those who are self-seeking and who reject the truth and follow evil, there will be wrath and anger. There will be trouble and distress for every human being who does evil: first for the Jew, then for the Gentile; but glory, honor and peace for everyone who does good: first for the Jew, then for the Gentile (Romans 2:5-10).

For anyone who eats and drinks without recognizing the body of the Lord eats and drinks judgment on himself. That is why many among you are weak and sick, and a number of you have fallen asleep. But if we judged ourselves, we would not come under judgment. When we are judged by the Lord, we are being disciplined so that we will not be condemned with the world (1 Corinthians 11:29-32).

Therefore judge nothing before the appointed time; wait till the Lord comes. He will bring to light what is hidden in darkness and will expose the motives of men's hearts. At that time each will receive his praise from God (1 Corinthians 4:5).

For you know very well that the day of the Lord will come like a thief in the night. While people are saying, "Peace and safety," destruction will come on them suddenly ... (1 Thessalonians 5:2, 3).

Judgment in Peter

For it is time for judgment to begin with the family of God; and if it begins with us, what will the outcome be for those who do not obey the gospel of God? (1 Peter 4:17).

Different Kinds of Judgment in the Old and New Testaments

1. Immediate.

Some judgments follow directly as consequences of sin. This may be punishment; it may be a warning, giving opportunity to repent; it may be assistance calling for resistance to a wrong direction. Some judgments may be shared by the innocent. This calls for patience and endurance on the part of the faithful.

2. Partial

Some judgments are delayed, giving further opportunity for repentance before retribution is demanded. In any event, the whole matter is not closed. The final verdict is still pending.

3. Corporate

Some judgments are on whole nations or groups. Consequences are suffered because of association only. Eternal salvation is not based upon corporate consequences, but partial judgments may be suffered by association, and consequences must be shared.

4. Personal

Particular judgment is exercised on the individual immediately upon death so that he will be going either to a place of peace and joy from the first moment or to a place of agony. Thus, an individual knows his fate immediately.

5. Final judgment

This is the official and public recognition of each individual's state in the general judgment of the great white throne.

> For God shall bring every deed into judgment,
>> including every hidden thing,
>> whether it is good or evil (Ecclesiastes 12:14).

Judgment in the Book of Revelation

As much as a book of Christ's second coming, the book of Revelation is the account of the judgments of God. It includes partial judgments given along the way and of the general judgment at the end time, which closes the books forever.

The three clear cycles—the seals, the trumpets, and the bowls—are three series of judgments that begin in the time of John and lead up to the very Day of Judgment, but fall back to follow the approach again on another path. Finally, the day is described when the twentieth chapter is reached. The dawning of that day is noted in passage after passage throughout Revelation:

> He said in a loud voice, "Fear God and give him glory, because the hour of his judgment has come" (Revelation 14:7).

> Take your sickle and reap, because the time to reap has come, for the harvest of the earth is ripe (Revelation 14:15).

> Then I saw a great white throne and him who was seated on it. . . . The dead were judged according to what they had done as recorded in the books (Revelation 20:11, 12).

This is the realistic moment everyone knows is indicated in human life. Nature suggests it, justice demands it, and in the book of Revelation, God most clearly declares it. This is a theme to pursue as one proceeds to study the Apocalypse of John.

Cyclical Interpretation of Revelation

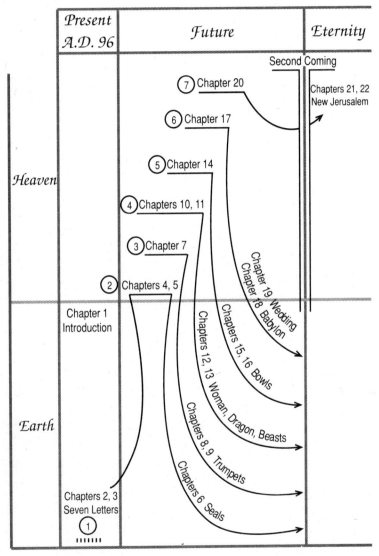

Numerals in a "○" indicate the seven cycles of Revelation

CHAPTER SIX

True Witnesses

Revelation 10:1—11:19

A little girl pleaded with her father to take her with him on one of his voyages. He was a rugged sea captain. Although he did not shrink from the occasional storms that made his trips dangerous, he was reluctant to risk the hazards with his daughter along. But finally he agreed to take her. Before many days had gone by, what he feared most is just what happened. A bad storm hit full blast. The captain determined he must take the helm himself. He was at his post steering the ship, when, to his horror, he saw his little daughter struggling to get across the wave-washed deck to where he was. After nearly being swept overboard several times, she finally reached her destination. The father held her securely in one arm as he kept the steering wheel in proper position with the other hand. He shouted to her above the noise of the storm, "What are you doing here?"

"I had to ask you a question," she replied. "Is the God of the land the same as the God of the sea?"

Without a moment's hesitation, he answered, "Yes, He is. Pray to God. He is the Lord of heaven and earth and both the land and the sea!"

The figures of Revelation vary greatly: the seals, the trumpets, the bowls, the beasts, the dragon, the sinful woman; but the message is the same. God is Lord over all.

Prelude

Overview

The opening of the seals has introduced the preaching of the gospel, the coming of tribulation in wars, persecutions, famine, pestilence, and death. But a window in Heaven shows the saved clothed in white robes by the altar of God and the lost on earth

137

actually seeking destruction rather than facing the inevitable judgment and its consequences. John must be viewing here in the sixth seal the time just before the end, and we expected the seventh seal would surely depict the coming of the Lord and the judgment. But instead, the opening of the seventh seal was delayed.

An interlude increased the suspense in anticipating the concluding scenes. The 144,000 had to be sealed on earth to insure their salvation no matter what came, and a scene was seen in Heaven showing the joy and rewards of those in Heaven following their trials on earth. Then, as though in answer to the prayers of the saints, a new series was begun. The trumpets announced one by one hardships that plagued the inhabitants of the earth who had rebelled against God. But still they resisted opportunities they had to repent. By the time of the sixth trumpet, the trials have mounted to the point that the end seems to be in view again. But instead of the seventh trumpet's following immediately, another interlude is introduced.

Chapter 10 begins with a powerful angel standing with one foot on the sea and one on the land and proclaiming in a loud voice that time has now run out. As he speaks, the voices of seven thunders are heard. It seems as though the seventh trumpet is introducing another series of seven. But John is told to seal up the messages of the seven thunders and not to write it down.

The voice gives further instruction to John. He is to take the little scroll from the hand of the powerful angel. He is supposed to eat the scroll. John does so, and it tastes sweet in his mouth, but turns sour in his stomach.

After this, John is told to measure the temple, but not the outer court that belongs to the Gentiles, for they will be in control of the holy city for forty-two months. During that time (1,260 days), two witnesses prophesy for God to the people of the city. Afterwards, a beast comes out of the Abyss and kills the two witnesses. Their bodies are left in the streets for three and a half days, and the inhabitants celebrate their death. At the end of this time, however, life returns to their bodies and they stand up to the amazement of all. Their enemies watch as the two faithful witnesses are taken up to Heaven. The conclusion of this action is marked by an earthquake. Seven thousand people die, and those who survive give glory to God.

Now the second woe is completed. The seventh trumpet is at last ready to sound. John has been on earth to view the things that took place in the holy city. Now, however, he observes what is taking place in Heaven. The triumph of Christ is praised. The twenty-four elders around the throne of God worship because Christ has begun His reign and the time for judgment has come. With the seventh trumpet, we have been brought again to the threshold of the end. Flashes of lightning, peals of thunder, an earthquake, and a great hailstorm mark the close of the seventh trumpet and the third woe.

Key Message

"The kingdom of the world has become the kingdom of our Lord and of his Christ, and he will reign for ever and ever" (Revelation 11:15b).

Glossary

Read through chapters 10 and 11 of Revelation. As you come to the terms listed below, note the explanation.

Chapter 10

Another mighty angel In Revelation 5:2, a mighty angel had sought someone worthy to open the seals of the scroll. This may be Gabriel (See Daniel 8:16; 9:21; 12:6f). *Another* here (Revelation 10:1) may indicate different from those sounding the trumpets, but be the same "mighty angel" met in 5:2.

Rainbow This is reminiscent of the description of God in His throne room (Revelation 4:3) and His divine mercy.

Fiery pillars The Israelites had been led out of Egypt by an angel in the pillar of fire and cloud (Exodus 14:19, 24). Here the fiery pillar is the appearance of the angels' legs, with one foot on the sea and one on land denoting the universal significance of his announcement.

Little scroll In view of what follows, this small book must have contained a message significant to the prophetic commission of John—perhaps a resume of the good news and John's role in delivering it.

Loud shout	The magnitude of the angel's announcement was matched by the volume of power used in its delivery—like the roar of a lion. It was echoed by the voices of the seven thunders.
Voices of seven thunders	These were intelligible to John but doubtfully so to anyone else.
Voice from Heaven	Perhaps this was the voice of Jesus, who was delivering this revelation.
Seal up	"Do not make the contents known. In fact, do not write it down." Compare this with Revelation 22:10 and Daniel 12:4.
No more delay (time*)	Time has run out.
Sweet as honey	The gospel is good news, and it is sweet as honey to our taste because of the salvation it brings.
Sour in the stomach	However, when the number of individuals who are lost and continue in rebellion against God are remembered, and the recognition of the tribulation suffered by both the wicked and the good along the way, the message brings pain to our stomachs.
Prophesy	John must continue to make known the message God has given him to deliver. It must extend beyond the churches of the province of Asia—about peoples, nations, languages, and kings, whether joyful or tragic.

Chapter 11

Measuring rod	A bamboo-like pole, six to ten feet long, used for measuring in order to do the following:
	1. build or rebuild (Ezekiel 40:5ff; Zechariah 2:1-3),
	2. destroy (2 Kings 21:13; Isaiah 34:11), or
	3. protect some and destroy others (2 Samuel 8:2).

---

*Translation in the King James Version.

The last fits best here. The whole section is symbolic, showing God preserving His own.

Temple If John is writing this in A.D. 96, the temple in Jerusalem is no longer standing. But this is a vision and does not involve the earthly temple. The word used here is the sacred center, equivalent to the old tabernacle (Holy of Holies, Holy Place and its furniture, court of priests and the brazen altar), but not the whole temple area with its court of Gentiles.

Outer court This denotes the area where Gentiles could enter without fear of expulsion. This was not to be measured and did not have the protection of the inner sanctuary.

Gentiles As the Gentiles (unbelievers) trample the outer court in the holy city (Jerusalem), they can take the physical lives of Christians, but they cannot touch the souls of the believers, measured and numbered in the sanctuary of the temple. See below for other interpretations.

Forty-two months This equals three and a half years. The Gentile reign of terror trampling on the holy city is described as lasting that length of time. See below for various interpretations.

Two witnesses Numerous attempted identifications are listed below. Moses and Elijah have more explicit associations with the two witnesses than any other suggestions.

1,260 days The length of the period the two witnesses prophesied. This is the same time period as forty-two months—counting thirty days per month.

Two olive trees In Zechariah 4:3ff, two olive trees are identified as the king Zerubbabel and the priest Joshua. They are standing on either side of a lampstand. The same type of figure is employed for the two witnesses.

141

Two lampstands	The one lampstand in Zechariah appears as two in John's vision representing the two witnesses.
Fire from mouths	As an attempt was made to arrest Elijah, fire fell from heaven and consumed the captain and his men (2 Kings 1:10). Another illustration comes from the Lord's word to Jeremiah (5:14): "I will make my words in your mouth a fire and these people the wood it consumes."
No rain	Like Elijah (1 Kings 17:1).
Waters into blood	Like Moses (Exodus 7:19).
Beast from the Abyss	Introduction of the antichrist met frequently from now on in Revelation. To be identified with the prophecies in Daniel (7:21), in Paul (2 Thessalonians 2:3ff), and in 1 John (4:1ff).
Great city	No doubt, the scene is figurative, but is it possible even to identify the symbol-city? Jerusalem is most likely intended, although some point out that Rome is regularly given the title "great city," and Babylon is often pictured for Rome.
Sodom and Egypt	Sodom represents the immorality of the people, and Egypt represents the oppression of the setting.
Lord crucified	The two witnesses were slain in the same city as the Lord was killed. This is what explicitly indicates Jerusalem as the intended site for the figurative teaching. But some still insist this is but further figurative language for Rome, where "every people, tribe, language, and nation will gaze on their bodies and refuse them burial." Not the place but the world of those rejecting Christ and resisting God is the significance.
Three and a half days	This number is used with the years of Elijah and drought (Luke 4:25, James 5:17, cf. 1 Kings 18:1). It also corresponds to the three and a half years calculated for Jesus' ministry, and is close to His three days in

	the grave. The prophecy of Daniel cannot be forgotten either (Daniel 12:11, see below, pp. 176-181). Here it is the length of time the bodies of the witnesses lie in the streets.
Loud voice	The voice from Heaven is associated with a call from God to a resurrection and ascension into Heaven.
Severe earthquake	God says, "I choose the appointed time; it is I who judge uprightly. When the earth and all its people quake, it is I who hold its pillar firm" (Psalm 75:2, 3).

One tenth of the city collapsed The loss is considerable, but by no means complete.

7000 people killed	If this tenth is indicated also in the 7000, it would be commensurate with some estimates of the population of Jerusalem in the first century A.D.[48]
Second woe passed	The passage of the first woe had been noted following the action of the fifth trumpet (Revelation 9:12). But this woe is not only preceded by the sixth trumpet, but by the episodes of the mighty angel and the two witnesses. Thus, all three scenes might be included in the second woe.
Seventh trumpet	Whereas the seventh seal was marked by silence in Heaven, the seventh trumpet is introduced by a big sound of many voices.

Kingdom of the world The rule of the unbelieving part of mankind.

Kingdom of our Lord Our Lord will take over the undisputed rule of the whole universe. Whether this is God or Christ or both, the conclusion is the same. Rebellious evil has been overcome. God will reign forever.

Your wrath has come As judgment over the condemned, this brings fearful desperation. To the saved, this brings joy.

---

[48]Joachim Jeremias, *Jerusalem in the Time of Jesus* (Philadelphia: Fortress, 1967), p. 83, n. 24.

Ark of the Covenant This is another indication that the description is figurative. Not only has the temple been destroyed for twenty-five years, but the ark had probably been missing for six centuries before that (since 586 B.C.). Yet the author could speak of them as though they were still in place. The lesson can still be given that in Heaven, the most sacred place of all, the Holy of Holies, will be open to the view of everyone and the ark, representative of God's presence, will no longer be hidden from view.

Lightning, thunder, earthquake, and a great hailstorm Once again, John has arrived at the threshold of judgment. "Each of the other cycles, the Seals (viii.5) and the Bowls (xvi.18), closes with a similar description."[49]

Content Notes

The Mighty Angel (10:1-11)

The Identity of the Angel (1)

In the interlude between the sixth and seventh trumpets, two episodes are given. In one, a mighty angel is the leading figure; in the other, two witnesses are at the center of the action.

All the way through the book of Revelation, comparisons can be made with visions and descriptive language recorded in the Old Testament. This is helpful; but, at the same time, one should be cautious concerning his conclusions. The fact that there are similarities does not mean John has lifted the material whole cloth from an Old Testament source. He may indeed be so familiar with a passage from the old Scriptures that the words describing that scene may influence his own description of the vision he has experienced. But it does not mean the experience was not a true part of John's vision. On the other hand, sometimes it almost serves as a Scriptural aid in one passage to understand another passage in Scripture a little better.

---

[49]C.A. Scott, *Revelation,* p. 226.

In the book of Daniel, we meet a figure reminding us of the mighty angel in Revelation 10:1:

> On the twenty-fourth day of the first month, as I was standing on the bank of the great river, the Tigris, I looked up and there before me was a man dressed in linen, with a belt of the finest gold around his waist. His body was like chrysolite, his face like lightning, his eyes like flaming torches, his arms and legs like the gleam of burnished bronze, and his voice like the sound of a multitude (Daniel 10:4-6).

> One of them said to the man clothed in linen, who was above the waters of the river, "How long will it be before these astonishing things are fulfilled?" The man clothed in linen, who was above the waters of the river, lifted his right hand and his left hand toward heaven, and I heard him swear by him who lives forever, saying, "It will be for time, times and half a time. When the power of the holy people has been finally broken, all these things will be completed" (Daniel 12:6, 7).

Since the angel Gabriel interprets Daniel's visions (Daniel 8:16-26; 9:20-27), this may be another reference to him. Likewise, it is possible that Gabriel is the mighty angel in Revelation. Two other passages in Revelation describe an angel with the same Greek adjective (translated "mighty": Revelation 5:2; 18:21). All three passages may well refer to the same angel, and this may be Gabriel. Since Revelation 10:1 specifies "another" angel, it must not be one of the four who had been bound at the river Euphrates (Revelation 9:14) nor one of the seven sounding the trumpets (Revelation 8:6). Nor should he be identified as Jesus Christ, as some identify him. Jesus is not of the created order of beings referred to as angels. The mere fact that some of the description of the angel is similar to words used to describe Christ does not mean the words are reserved for deity.

The Announcement (2-7)

The mighty angel makes a most imposing figure. He must come directly from the throne room of God. The use of the words *cloud, shining face, pillars of fire for legs,* and *rainbow* does not make a person divine, but it certainly associates the angel with a divine mission and an important one.

145

The angel takes his stand with his right foot on the sea and his left on the land. Here is a Heavenly being delivering a message on the earth, with his posture including both land and sea. His mission must be of universal significance. His opening shout can only be likened to the roar of a lion, but no words communicate what he says. It awakens the voices of the seven thunders, but again, no words communicate what is said. Evidently this has some meaning to John because he is prepared to take notes on the occasion. But the voice of instruction from Heaven prohibits him from writing anything down or making known anything that is said. This naturally raises questions in our mind. Why the secrecy at this point? Granted, any suggestions are pure speculation, but listing possible explanations may be useful for our attitude in viewing the future. This may be the very purpose for which the incident is recorded but its message, its figures or meaning, are not divulged. This emphasizes a continual limitation to the understanding of man and the amount of information he has to go on.

As in the case of God's speaking to Job, He convinces Job he has gone beyond his depth and does not have all of the answers to the problem of suffering. Nor does God assure Job that He will make all the answers plain. Because of Job's limitations, he is simply asked to trust in God (Job 38-42). This lesson from the seven thunders is sufficient in itself: there is much more we do not know, and it is best that we do not know it, for if we were told, we still would not understand, and we might get the wrong impression that we understand when in fact it is beyond our understanding. In the final analysis, we must have simple faith and trust in God.

Then there is the example Paul gives of the man caught up into the third Heaven (almost certainly Paul is speaking of himself). In Paradise, he saw things he was not permitted to tell (2 Corinthians 12:1-10). Associated with this limitation was his thorn in the flesh, and this weakness increased his dependence on the Lord and ultimately resulted in far greater strength than he had from himself. When we are forced to recognize our limitations, our trust and strength in the Lord are increased.

Still further possible reasons suggest themselves for the silencing of the thunder cycle. The very figure of the thunder suggests severe judgment. The opening of the seals has revealed many tribulations: the sounding of the trumpets has brought another cycle of catastrophes involving the world of nature as well as human society. If anything, the second becomes still more severe than the first in its description, and more encompassing. What if the third cycle shows conditions so fearsome that the sudden portrayal of such prospects for the future will be too much for some to bear? To move into periods of hardship one step at a time, trusting in God at each step, is better than knowing at the beginning the full extent of the suffering involved. A person grows stronger in his endurance as he endures. In his wisdom, God knows what is better for us to know and what is better for us not to know. He wants us to recognize this area exists rather than assume we know all the details of the foreknowledge of the conditions of our lives.

In fact, there must be a limitation to what God can tell us of the future without infringing on the freedom of choice. If you knew for sure what was going to happen tomorrow, this would be certain to influence the way you would choose to spend that day. This would be taking away the responsibility of our response to God in freedom of choice. Perhaps the message of the thunders contained prophecies so explicit that they should remain unknown to us now. The period covered in the third cycle may also be concurrent with that already given in the first two. This may be well for John to bear in mind as he gives record of his visions, but too heavy for all to bear down through the ages. So the message of the seven thunders is sealed up and remains unopened.

While this exchange takes place between John and the voices of the seven thunders, plus the interruption by the voice from Heaven, the mighty angel has remained at his station on land and sea. One dramatic scene after another is found in the book of Revelation, but this view of the mighty angel in all his splendor, ready to make his proclamation, rivals them all. Where was this spot on the earth? Was this on the shores of Patmos where John was in exile? Or was John transported in his vision to another part of the world? It must be a transportation far beyond his day in time, beyond this day as well. How many more days no one knows. Who will hear this pronouncement? Will there be a crowd? Will they understand the words, or will it be as Jesus heard the voice in the temple area the last week of His life, and the crowd heard it only as the sound of thunder (John 12:28, 29)? Or will the whole world hear the pronouncement? When will this be in relation to the Lord's second coming and the judgment? Regardless of how close this scene is to the final days, most would agree that his words describe something in the future as though it is already present. *Proleptic* is the word exactly fitting this situation and many scenes in the book of Revelation. *Prolepsis* is defined as "the representation or assumption of a future act or development as if presently existing or accomplished."[50]

The mighty angel raised his right hand to Heaven and made his proclamation still more solemn by swearing by the person of God the truth of what he was to affirm, that "there should be time no longer" (KJV), or, "there will be no more delay" (NIV—Revelation 10:6). The Greek word used in the statement can be translated either "time " or "delay." If one conceives of time as a measurable segment taken out of eternity, then this period will end at the coming of Christ, the resurrection, and the judgment. Eternity will continue as time ends. Rather than such a meaning as that, the context seems to indicate that there is not much time left; it is running out. But the word *delay* sounds rather weak for the momentous announcement of the mighty angel. Perhaps "No more time remains" would convey the meaning better. John joins the statement the angel made to his own comment on what would happen in the days of the seventh trumpet that is being introduced. Then the mystery of God will be accomplished. The secrets that have been worked out through the ages will be fulfilled and made known in His victory over Satan, the settling of the accounts in the judgment of mankind, and the final order of eternity put into effect. Just as Christ's birth was announced to the shepherds at His first coming, so the final trumpets will herald His second coming, and it may be Gabriel who shares in that scene as well as the announcement of the first to Mary and to Zachariah.

The Lesson (8-11)

More action is added to the drama. John has been standing by as a spectator, but now he is told to go onto stage and participate in the scene personally. The angel holds in his hand a little scroll. This is not the scroll with the seven seals (Revelation 5:1). The words are different in the Greek. The one used here is a diminutive form, a *little* scroll. Its contents are not described. A good suggestion is the gospel, the Word of God, and the judgments that

---

[50] *Webster's New Collegiate Dictionary* (Springfield, MA: G. & C. Merriam Co., 1981), p. 913.

go with it. "And the gospel must first be preached to all nations" is associated by Jesus with the signs of the last times (Mark 13:10).

The voice from Heaven instructs John to take the scroll, which is lying open in the hand of the angel. When John asks the angel to give him the little scroll, the angel insists, "You take it and eat it." It seems that both the voice from Heaven and the angel want John to take the scroll by his own effort rather than have it delivered to him or forced on him.

After John has eaten the scroll, he finds it just as the angel had said—it was sweet in his mouth but is sour in his stomach. What then is the lesson? Many conjectures are made, but when you follow the interpretation that the scroll includes the gospel, a meaning can be seen for the sweet and sour.

When a person accepts the gospel, the good news, his response to God brings joy and blessing to his life. He is freed from the shackles of sin and also from the guilt and consequences of sin in the second death. He is even freed from the rules and regulations of the old law. As time goes on, however, he finds that all is not easy in the life of a Christian. Satan continues to tempt him. Things he could do before are outside his way of life now. But more than that, the friends of the world are at enmity against Christ and all who are His. Persecution makes his stomach turn sour.

Not only are hardships brought because he is a Christian, God also brings judgment upon the world in its sin and its need for repentance. Oftentimes when the world suffers because it has sinned, the Christian suffers, too, because he is a part of human society. His grief, however, is not simply because he is forced to suffer with the world, but because so many people are lost without hope. The broad way leads to destruction, and the majority of the world is traveling in that direction. This has to bring bitterness to the heart of the Christian. Not long after he was rejoicing in the good news, he is saddened by the blows of persecution, judgment, suffering, and concern for the plight of the unsaved. The sweetness in his mouth has turned sour in his stomach.

But John is told to prophesy again, to be God's spokesman to peoples, nations, languages, and kings. This does not sound like time has run out, but instead the gospel is being proclaimed—worldwide. This is part of the lesson. Do not try to force Revelation into a neat chronology with one event following the other. This last statement about witnessing as a prophet prepares us for the next scene and links these two montages together as the interlude between the sixth and seventh trumpets.

The Two Witnesses (11:1-14)

Measure the Temple (1, 2)

The basic purpose of this interlude between the sixth and seventh trumpets is to bring assurance and encouragement to the Christians after the heavy tribulations of two woes and the last trumpet on the road to final judgment. How does this order to measure the temple fit into the total picture? It serves two purposes:

1. These two verses provide an introduction for the upcoming two witnesses.
2. The temple analogy supplies an assurance in the face of danger that God preserves a refuge for the Christian.

The temple is to be measured in order to be protected and spared. This place would be marked with God as its owner and anything within its walls would be assured of His care. Its worshipers would be measured as well. This would make sure of their genuine lives, and they could be assured of the grace and care of God. Ironically, however, the temple had been destroyed some twenty-five years before. This would scarcely provide much assurance—God's having him measure a temple that was not there because it had been destroyed by the enemy. On second thought, the point that John is establishing is that the Heavenly model of this temple still does exist (see Hebrews also). In other words, there is a protection beyond the reach of human hands and beyond the clutches of natural calamities. Despite martyrdom, there is security. Besides the body, there is the soul. We need not fear losing the physical life, rather fear "the One who can destroy both soul and body in hell" (Matthew 10:28).

But besides the inner portion of the temple proper, there are the outer courts. These are not to be measured. They will not have the protection the Holy of Holies, the Holy Place, and the altar have. Sure enough, the outer courts are occupied by the Gentiles as they trample on the holy city for forty-two months.

This number equals three and a half years. Antiochus Epiphanes occupied Jerusalem and sacrificed swine on the altar of God in 168 B.C. He was in control there about three and a half years. But the Romans took Jerusalem in about three and a half years in A.D. 70, when they destroyed the temple as well. So details do not fit the prophecy in a literal way, but it obviously was not intended to be taken that way. So what is essential to the episode?

(1) Those worshipers who are in the inner sanctum of the care of God need not be afraid; they are safe. The temple and the worshipers have been measured.

(2) The outer courts of the temple will be overrun by the unbelievers. They will trample on the whole city. This may mean Christians will suffer hardship, even loss of physical life; but the persecutors cannot penetrate to the soul and eternal life. God is their refuge there, and beyond the reach of man or Satan. The martyrs are safe beneath the altar of God, which has been measured, and their lives have been numbered.

(3) The period of these conditions is temporary. The time is limited.

(4) Details concerning this period are continued in the next montage of the two witnesses. Both scenes cover the same span of forty-two months or 1,260 days, each of which equals three-and-a-half years. Whether this is a literal three-and-a-half-years in this scene or whether it is a number symbolic of a calamitous period is a part of the puzzle. Whichever, it remains under God's control.

The Witnesses (3-6)

In the midst of, or more likely toward the close of, the Gentile trampling in the city, two witnesses appear in deep contrast to the attitude and actions of the unbelievers. The witnesses deliver their testimony in sackcloth, mindful of the sin and degradation, the rejection of God and His ways, that have marked these days. H. B. Swete describes this scene, "the two prophets . . . 'tortured' the world by setting men's consciences at work."[51]

Have these things already happened or will they happen some time in the future? Or will they happen time and again throughout the history of man? Or will they happen just before the final end? The answers to these questions would be much easier to determine if we could identify the two witnesses.

Who are they? If they are Peter and Paul, then this must refer to a time in the past. Truly, both Peter and Paul died in giving

---

[51]*Commentary on Revelation,* p. 139.

their testimony, but this does not mean that John is receiving a vision about something that has already happened before in his own lifetime. What about Moses and Elijah? They were in the more distant past, but they did the very things that are associated with the works of these two witnesses. They had the power to cause the rain to cease, as Elijah did. They had the power to turn water into blood and bring plagues, as Moses did. Then, too, Moses and Elijah came back to be with Jesus on the Mount of Transfiguration. Why could they not come back at some future time to serve as the two witnesses in a time of gross rebellion against God? Certainly, they could, and one would not want to say that God could not cause just that to happen. However, there are other possibilities.

An important prophecy, remembered in the time of Jesus, predicted that before the Day of the Lord would come, Elijah would return. Jesus taught explicitly how this prophecy had been fulfilled. John the Baptist fulfilled it. He had come in the spirit and power of Elijah. Perhaps, then, these two witnesses were not Moses and Elijah returned in the flesh, but they were like Moses and like Elijah as they witnessed. From early times, one suggestion after another has been made to identify these two in a similar fashion: for example, Elijah and Elisha or Enoch and Elijah have been recommended as candidates for these two witnesses.

Others have insisted this is looking in the wrong direction for the answer. They insist it is being too literal to tie the figure to individuals. This is symbolic. The allegorists submit their views: some say the witnesses stand for the law and the prophets. Others prefer the law and the gospel; still others, the Old and New Testaments or the church and the Word of God. Perhaps the two are specified, not because it is important to identify the two who are actually involved but because two witnesses were demanded under the law (Deuteronomy 19:15) and this whole scene speaks of the testimony of the church to the world in its two aspects, as witness to things of the past and as prophetic of things pertaining to the future.

So what is the sure message of the two witnesses? Conclusions should be withheld until all of the passage is in view, and even then the identity of the witnesses and the time of the action may remain in uncertainty. But one question cannot be put off: "Would you dare to be a Daniel?" Or, "Would you dare to be a witness?"

How are the times we are living in? How will our lives register as witnesses in the time and place in which we live? The message of Revelation was not written to tell when the judgment will be, but to present a challenge for faithfulness and witness all along the way, for every generation until it comes.

These two witnesses are likened to two olive trees and two lampstands. The Old Testament passage most closely associated with these figures is Zechariah. (See Zechariah 4.) Two essential messages in this vision focus on the source of sustaining power. "'Not by might nor by power, but by my Spirit,' says the Lord Almighty" (Zechariah 4:6), and, "These are the two who are anointed to serve the Lord of all the earth" (Zechariah 4:14). This is an apt commentary on the two witnesses who stood up for the Lord when evil was rampant. Their power was from the Spirit of God.

The Attack of the Beast (7-10)

The life and death struggle of these two witnesses has taught many lessons. First, they are invincible as long as God chooses to use their lives in their service to Him. Not until they have finished their testimony does God allow the beast to come up from the Abyss. This is the second lesson. Even though God is in control, Satan and his emissaries are allowed their day. For all our reasoning at that point, we appeal ultimately to faith and trust in God, accepting this trial that comes. And this is why we are told about it, so we will not be surprised when it happens to us. But the episode continues in the unexpected. The two witnesses are overpowered and killed. But we thought this was an interlude to bring relief from the heavy tribulations of the seals and the trumpets. This does not sound like much encouragement. In fact, the tragedy grows still more grim as the world does not even allow decent treatment for the dead bodies. Gleeful parties are enjoyed, celebrating the silencing of the only voices calling to their consciences to resist the anti-Christ and follow God. In this second lesson, we grow in our respect for God's openness with us. He does not paint a delightful, unrealistic scene and say all of life is like this when you follow Him. He does not list all of the special blessings these witnesses had received while they were serving Him.

Resurrection (11, 12)

The third lesson is again unexpected. It comes with inescapable realization. This is not the end, there is more. The witnesses come to life. Before the eyes of all, they are removed alive beyond the reach of human hands—in an ascension into Heaven. In the same moment, the work of the beast and the evil of his followers are seen for what they really are—their momentary triumph and care-free celebration return to haunt them in the face of pending consequences. They are struck with terror. No further deceit can cover the plain truth. They have killed the witnesses, but now they have been resurrected and have been victoriously taken to be with God. The deep implications of this vision are highlighted by one subtle detail added as the bodies of the witnesses lie in decomposing disgrace before the gloating inhabitants of the earth. The place is described as the city "where also their Lord was crucified" (Revelation 11:8). This confirms the unmistakable indication that the witnesses were traveling the same path that Jesus took to the cross: His suffering for the sins of others, His death, His resurrection, His ascension into glory. The differences are enough to tell us it is not an exact copy, but similar. Three and a half days to the resurrection, not three; no burial, instead of a rock-hewn tomb—this is to be expected because no witness, no sacrifice, could duplicate the vicarious atonement of Christ's death, but the life of a witness is lived for a purpose and will end in victory. And this victory includes more than the personal salvation of the witnesses as they are taken to Heaven.

Earthquake and Destruction (13, 14)

This is the fourth lesson of the vision. Judgment comes on the unbelievers. A tenth of the city is destroyed, seven thousand lose their lives, but then the unexpected happens again: the remnant turn to give glory to God. Commentators dispute whether this is in repentance or simply in terror, but it is still a recognition that God is greater than the beast, and it stands in contrast with the times after severe tribulation. The report then was simply, they "still did not repent" (Revelation 9:20). This was the purpose for which the witnesses had given their lives—that people might come to give glory to God and recognize Jesus as Lord.

Many questions are left unanswered. Is this vision still speaking of literal, old Israel on one hand and Gentiles on the other? Or is this speaking of old Israel with the Gentiles outside the protected walls of the temple suffering because it has continued to reject God and His Son? Then does this indicate that the remnant will turn after a tribulation and give glory to God? Or rather is this speaking of New Israel made up of those who believe on Jesus as the true Messiah, the Christ, whether Jew or Gentile in their genealogy. They are the believers, the worshipers inside the temple proper, who are measured and protected. In the outer courts where the two witnesses are doing their work and the unbelievers, the Gentiles, are trampling on the city, the whole of the population is pictured as non-Christian. But these are from "every people, tribe, language and nation" (Revelation 11:9). They are the unbelievers, referred to as "the inhabitants of the earth," who gloat over the bodies of the martyred witnesses. This includes the unbelieving Jews but are many more as well. The believers, whether Jews or Greeks, then are inside the temple and the unbelievers are outside. The believers are protected, but this does not mean they will never lose their physical lives in their witness for the Lord. The two witnesses did, but they were taken to Heaven to a glory beyond the reach of evil hands. The promise of like protection extends to all believers.

Thus the application of this passage to the sparing of the remnant of Israel becomes difficult as well as any treatment of time, whether three and a half years at the beginning of tribulation or the end or any particular period at all. In fact, we need to be mindful of the place of the figures. They are the path that leads to the truth, not the final truth itself. The Lamb on the throne with God is not an animal lamb but represents Jesus, who was sacrificed for our sins but is now alive and victorious. So also with this vision of the measuring of the temple and the two witnesses. The three and a half years of the Gentile domination of the outer courts is a path that leads back to Daniel, then it leads to a fulfillment in Antiochus Epiphanes. But that same path leads also to the predictions of Jesus and the destruction of Jerusalem in A.D. 70. But again this is not all. John is receiving a vision about A.D. 96, and these same paths are used to lead to something further. They are like the lamb—do not stop with the animal lamb, but go on to the truth behind the figure. Even so with the identity of the two witnesses. The rain that is held back for three and a half years—this is a path that leads to Elijah, but maybe Elijah is still part of the path and not the final truth (like the lamb). So also with turning the water into blood and using all kinds of plagues. This path leads to Moses, but Moses may well be a part of the path that leads ultimately to someone else who is like Him. In fact, this prophecy of John may have been fulfilled

155

several times through the centuries, just as Daniel's prophecy was fulfilled both in the time of Antiochus Epiphanes and in the Roman Titus. Or it may be that the very end time will witness the capping fulfillment of all.

Meanwhile, a person reading the book of Revelation can hear the message whenever he is living.

> Nevertheless, God's solid foundation stands firm, sealed with this inscription: "The Lord knows those who are his," and, "Everyone who confesses the name of the Lord must turn away from wickedness" (2 Timothy 2:19).

The Seventh Trumpet (11:15-19)

The seventh seal, instead of continuing into judgment from the final days pictured in the sixth seal, provided a linking introduction to the seven trumpets. Now the seventh trumpet serves a similar linking role. The sixth trumpet had come again to the threshold of the judgment, but as with the seals, the judgment is not presented. However, another series of seven does not follow immediately, so the joining together is done in a different way. The words of the song sung by the twenty-four elders (Revelation 11:16-18) briefly outlines the whole book of Revelation beginning with the throne room (Revelation 4:9; 5:8).

1. Thanksgiving and praise were given at the beginning. (See Revelation 7:12.)
2. The heathen (nations) were angry and Satan was filled with fury (Revelation 12 and 13).
3. God's wrath follows (Revelation 14—16).
4. The judgment finally comes (Revelation 20), with rewards for the servants of God (Revelation 21, 22), but destroying the destroyers (Revelation 17—19).

The seventh trumpet closes with the sighting of the ark in Heaven. An old tradition, whether true or false is uncertain, said that the ark had been taken to Heaven by Jeremiah and hidden away until the coming of the Messiah. However, it is there in John's vision, and it is open for all to see.

The scene is marked at the end, as the other series of sevens, by earthquakes, thunders, and lightning. These are among the signs of the immediate end at hand.

Special Subject #6

The Kingdom

After Jesus had taught the disciples for over three years, had died and been raised again, they asked a question about the kingdom. The way they worded the question makes a person doubt they understood all that Jesus had been teaching on this subject of "kingdom." They asked, "Lord, are you at this time going to restore the kingdom to Israel?" (Acts 1:6). In Jesus' reply, He did not probe further by asking what they meant by "restore," or what their idea of "kingdom" was, or what they included in "Israel." Instead, He rebuffed them, saying they should not be asking "when": it simply was not intended that they know the appointed times or dates the Father has decided.

We fret about how the disciples misunderstood Jesus' teaching on the kingdom, but we still hang up on the "when," which is the very point Jesus explicitly warned us not to try to anticipate God.

The expectation the Jews had for the coming of the Messiah is clear. They looked forward to His ushering in the messianic age with all its blessings. This meant material wealth, political power, religious assurance, and general supremacy for the Jews. They had various traditions about its coming. Some maintained if every Jew in the whole world would keep just one Sabbath day in perfect fulfillment of the law, then the messianic kingdom would come. Others were inclined to force God's hand by boldly going out in military attack against Rome. Risking their own lives and the lives of their loved ones, they expected God to protect them and bring the messianic age to rescue His militant defenders from defeat.

Surely the disciples knew this was not the kind of kingdom Jesus had in mind, nor the way He proposed it would come. In fact, He had done so much teaching about the kingdom one gets the impression that this is no old kingdom to be restored but something entirely new. Mark sums up Jesus' preaching at the outset with the words: "The time has come. . . . The kingdom of God is near. Repent and believe the good news!" (Mark 1:15). Matthew alone uses the terminology "kingdom of heaven" in parallel passages to "kingdom of God" (Matthew 4:17), showing the phrases can be used interchangeably. But after this, Jesus had preached the kingdom was already present in their midst (or within them—Luke 17:21). Then besides that, Jesus had stated:

"I tell you the truth, some who are standing here will not taste death before they see the Son of Man coming in his kingdom" (Matthew 16:28). On the other hand, we are still praying the Lord's model prayer: "Thy kingdom come, thy will be done on earth as it is in heaven." Did the kingdom come while Jesus was here, or did it come soon after? Or is it still to come some time in the future? No wonder the disciples at the crossroads of time, when Jesus was here at the close of the former days and the beginning of the latter days, were struggling to understand where and when the kingdom would exist. Jesus told Pilate (in John 18:36) that His kingdom was not of this world—so should we expect to see any signs of it on earth? Will we see any kingdom of God this side of His throne on high? The disciples lived too early to be pre-or post-or amillennialists, but perhaps their problem was more like pre-or post-or a*royalists*. Was there a kingdom before Christ came the first time or did it come after His earthly ministry or did it exist only in Heaven all the time? When we put together the Scriptures' teaching about the kingdom of God, one major truth must be recognized at the outset: different aspects and different forms are indicated in different times, and to determine which is intended for each passage is a necessity.

The Kingdom of God in the Old Testament

The reign of God is eternal. His kingdom is eternal to our past and will be eternal to our future. "Your kingdom is an everlasting kingdom, and your dominion endures through all generations" (Psalm 145:13). The word *kingdom* is rather misleading, however, because we immediately begin looking for boundaries to a certain sphere or for a clear center on earth with its palatial gardens and palaces. Rather, the word connotes kingship or authority. Because of the rise of godless ways among men, the kingship of God became less manifest on earth. God predicted a coming time when He would rule through His anointed one, the Messiah. This would usher in a new period of the kingdom. In fact, there were to be different phases to His kingdom.

The Kingdom in the Time of Jesus

The Messiah came in the person of Jesus, but He did not bring with Him the type of messianic kingdom the Jews expected. Since Jesus was the king, while He was here, the kingdom was itself present in His very presence. "But if I drive out demons by the

158

Spirit of God, then the kingdom of God has come upon you" (Matthew 12:28). This is the reason He could tell the Pharisees, answering their question about when the kingdom of God would come, "The kingdom of God does not come with your careful observation, nor will people say, 'Here it is,' or 'There it is,' because the kingdom of God is within you [or, among you]" (Luke 17:20, 21). So Jesus taught for one aspect of the kingdom it was already here when He was here.

Perhaps Jesus taught more about this aspect of the kingdom than has been preserved for us in the Gospel narratives, because it was more important that the preparation for the church be emphasized with its teaching for all the centuries and for all places. This was the essential proclamation, "The kingdom is at hand"— soon to come, but not here now.

Then there was still another aspect of His preaching about the kingdom that would come at the end of time—the eschatological kingdom—when He, God's anointed, would return and the Judgment Day will have arrived. These are clearly three different aspects of the kingdom of God that Jesus included in His teachings—the present, the near future, and the final. He could say the present was already here, the one to be soon would be before the death of some in the sound of his voice (Matthew 16:28), and the final one would come after growth and waiting, such as in the parable of the tares or the ten virgins, and in His teachings about His second coming, judgment, the resurrection, and eternal life.

The Kingdom as the Church

Although Jesus was preparing His disciples to be leaders in the coming church, His recorded words show infrequent use of the word for church (only three times, once in Matthew 16:18 and twice in Matthew 18:17). It becomes apparent, however, that He used the word *kingdom* often times meaning the church. His parables of the kingdom are more often than not His teaching about the coming church. His promise of giving the keys of the kingdom to the apostle Peter is immediately followed by His affirmation concerning the foundation he was using for the building of the church. The church and the kingdom are the same in the context. This makes entirely understandable His promise that the kingdom would be coming in the lifetime of those hearing His voice as He spoke to them in His earthly ministry. It was only a matter of days after His ascension that Peter used the keys to open the kingdom

Coins of Roman Emperors
Claudius (41-54)

Head of Claudius (obverse).
Female figure, Constantia (Courage, Resolution), helmeted in military dress, holding spear (reverse).
Acts 11:28 reports a famine during his reign.
During one period, Claudius ordered the Jews to leave Rome (Acts 18:2).
Coin issued A.D. 41.

Nero (54-68)

Head of Nero (obverse).
Temple and figure of Vesta (reverse).
After the burning of Rome (64), Nero blamed the Christians and persecuted them.
Paul was beheaded during his reign (c. 68).
This coin was issued A.D. 64-68.

*in the First Century**

Titus (79-81)

Titus Caes[ar] Vespasian (obverse).
Two captives seated back to back between trophy of breast plate, helmet and two oblong shields.
Titus conquered Jerusalem A.D. 70.
This coin was issued ten years later in a mint at Rome.

Domitian (81-96)

Head of Domitian, radiate, depicting the rays of Sol (obverse).
Virtus (Courage, Valor), draped and helmeted with one foot on a helmet and holding a spear (reverse).
Domitian was emperor when John was exiled to Patmos.
This coin was probably issued within five years of when John wrote the book of Revelation.

*All coins shown here are held in the Ancient History Teaching Collection of Macquarie University, Australia. Used with permission.

as he proclaimed the first full gospel message, and three thousand answered the invitation. This is what Jesus was talking about in His words recorded by Mark, "I tell you the truth, some who are standing here will not taste death before they see the kingdom of God come with power" (Mark 9:1).

The Kingdom of God on This Earth

Even though an individual is still living on this earth, he can enter the kingdom of God now and enjoy privileges that unbelieving inhabitants of the earth cannot know. Augustine pictured it as the City of God versus the earthly city. Paul gives us confidence when he states, "For he has rescued us from the dominion of darkness and brought us into the kingdom of the Son he loves" (Colossians 1:13). Paul spells this out in his epistle to the Romans, "For the kingdom of God is not a matter of eating and drinking, but of righteousness, peace and joy in the Holy Spirit, because anyone who serves Christ in this way is pleasing to God and approved by men" (Romans 14:17, 18). This is not the ultimate manifestation of the kingdom, for a life of struggle is still necessary to be faithful to the Lord in the face of Satan and adversities. This is the church militant in its service to God and opposition to the pull of the world.

The Kingdom in Heaven

When a Christian dies, he exchanges his place in God's kingdom on the earth, the church militant, for a place in God's kingdom in Heaven, the church triumphant. This is the same kingdom in a new power and glory not known before. It lies beyond the reach of evils and woes still known on earth. This is the sanctuary that was measured for the protection and assurance of the faithful while the battles still waged in the outer courts of the temple. This is the manifestation of the kingdom where the two witnesses were taken from their deaths in the street and the attackers could no longer submit them to torture and shame. This is where they saw the full majesty and power and love of God and the Lamb. And God will wipe away every tear. But this still is not the eschatalogical kingdom.

The Kingdom as Final and Eternal

God has reigned eternally, the church has been in existence for almost two thousand years, the church kingdom has had its history on earth and its triumph in Heaven, but still the final manifestation of the kingdom has not yet come. This is why we still pray, "Thy kingdom come, thy will be done on earth as it is in heaven." This has reference to the final days when the Lord returns, when the resurrection comes, when the general judgment of all is announced, when all will bow in recognition and honor before Christ (Philippians 2:9-11), and finally Christ will return to God the full authority God had granted to Him for the fulfillment of His task:

> Then the end will come, when he [Christ] hands over the kingdom to God the Father after he has destroyed all dominion, authority and power. For he must reign until he has put all his enemies under his feet (1 Corinthians 15:24, 25).

And God's kingdom will endure for ever and ever.

The Kingdom in the Book of Revelation

When one speaks of the book of Revelation, most people think immediately of the end times. A study of the kingdom of God helps balance our view. The book treats first the plight of the seven churches of Asia. They were a part of the kingdom still on earth and what they were suffering. Then we are given a glimpse of the redeemed in Heaven. They were a part of the triumphant kingdom in Heaven, but still not of the final kingdom, not of the end times. The martyrs under the altar were concerned about the injustices still going on against their brothers on earth. We have come all this way in Revelation, but most of the material tells us of conditions short of the final time. It concerns much more than exclusively on the time of the second coming.

At this point in Revelation, note these four observations about the kingdom:

(1) In Revelation 1:9, the author makes an introductory statement, "I, John, your brother and companion in the suffering and kingdom and patient endurance that are ours in Jesus...." These three words—*suffering, kingdom,* and *patient endurance* —have been underscored as important themes to the whole of the book. To trace the role of the kingdom through the message of Revelation will help our understanding of its truths.

(2) Also in the first chapter (Revelation 1:5, 6), the first doxology reads,

> To him who loves us and has freed us from our sins by his blood, and has made us to be a kingdom and priests to serve his God and Father—to him be glory and power for ever and ever! Amen.

Does this mean a kingdom of priests? or of royal priests? or of rulers and priests? In any event, we are describing here the kingdom triumphant in Heaven, not the final stage of the kingdom but perhaps very similar. What is characteristic of the redeemed is that if they have suffered with Him, they will also reign in His kingdom with Him. Above all, they want to serve God. The kingdom aspect is the ruling and the priestly aspect is the serving. The next reference to the kingdom is like this also: "You have made them to be a kingdom and priests to serve our God, and they will reign on the earth" (Revelation 5:10). But here the earth is given as the place where this privilege begins. This is reminiscent of Matthew 5:5, "Blessed are the meek, for they will inherit the earth."

(3) Another passage that couples reigning and priestly service is Revelation 20:6: "Blessed and holy are those who have part in the first resurrection. The second death has no power over them, but they will be priests of God and of Christ and will reign with him for a thousand years." This is the one chapter of the Bible that makes reference to the millennial reign. Where does this fit the church kingdom on earth or the church kingdom in Heaven or the eschatological final kingdom? Why have we waited until now to hear about it? Is it identical with one of the other kingdoms already identified? At this point, we acknowledge the problem, anticipate making some decision in the study of chapter 20, and propose to watch for clues along the way.

(4) The last observation calls attention to a statement important to the understanding of the cycles in Revelation. The seventh trumpet sounded the arrival of the final stage of the kingdom. The prayer, "Thy kingdom come," was answered:

> The kingdom of the world has become the kingdom of our Lord and of his Christ, and he will reign for ever and ever (Revelation 11:15).

CHAPTER SEVEN

War in the Heavens and on Earth
Revelation 12:1-17

In the borderland of Thailand, almost within sight of Laos, lived a woman enduring one trial after another. Her husband had cancer and required constant care. One of her sons had been seriously wounded in the continuous state of war in the area; he will never be able to work or regain a normal existence. Her daughter had married, but because of a series of tragic events, and through no fault of her own, her husband chose to desert her. She had no recourse but to return home and live with her mother. There was one son, however, who was the pride and joy of the family. He attended a Christian mission school some miles away, and showed every promise of becoming an outstanding success. He was bright, he was ambitious, and he had high Christian ideals and worthy goals. He wanted to go to a university and become a lawyer some day—but first and foremost, he was a Christian. One weekend he returned home to visit his family. In a freakish accident, he fell from a tree and was killed. The grief of the mother was almost beyond control. She traveled the miles to see the missionary. She had one request to ask of her. "Will you please lend me another tape about Jesus. He is the only One who can give me peace and strength."

> Who shall separate us from the love of Christ? Shall trouble or hardship or persecution or famine or nakedness or danger or sword? ... No, in all these things we are more than conquerors through him who loved us. For I am convinced that neither death nor life, neither angels nor demons, neither the present nor the future, nor any powers, neither height nor depth, nor anything else in all creation, will be able to separate us from the love of God that is in Christ Jesus our Lord (Romans 8:35-39).

The apostle John was able for just a little while to see what was going on behind the scenery of life. He was able to see causes and results we only guess at and suppose. Despite the battles and the powers, the hardship and the losses, God in Christ, with the people of God, will win out.

Prelude

Overview

Something more than another interlude begins in the twelfth chapter of Revelation. For the time being, visions in the form of series of sevens are set aside. This montage demands the very sky as the screen for its action. Although the series of seven is broken, the cyclical pattern of the apocalypse is still retained, for this episode coming up travels again the course just covered by the scenario of the two witnesses, and that in turn retraced the period when the temple was measured but not the outer court. The key to this is the length of time indicated in each instance. The outer court will be trampled under foot for forty-two months; the two witnesses will prophesy for a thousand, two hundred sixty days; and in this chapter, the woman will be nourished in her refuge in the wilderness for the same number of days (Revelation 12:6), which is also designated as "a time, times and half a time" (Revelation 12:14). This may not be a literal period of three and a half years, but having been established in the past as a literal period of distress, the period may have retained its tribulation-significance by its code as the length of time—although the meaning was not dependent on a literal length of time. Each of these scenes—the measuring of the temple, the testimony of the two witnesses, and the woman and the dragon—may well represent the whole sweep of time from Jesus' first coming to the period of His second coming.

The mural in the sky introduces three figures: a woman, a dragon, and a baby. The woman is beautifully adorned with the sun around her, the moon at her feet, and stars as her crown. She is about to have a child. In front of her stands the red dragon, a horrible, ferocious sight. He has seven heads and ten horns, and each head has a crown. His enormous outline in the sky can be imagined because in the swish of his tail he collects a third of the stars and casts them to the earth. He keeps his position in front of the woman because he wants to consume the child as soon as it is born. The child is a son, destined to be a ruler. In a flurry of action, the child is snatched into Heaven, the woman flees on the wings of an eagle to a hiding place, and the dragon gives pursuit to Heaven.

The dragon is explicitly identified as Satan; the child must be the Messiah; and the woman must be representative of someone more than a single individual. Who will best answer the clues for the woman's identity? The people of God through the centuries: Israel under the Old covenant and the church in the New Covenant period. In this opening scene, Satan has lost the first round of the conflict. The child is with God on His throne, and the mother is safe in her place for 1,260 days.

The next scene is in Heaven. A full-fledged war is waged between Michael and his angels against Satan and his angels. Again Satan loses. He and his forces are thrown out of Heaven down to earth. A loud voice makes detailed announcement of the victory in Heaven.

The third scene is on earth. Filled with fury, the dragon returns to his pursuit of the woman who has borne the son. He tries to overwhelm her with a torrent of water, but the earth opens up and consumes the river. Satan has been defeated again.

This section of Revelation is not a report of conflict between Satan and the Messiah. It is the enumeration of three defeats against Satan. This is for the encouragement of the people of God.

Unable to reach the offspring of the woman in Heaven, unable to reach the woman on earth, Satan redoubles his efforts to crush the rest of her individual offsprings on earth. Satan stands on the seashore, ready to summon assistance for his works of evil.

Key Message

"They did not love their lives so much as to shrink from death" (Revelation 12:11b).

Glossary

Read through chapter 12 of Revelation. As you come to the terms listed below, note the explanation.

Sign   An extraordinary event, usually a miracle, with a special meaning. Here a tableau displayed across the sky. *Sign* is used seven

	times in Revelation, three times indicating signs from God (Revelation 12:1, 3; 15:1) and four from Satan in deception (Revelation 13:13, 14; 16:14; 19:20).
Woman . . . sun	Various interpretations have been offered, including the Virgin Mary, the Jewish nation, and the church. The best answer is the people of God. (See the explanation below, pp. 170-172.) For "clothed with the sun," see Psalm 104:2; Song of Songs 6:10.
Moon . . . footstool	The moon gives less light than the sun but more than the stars. Perhaps this represents the Mosaic law, i.e., the old dispensation.
Twelve stars, crown	Perhaps the number twelve is suggested by the twelve tribes of Israel, the Patriarchal period. The stars are associated with the sun and moon, but are lesser lights. There is nothing here to indicate association with the twelve signs of the Zodiac or the stars of the pagan gods.
Another sign	The scene was in one panorama, but two opposite signs. This was the hostile, evil sign to be in conflict with the good.
Red dragon	Described as "an enormous [powerful] red [murderous] dragon [ferocious]." It is identified as the devil, Satan, the ancient serpent (Revelation 12:9).
Seven heads	This may indicate the height of intelligence, craftiness, and deceiving shrewdness (2 Corinthians 11:3). Seven indicates fullness.
Ten horns	A symbol of enormous power. Some animals have their strength to attack in their horns, so ten horns would be exceedingly strong.
Seven crowns	The word here for crown is not *stephanos* (the victor's honorary wreath, used eight times in Revelation), but it is *diadema,* the crown of the ruler, only used three times (Revelation 12:3; 13:1; and 19:12-16) and nowhere else in the New Testament. Seven crowns would indicate royalty, kingship,

Stars (¹/₃)	over all the kingdoms of this world or through kings, Satan exercises his power. This shows the enormity of the dragon as he moved about lashing his tail. Perhaps it also shows his fury at confinement to his activity and is symbolic of Satan's interruption of the natural order in God's universe—he flung these stars to the earth. (See Daniel 8:10.)
Birth of a son	There is general agreement to the identity of the Son as the Messiah-king. But the birth in this drama should not be reduced to a night in Bethlehem. Birth here arches from that first night all the way to the ascension of Jesus and His taking His place beside God on the throne in Heaven.
Iron scepter	A firmness is denoted in the Messiah's reign, not necessarily tyrannical. A close parallel is seen in Psalm 2 (esp. v. 9), which associates the reign with judgment and the Messiah. (See also Jeremiah 19:11.)
1,260 days	Equivalent to three and a half years, the same as the time the church was persecuted in the figure of the two witnesses and now in this figure as well.
Michael (and angels)	A third scene finds the archangel Michael (see Jude 9) at the head of the fighting forces of Heaven.
Dragon (and angels)	Satan has his forces likewise, but they cannot penetrate to the heart of Heaven, but are defeated and cast down to the earth.
Blood of the Lamb	The effective defeat of Satan was ultimately achieved in Christ's death.
Word of their testimony	The proclamation of the gospel is the power of God to salvation.
Great eagle	Since Satan cannot get to the Son in Heaven, he directs his attacks against His body of followers on earth. The figure of the eagle provides a picture of the speed and ease with which the church retires to safety.

Time, times and half a time This is a way of designating a period of time in Daniel (12:7) equivalent to three and a half years ("time" = one year; "times" = two years; "half a time" = one half year; total = three and a half years) or the same period as the 1,260 days. It is a symbolic way of designating a limited period of concentrated attack from Satan upon the church, but the deliverance provided by God.

Content Notes

Three Signs in Heaven (12:1-9)

This section begins with an introduction of figures that will continue in significance throughout the rest of Revelation: the woman, her male child, and the dragon. The same three are found in the first book of the Bible as well as the last. In Genesis 3:15, God informed the serpent: "I will put enmity between you and the woman, and between your offspring and hers; he will crush your head, and you will strike his heal." The dragon in Revelation 12:9 is plainly identified as the ancient serpent, Satan, the devil.

Sign 1: A Woman About to Give Birth (1, 2)

What of the woman and the offspring, who are they? Despite all of the fluidity of apocalyptic figures, the application of the woman as a reincarnation of Eve does not satisfy the scene or the lessons. Perhaps it would be best to identify the child, and then the mother would be indicated. The marks of the child are clear: He is a male child, and His life is characterized by a rule with an iron scepter (Revelation 12:5). This is language found in one of the outstanding Messianic Psalms:

> He said to me, "You are my Son;
>   today I have become your Father.
> Ask of me,
>   and I will make the nations your inheritance,
>   the ends of the earth your possession.
> You will rule them with an iron scepter;
>   you will dash them to pieces like pottery" (Psalm 2:7-9).

170

This indication that the child is the Messiah is confirmed in the next step—He is taken up to God and to a place at His throne. The identification is further borne out in that Christ won out over the great dragon "by the blood of the Lamb" (Revelation 12:11). All of the pieces fit together perfectly, the child is Jesus, born in Bethlehem, crucified but raised again, ascended into Heaven and seated at the throne of God on His right hand.

Then does this mean that the woman is the Virgin Mary, the mother of Jesus? Not necessarily so. If we find a literal figure to fill the role, it may be that we make the role too small and choke out the lessons of application that are being taught. Truly, Herod was waiting to cut short the life of the baby Jesus, and Joseph and Mary fled to a place of refuge in Egypt. But this scarcely matches the proportion of Satan's attempt to overcome the child, to storm Heaven itself, and to wipe out the woman in her place in the desert. This is something bigger than one individual, Mary, and one single generation in time.

Who could represent the mother and be of greater significance than an individual? Israel has been suggested. Here is a chosen nation God raised up for the very purpose of bringing forth His Son from their number, the Messiah, the Son of David. How apt a figure to call Israel the mother who brought forth Jesus! On the other hand, most of the action, and the lessons from it, come after the birth of the child and the mother figures prominently in this action. Jesus came to His own and those who were His own received Him not. Israel the nation rejected Him; they did not receive Him as Messiah. So it seems wrong to say that all these efforts to destroy the mother was a pursuit of Israel on Satan's part.

In the years following the establishment of the church, Satan did not persecute Israel in his conflict with Christ; he pursued the Christians. Because of this, some insist the mother must represent the church rather than Israel. This, however, poses problems chronologically. The church was not established until after Jesus had ascended to Heaven, and this does not fit His being born of the church as His mother before the church had an existence. But this is figurative language, we are reminded, and perhaps we should not be bothered with sequence in time.

Why not, however, use a terminology that would rise above these difficulties and at the same time recognize the truth in each? We need not speak of the people of God in Old Testament times as the church in the Old Testament. Neither need we speak of the church as Israel in the New Testament. We can, however, speak of both as the "people of God," depending on when they lived to determine whether they are Israel or the church. What Satan is striving to destroy is the people of God. These are the mother of Jesus in the panorama written in the sky—the people of God. This is the great conflict between Christ and God's people versus Satan and his forces. The results are summed up in the statement:

> They overcame him [Satan]
>> by the blood of the Lamb
>> and by the word of their testimony;
> they did not love their lives so much
>> as to shrink from death (Revelation 12:11).

Sign 2: A Red Dragon (3-6)

Dragons appear in a great variety of roles throughout antiquity and have passed into the lore of our present day. They also have a place in a figurative use in the Old Testament. Regularly, they depict vehement enemies of God and of Israel (Psalm 74:14; Isaiah 27:1; Ezekiel 29:3). This is a case where a use common to inspired men of old has been included in a symbolic way for the vision to John. It is far more reasonable that the figure is related to the Old Testament than to any of the mythologies of the surrounding peoples.

John sees that the dragon in the sky is determined to devour the child at birth. Instead, the son is "snatched up" to God the moment He is born. This is the same word used to describe the taking up of the Christians at the Lord's second coming (1 Thessalonians 4:17). At the same time that the child is taken to the throne of God, beyond the reach of the dragon, the mother flees to a place prepared for her in an isolated spot. (*Desert* does not mean a waterless place, but an uninhabited area.) She is to be cared for a definite period of time. Usually the three-and-a-half-year unit of time is associated with a period of intensive tribulation, but this time it denotes a period of special protection.

Sign 3: A War in Heaven (7-9)

The scene now changes. The action previously has been portrayed in the sky, but ends in a place of refuge evidently on the earth. The dragon, however, seems more intent to overcome the

172

child than to pursue the mother at the moment. So the action shifts to war in Heaven. Some picture this as Satan's concerted attempt to storm the very heart of Heaven to reach the child on the throne. Others see the warfare as taking place in some lower realms of Heaven and not reaching the throne room of God itself, and the scenes we have been seeing through the eyes of John in this report.

In fact, as the report is given, it would seem that the fighting is initiated by Michael and his angels rather than a move instigated by the fury of the dragon. In any event, Satan and his forces "lost their place in heaven" (Revelation 12:8) and were hurled out. Some express surprise that Satan had a place in Heaven. Yet even after his first rebellion, it seems that he had the privilege of intermingling with the angels at their councils. (See Job 1:6ff; 2:1ff.) This, however, seems to be a crossroads when Satan no longer has any access to Heaven whatever. Michael's victory is complete. This is the archangel whose special duty is leading in war. (See Daniel 12:1.) Satan is hurled to the earth, and his angels with him.

The time of this event remains uncertain. Perhaps this occurred some time in the distant past and is simply inserted now to emphasize the ultimate defeat of Satan. Jesus had told of seeing Satan fall as lightning from the sky (Luke 10:18) when the seventy reported concerning one of their evangelistic campaigns. But even here one cannot tell whether this is a proleptic announcement of something still in the future.

The Results of the Battle (12:10-17)

Satan's Defeat (10-12)

The victory over Satan gives rise to another outburst of praise to God. The victory is not complete because Satan is going to continue his work on earth. *Satan* in the Hebrew means "accuser" or "adversary." The word *devil* in the Greek means "slanderer." The most loathsome person in Roman society was the paid informer who profited by accusing people before the Roman authorities. Satan operates in a similar way for his own advantage and pleasure. He accuses and slanders men before God as he did in the case of Job. In addition to this, he goes about deceiving the whole world.

The Heavens rejoice that Satan has been cast down. The book of Revelation uses the Greek word for Heaven *(ouranos)* fifty-two times, but in this verse (Revelation 12:12) the form is plural for the only instance. Perhaps the plural is used here to recognize there are different parts to Heaven and in the area that Satan was present and where the battle was waged was separate from the throne of God and the altar of the saints and all the redeemed. When the battle is won, the rejoicing includes all the Heavenly places—the Heavens.

Woe, however, to the earth because Satan's fury is great, both because of his defeat and because further limitation put upon his field of operation. He now concentrates still more on the world of mankind, and he knows his time is short. The Greek has two popular words for "time." The one *(chronos)* has to do with the sequential passage of time. The other *(kairos)* has to do with the opportune moment, the proper or fitting time. This latter word is used in this passage. Perhaps the meaning is not so much the time is limited as that the opportunities have been narrowed down. In any event, time is a relative term and in some ways a thousand years can be short whereas one day may be too long. And still the evil activity of the devil is feverish.

Satan's Continued Rage (13-17)

Satan has been thwarted at his attempt to stop the work of the Messiah at His appearing. He has been dislodged from his association with Heaven at all, and has been cast down to earth. Now Satan renews his work on earth and concentrates his efforts in an attack on the people of God, symbolized as the woman who had borne the Messiah. She had been carried to a place of refuge on the wings of an eagle. This is reminiscent of the language in Exodus recording the words of God to Moses:

> You yourselves have seen what I did to Egypt, and how I carried you on eagles' wings and brought you to myself. Now if you obey me fully and keep my covenant, then out of all nations you will be my treasured possession. Although the whole earth is mine, you will be for me a kingdom of priests and a holy nation (Exodus 19:4-6).

This parallel does not establish the woman as exclusively Israel nor does it identify this scene in John's vision with the Exodus from Egypt. What can be concluded is that similar figures can be used more than once. Two other conclusions are helpful.

1. The parallel passage may provide an example useful in seeing the direction of the fulfillment in the later passage.
2. The parallel passage may give indication that the lesson is recurring and could be applied on different occasions.[52]

Ironically enough, some commentators are disturbed when they can find no parallel references to the dragon's attempt to destroy the woman by sending a river of water to sweep her away, but the earth simply swallowed the torrent. Some even maintain this must come from a legend we do not know about. Whether we can find something like it or not (for example the river at Colosse that disappears), the lesson is clear, and its claim to be a part of John's vision is trustworthy. Satan was unable to overwhelm the people of God (the church in this period). It denotes in one period times of distress and protection.

Thwarted again, Satan sets out in a rage to deceive and make war against the people of God one by one. But if the woman is the people of God, how can his attack on those who are obedient to God be any different from his attack on the woman?

In many computer programs, there is a way to give a "global" command; that is, in one stroke, a change can be made all the way through a document no matter how many words or pages are involved. Without this possibility, the individual must go through the whole of the document and make the changes one by one. Satan wanted to wipe out the church in one "global" attack, but he could not shake it any more than he could reach Christ to annihilate Him. Not having the power to destroy the church—the very gates of Hades could not prevail against it—he has to pursue his program of making life difficult, of deceiving, of leading astray each one of the people of God: those who obey Him and keep the gospel of Jesus Christ. No global stroke could fell the church, only one by one can Satan make his inroads on the people of God. Even then, the devil cannot snatch one from the fold. The individual has the choice; he can choose to remain faithful to

---

[52]A long list of examples of the enmity between the serpent and the woman and her seed is given in W. Hendriksen, *More Than Conquerors,* pp. 163-173. He does not mean, however, that each instance can be shown to be the exclusive fulfillment of the figure in Revelation. To the contrary, he is showing that the same hostility that is seen in the history of Israel is found in the course of the church from the birth of Jesus in Bethlehem to His coming again.

Jesus no matter what transpires; but if he succumbs to the trials and temptations of the deceiver, he forfeits his place in Heaven. This is what the book of Revelation is all about—"be faithful to the point of death."

At the close of chapter 13, variant readings in the manuscripts make possible the translation, "I [i.e., John] stood on the shore of the sea." But the reading is much to be preferred that states: "And the dragon stood on the shore of the sea." In his defeat and his fury, Satan is about to call forth from the sea reinforcements for his evil work.

Special Subject #7

The Book of Daniel

The book of Daniel calls to the reader of the book of Revelation for a special study. Good reasons for this are evident:

(1) Both books make use of apocalyptic expressions not ordinarily used in the narrative or doctrinal parts of Scripture. This vision-type literature reports these direct revelations to the writers. What the book of Revelation is to the New Testament, Daniel is to the Old Testament. Not only do they have prophecy in common, but they have truths expressed in a figurative language, representing the real. Not only do they speak of earthly events, but they describe Heavenly scenes as well. They treat not only the future, but the future to the very end of time (*eschatos,* last). The fact that both these books are apocalyptic is reason enough to put them alongside one another as we study.

Daniel is not the only book of the Old Testament that has apocalyptic sections. Isaiah, Ezekiel, Zechariah, and Joel, for example, all contain some. But Daniel is the best single example. It will help broaden our appreciation of the apocalyptic and sharpen our understanding of its interpretation to use Daniel as an added example.

(2) The messages are so much alike; they corroborate one another. Each adds to the understanding and assurance of the other. Differences are so apparent that it must not be a case of copying what the other had, but the similarities supply us with two witnesses for the same truth. Just as two eyes are better than one— our judgment of depth is assisted, our peripheral vision is broadened, and our total vision is strengthened—so Revelation and Daniel work together.

(3) Yet when the two are used together, dangers surface that must be guarded against. To use a book one verse at a time disregarding the context and the sweep of the book's message is wrong. Too often, we see a similar figure or wording in Daniel and we lift that verse to put it into the context of a passage in Revelation. Another related danger is to fail to see the possibility of dual fulfillments to a prediction (such as both Antiochus Epiphanes, 168 B.C. and the fall of Jerusalem in A.D. 70 as the abomination of desolation predicted by Daniel), or the repeated fulfillment throughout history rather than a single historical incident. We must strive to be faithful to the intended meaning of the inspired author for his own message. On the other hand, the prophet himself may not be aware of the full import of a figure or prophecy he is delivering for God. But to help avert an unfair piecemeal use of Daniel, this brief overview of the book of Daniel is being included.

(4) Another bonus to reviewing the material on the book of Daniel is that one learns a great deal about the commentator and his starting points from the way he treats Daniel. If he says the book must have been written no earlier than 165 B.C., you know that he is likely to feel predictive prophecy is an impossibility, and this becomes a basis for his rejecting Daniel, in the time of Darius, as the true author of the book that bears his name. Scholarship has polarized so clearly on the problem of Daniel's authorship that it helps identify the liberal who denies that the person Daniel could have written the book in the time he lived during the Babylonian captivity. This denial is maintained because the prophecies are so clearly descriptions of what happened, especially in the time of Antiochus Epiphanes four hundred years after Daniel lived. Those who deny predictive prophecy maintain that no one could have written this before the time described had been reached and the very happenings had already transpired. Denials by such scholars, made more subtly in other books, become clear in the study of Daniel.

Overview of Daniel 1—6

The book of Daniel is the account of a man's life and a series of visions he had in his latter days. The first half of Daniel tells how he was taken as a young Jew from Palestine to Babylon for the captivity from 606 to 536 B.C. He was a loyal, dedicated young man, and his experiences have captivated readers through the centuries.

Daniel and three other young men were faithful to the God of their fathers, and God enabled them to know literature and learning, and to interpret visions and dreams of all kinds. In the second year of Nebuchadnezzar, Daniel interpreted a dream for him: it was a statue with a head of gold (representing Nebuchadnezzar himself and the Neo-Babylonian kingdom), chest and arms of silver (Medo-Persian kingdom, established by Cyrus, 539 B.C.), bronze belly and thighs (Greek empire, established by Alexander the Great, d. 323 B.C.), and iron legs and feet (Rome, which conquered Jerusalem in 63 B.C.). A rock smashed the feet and then became a mountain and filled the whole earth (the kingdom of God—the church). Upon Daniel's recounting the dream and giving the interpretation, the king made him ruler of the province of Babylon.

After this, Nebuchadnezzar made a ninety-feet-high image plated with gold and required all to worship it. Shadrach, Meshach, and Abednego would not obey, and they were thrown in the fiery furnace, but they were miraculously spared.

Then Nebuchadnezzar had a dream about a tremendous tree whose top touched the sky, but it was cut down. Daniel interpreted the dream: the tree was Nebuchadnezzar, and he would be cut down from his high place and live like a beast of the field. This came to pass.

The next scene was the night before Babylon fell to the Medes and Persians (539 B.C.). Belshazzar was the grandson of Nebuchadnezzar (Nabonidus was his son, but he was not in the city, and his son Belshazzar was ruling in his stead). In the middle of a riotous party, a handwriting on the wall predicted his ruin. That very night, he was killed and the city was taken by Darius the Mede.

Daniel was made a satrap in the reign of Darius, and he was so successful as to draw the jealousy of other administrators. Probably the most popular account in the book is Daniel's night in the lions' den. After he had defied the orders of Darius not to pray to any god but to him only, Daniel was thrown into the den of lions. When God spared him from the lions, Darius praised Daniel and his God, and restored Daniel to his former place. The prophet remained faithful and prospered during the remainder of his life under the rule of Darius and Cyrus.

With chapter 7, the second half of Daniel's book begins as he describes one vision after another. The first occurred in the opening year of Belshazzar's reign (about 553 B.C.). So the experience in chapter 7 took place before the incidents recorded in 5 and 6. Daniel had a dream, and visions passed through his mind as he was lying on his bed (Daniel 7:1) Four beasts came out of the sea. They seem to represent the same kingdoms seen in the dream Nebuchadnezzar had (Daniel 2:24-47). The lion represented the Neo-Babylonian. The bear was the Medo-Persian federation (Lydia [546], Babylon [539], Egypt [525]). The leopard was the lightning conquests of Alexander the Great (334-323), which ended up in a division into four areas or kingdoms. The fourth beast was frightening to behold, and its ten horns showed its universal power. This was Rome. A little horn grew up in the midst of the others. He was the boastful antichrist who was eventually slain. One like a Son of Man came on the clouds of Heaven to the Ancient of Days and received power and authority from all that would last forever. The vision was assisted by an explanation from an angel standing by. Daniel learned about the beasts—that they were kingdoms and that from the fourth kingdom one would rise who would oppress the saints "for a time, times and half a time" (Daniel 7:25). But his power would be taken away and the sovereignty of all the kingdoms would be handed over to the people of God, and His kingdom will be an everlasting kingdom.

A ram and a goat were the main figures in the second vision (Daniel 8). It came two years after the first one. The ram fits best to the second beast of the first vision—this was the Medo-Persian empire. The charge of the powerful goat was the coming of Alexander the Great. A little horn grew up in the midst of the four horns coming from the goat. He brought the abomination that comes from desolation to the sanctuary of God. This was most likely descriptive of Antiochus Epiphanes. How long will this be? The answer was 2,300 evenings and mornings. Gabriel was called to give explanation to Daniel. The vision was so devastating that Daniel was exhausted and lay ill for several days afterward.

Chapter 9 records how Daniel pleaded with the Lord in prayer and petition. He confessed the unfaithfulness and rebellion of Judah. He admitted they deserved the disasters in Jerusalem and the exile in Babylon, but now, not because of Judah's righteousness, but because of the Lord's mercy, he asked that God would not delay His relief. Daniel was puzzled about the prediction of Jeremiah. He knew that Jeremiah had specified that the exile would last no longer than seventy years (Jeremiah 29:10), but he wanted to know when the Lord was counting the beginning of the exile that he might be sure of the end. Gabriel was sent to Daniel to tell him more. He gave the mark of the end of the exile, the issuing of a decree to restore and rebuild Jerusalem. But this was also to mark the beginning of more series of sevens. This time it was seventy sevens—from then all the way to "finish transgression, to put an end to sin, to atone for wickedness, to bring in everlasting righteousness, to seal up vision and prophecy and to anoint the most holy" (Daniel 9:24). This passage of explanation has introduced more myriads of interpretation than any other single passage of Scripture. Whether this refers to seven days, weeks, or years is a matter of dispute. Whether this leads to Antiochus Epiphanes, the Romans, the time of the Messiah's first coming, to His second coming, to the antichrist and the millennium—the assurance is left that God knows how and when these things will come to pass, but man must be ready to believe and follow.[53]

In the third year of Cyrus, another vision came to Daniel (chapter 10). This time he saw a man very similar in appearance to Jesus as described in Revelation 1:12-16. He told him of the coming of the prince of Persia (going back to the time of the Medes and Persians again), and the prince of Greece (referring again to Alexander the Great). Then he told of the king of the South and the king of the North and of their enmity with one another. From the details in the eleventh chapter of Daniel, it is evident that the Ptolemies of Egypt are the forces in the South and the Seleucids of Syria with its capital at Antioch are the armies from the north. Finally, again, Antiochus Epiphanes comes to the fore and establishes himself in the temple fortress and abolishes the daily sacrifice. The abomination that causes desolation is described in this vision as well. "Yet he will come to his end, and no one will help him" (Daniel 11:45).

The last chapter of Daniel (12) records how Michael, the great prince, will protect Daniel's people. A terrible time of tribulation

---

[53]For a convenient listing of variant beliefs on this passage, see Edward J. Young, *The Prophecy of Daniel* (Grand Rapids: Eerdmans, 1949), pp. 191ff.

will follow. The time of the resurrection will come, and judgment. Daniel asked how long it would be before all these things would come to pass. "It will be for a time, times and half a time," was the answer (Daniel 12:7). Then at the end of the book, the man clothed in linen added, "From the time that the daily sacrifice is abolished and the abomination that causes desolation is set up, there will be 1,290 days. Blessed is the one who waits for and reaches the end of the 1,335 days" (Daniel 12:11, 12).

Daniel is told to continue his way to the end. He would rest, "and then at the end of the days you will rise to receive your allotted inheritance" (Daniel 12:13).

Conclusions

The reason this review of Daniel has been inserted is to help understand Revelation. What can we conclude from comparison of the two?
1. Similar figurative language is used to convey lessons.
2. Historical applications were made to the figurative.
3. Lessons were sometimes repeated in a cyclical manner.
4. Lessons may be repeated in more than one fulfillment (Antiochus Epiphanes and Fall of Jerusalem).
5. Similar figures may have variant applications in different books; the context of the individual book is more important than a similarity with another book having a different context.

The study of Daniel and Revelation together helps the understanding of both. The same God has inspired the writing of each. He was in control in the time of Daniel and in the time of John, and He is still in control in our own time. He will be the complete victor in the end that will be eternal.

CHAPTER EIGHT

Evil Runs Rampant
Revelation 13:1-18

The year after the apostle John returned to Ephesus from his exile on Patmos, Tacitus was consul in Rome. He later became an historian of his times. His summary description of Rome in the months following the death of Nero (A.D. 68) is given below:

> The history on which I am entering is that of a period rich in disasters, terrible with battles, torn by civil struggles, horrible even in peace. Four emperors fell by the sword; there were three civil wars, more foreign wars, and often both at the same time. There was success in the East, misfortune in the West. Illyricum was disturbed, the Gallic provinces wavering, Britain subdued and immediately let go. The Sarmatae and Suebi rose against us; the Dacians won fame by defeats inflicted and suffered; even the Parthians were almost roused to arms through the trickery of a pretended Nero. Moreover, Italy was distressed by disasters unknown before or returning after the lapse of ages. Cities on the rich fertile shores of Campania were swallowed up or overwhelmed and the very Capitol fired by citizens' hands. Sacred rites were defiled; there were adulteries in high places. The sea filled with exiles, its cliffs made foul with the bodies of the dead. In Rome there was more awful cruelty. High birth, wealth, the refusal or acceptance of office—all gave ground for accusations, and virtues caused the surest ruin. The rewards of the informers were no less hateful than their crimes; for some, gaining priesthoods and consulships as spoils, secret influence at court, made havoc and turmoil everywhere, inspiring hatred and terror. Slaves were corrupted against their masters, freedmen against their patrons; and those who had no enemy were crushed by their friends. . . .

For never was it more fully proved by awful disasters of the Roman people or by indubitable signs that the gods care not for our safety, but for our punishment.[54]

This was written by a non-Christian in a time when he recognized that evil was running rampant.

Prelude

Overview

This chapter outlines in symbolical, visionary form the program of Satan. The figures used to do this were not chosen by Satan or by John. These are claimed to be revelations from God shown to John. The reason a description of the Roman world in the latter half of the first century was given above is not because this chapter must have these people and occasions to understand its meaning, but because these were the times of John the writer and the first readers to see John's book. We learn from Daniel that at least on some occasions the prophet begins his prophetic visions in his own day and then progresses into the future from there (the four beasts of Daniel begin with the neo-Babylonian kingdom where Daniel was in exile at that very time, but it goes on to the antichrist in a future kingdom and finally to an antichrist at the time of judgment). This is a lesson to be remembered as we view the context in Revelation. John was in exile by order of a Roman ruler. The world had tried to crush the Christian religion just over thirty years before. Now by John's own testimony from a place in exile, persecution was rearing its ugly head again.

The drama of the dragon, Satan, and his beastial helpers could have no more fitting setting than on a stage with the Roman power and persecution as the backdrop. But then a danger becomes evident. What if the viewers give all their attention to the backdrop and fail to watch the action of the performers and see the message there? It is well that we recognize this is only scene 1. There are more scenes to follow when the outcome is more clearly seen. It is better not to tie the lessons so tightly to the backdrops that we fail to see the same scenes are to be played out through the ages in front of one backdrop after another before the end finale.

---

[54]Tacitus, *Histories,* I.2,3.

The danger is greatly increased, however, when we find there are those who devote themselves to the study of Revelation, but refuse to accept the place of God in its truths, seeing only the ideas of John (or some other author of the time), apocalyptic sources of that period, and a knowledge of Old Testament terminology. Such a combination of emphasis on local coloring and a denial of divine insight leaves the whole book of Revelation earthbound, chained to the first century and a thoroughgoing preterist interpretation. On the other hand, one must not dismiss lightly any of the details found in Revelation. As we proceed, we want to profit by God's choice of the figures, appreciate the dimension supplied by the times and places reflected in the action, and be prepared to follow the lessons clearly intended.

The host of insistent views on this chapter is simply incredible. Two beasts, one from the sea and one from the land, are helpers to Satan—this much is agreed upon. Who each is remains unsolved. Many advocate that the first is a civil, political leader, or the world power he represents, some say in the first century, some in the end time, some say both. These usually look upon the second beast as more of a religious leader (he is called a false prophet), or the apostate religious body he represents. Even disagreement reigns as to which one of these should be considered the "antichrist" (see Special Subject #8 at end of this chapter).

The imitation that Satan practices in his deceitful ways becomes evident as the chapter unfolds. Just as the one on the throne is associated with the Lamb and the sevenfold Spirit, so the dragon enlists the two beasts to work with him.

Key Message

"This calls for patient endurance and faithfulness on the part of the saints" (Revelation 13:10b).

Glossary

Read through chapter 13 of Revelation. As you come to the terms listed below, note the explanation.

Dragon	The dragon, Satan, waited on the shore for help to carry out his evil work.
Beast (from the sea)	From the sea (which may symbolize the turbulent unrest of the wicked—Isaiah 57:20f) or from the location of the sea (in

the Mediterranean area), a beast emerges. Agreement on the character represented by this beast is hard to find. Some say the antichrist (see below, Special Study #8). Others say Rome, Nero, some future secular power like Rome, or the general influence of the world as it is opposed to God. It seems to be the same beast as in Revelation 11:7 and related to the four beasts of Daniel 7:2-7. See below pp. 118ff.

Ten horns

Horns are the basic symbolism for power, and ten means complete. Ten kings, yet to come (Revelation 17:12); some maintain they are ten rulers of the Roman empire.

Seven heads

Basic symbolism for intelligence. Some maintain these are the first seven emperors of Rome, from Augustus to Domitian. The blasphemous names on the heads have been associated with the divine titles used by the Roman emperors.

Ten crowns

The ruling crown, *diadema,* is pictured on each of the horns. This differs from the dragon, who has seven crowns on each of the seven heads instead (Revelation 12:3).

Leopard

The beast was like a leopard, the third of the four beasts in Daniel's vision. He is swift and fits the advance of Alexander the Great (Daniel 7:6).

Bear

The feet were those of a bear, the second of the four beasts of Daniel. This was the Medo-Persian kingdom, but here it is only a part of the animal figure.

Lion

The mouth was like a lion's, and this beast was the first of Daniel's vision (the Neo-Babylonian kingdom, Daniel 7:4)

Fatal wound

The death blow to one of the heads had been healed. Probably a travesty on the crucifixion and resurrection of Christ. Some try to apply this to Nero and a belief he would return after death—which did not happen.

Forty-two months	The same length of time designated four other times for tribulation and protection (Revelation 11:2, 3; 12:6, 14). It may be a figurative number indicating a period of severe persecution for Christians. It is literally three and a half years. Dispensationalists identify it with the "Great Tribulation."
Book of life	This is referred to six times in Revelation and once in Philippians (4:3). It contained a list of all those faithful followers of the Lord. They would not worship the beast, but all others, "the inhabitants of the earth," would worship him.
Another beast (from the earth)	As the first beast helped the dragon (Satan), so the second beast helped the first beast do his work. Some would see a secular power in the first beast and a false religious force in the second beast—the false prophet referred to in Revelation 16:13; 19:20; 20:10.
Two horns	This is not Jesus, the Lamb with seven horns (Revelation 5:6), but similar. Jesus warned of wolves in sheep's clothing (Matthew 7:15).
Miraculous signs	Remarkable wonders that deceive unbelievers. Jesus and Paul warned against them (Matthew 24:24; 2 Thessalonians 2:9).
Fire from Heaven	The similarity to Elijah is unmistakable (1 Kings 18; 2 Kings 1), but the times, motives, and source of power are different. The second beast could only do what it was given him to do. One does not know to what extent this was magical trickery.
Beast's image	An image of the first beast was constructed, and, whether by ventriloquism or magical skills, it was made to operate for the forces of evil so that death was the penalty for failing to worship it.
Mark of the beast	This mark is another imitation introduced on Satan's part, countering God's sealing of the redeemed (Revelation 7:3; 9:4; 14:1).

The beast required a mark of his own on the right hand or upon the forehead. This does not require a visible sign.

Number of the beast, 666 The mark of the beast is associated with the number of a man's name. Since the letters of the alphabet are also used as numbers in the Greek, Hebrew, and Latin, the numerical value of the letters in any word can be added up to give a numerical value of that word—or name. Many have used this fact to attempt to determine the identity of the beast.

In the last century, Nero has been suggested as a candidate for the name indicated here. This is most unlikely, for the solution demands the wrong language (to get this answer, Hebrew letters must be used, but John was writing in Greek); it demands a different spelling (the Hebrews ordinarily spelled Caesar with a *yodt* in the Talmud, and in the Latin it does not have a final *n (Neron)* form for the Hebrew ending needed to get the right numerical number); and Nero was already dead when John was writing about seeing this beast come forth. There was a myth, however, that Nero would come back leading an invasion of the Parthians. But this never occurred. Without a great stretch of the figurative, Nero does not fit.

But each generation has offered hundreds of suggestions, and none has proved satisfactory for long. (See below pp. 196ff.)

Content Notes

The Beast From the Sea (13:1-10)

The Appearance of the Beast (1-4)

The visions of John are continuing to trace the work of Satan. As the dragon, the devil had attempted to forestall the plan of

188

God by destroying the Messiah at His birth. Satan failed; so he assailed Heaven itself to stop the rule of God and the Messiah on the throne together. He failed and was cast out of Heaven. Then he tried to overwhelm the church in one tremendous gush, but the rushing flow failed even to reach the protected woman. Now Satan turns to annihilate her children, the faithful followers of the Lord Jesus, the body of the redeemed. To do this, he seeks support. In some ways, it seems as though he deliberately follows God's example, trying to imitate the very nature of the Godhead and the work of the three: the Father, the Son, and the Holy Spirit. Just as opposite as one can comprehend, Satan stands for everything that is evil and God for the pure and holy. Akin to himself, the dragon has his associates in two beasts, one from the sea and one from the land. From now on, Satan does his work through the beasts, and we hear no more of Satan's activities directly until the twentieth chapter.

The beast from the sea is the antichrist in every way. Not only is he against Christ, but he is His counterpart, just as opposite as he can be. On each of his seven heads, he has a blasphemous name. This could be an attack upon God, an insult against Him, a claim to be God, or a boast about doing things God alone has the prerogative to do. Later, we are told these heads are kings (Revelation 17:10), and without doubt the first readers of Revelation would think immediately of the honor as deity given to the emperors of Rome on the temple inscriptions and the statues set up in the provinces around the Mediterranean. But there is more involved in the claims and work of the beast from the sea than the first seven emperors of Rome.

A difficult description to explain is that one of the heads of the beast has a fatal wound that has been healed. The Greek is really saying this was a death blow from which he has been raised. This is a counterpart to the Lamb's looking as if it had been slain (Revelation 5:6) and yet standing victorious beside God on the throne. We know the allusion to Christ and His resurrection, but what is this claim for a head on Satan's beast? A common explanation is that Nero killed himself, but a story arose that he was going to return, leading the feared armies of the Parthians against Rome. This is scarcely satisfactory. If these heads are the early emperors of Rome, the majority of them should have shown a death wound because most of them died a violent death. The interpretation continues, however, with the insistence that Nero was the only one of them who was supposed to come back. In fact, one can readily see why the people were slow to admit his death. On at least two occasions, Nero had sent false reports to the senate that he was dead. His spies were watching to see who would cheer for joy at the news. Of course, those who did met their deaths shortly. So by the time Nero was really dead, everyone was afraid of being tricked and would not have been surprised to see him turn up again. Several pretenders tried to get something started in 69 and in 79 and also in 88,[55] using Nero's name, but they were stopped and recognized as frauds. By the end of the century, Dion Chrysostom (orat. xxi.9) scoffed at such a belief as foolishness.

The problem of Nero and the numbering of the Roman emperors will be renewed in the seventeenth chapter, but at the present, note the importance of the fatal wound that has been healed. The beast is identified in this way two more times in this chapter. This seems to be the drawing factor that leads the "whole world" to follow him and worship the dragon. They worship the beast as well. They are so awed by the beast's presence that they declare, "Who is like the beast? Who can make war against him?" (Revelation 13:4). On the one hand, hearing these words would cause the non-Christian world of the first century to think immediately of Rome and its power. On the other hand, the people of God would remember the words of David: "Who is like you, O Lord? You rescue the poor from those too strong for them, the poor and needy from those who rob them" (Psalm 35:10), or the words of Moses: "Who among the gods is like you, O Lord? Who is like you—majestic in holiness, awesome in glory, working wonders? You stretched out your right hand and the earth swallowed them [the enemy]" (Exodus 15:11, 12). Down through the ages, different beasts have arisen as world powers have made their threats, but still the Christian looks to God and the Lamb. The beast offers only an empty imitation, which leads to destruction.

In all of this, the lasting impression left by the beast is his imitation of God and Christ. Whether we can identify the head of the beast with the mortal wound and yet lived, we get the lesson—it is a feeble imitation of the heart of the gospel in Jesus. It may be a Nero who never came back. Or a Domitian who carried on his

---

[55]Tacitus, *Histories,* 1.78, ii.8, Zonar. xi. 18, Suetonius, *Nero,* 57.

work of persecution for him, or the heads could all be seven anti-God powers that rise in opposition to the people of God—but Satan tries to draw the world away through counterfeits in power and authority, similar in ways and means.

One needs to note also the association of the first beast from the sea and the four beasts of Daniel (7:2-7). The three first beasts of Daniel—the leopard, the bear, and the lion—are all combined in the one beast that came up from the sea in John's vision. The fact that the fourth beast of Daniel represented the Roman power may be the very reason the combination stopped with three. Another significance than simply the identification of the kingdoms emerges when one notes the time the earliest one was in power. Daniel's first kingdom was neo-Babylonian, the time in which Daniel was living. But his message projected into times beyond his own, and even to the end of the ages. So we should not be surprised if John's vision should draw symbols from John's own day and have its message extend to later times. Thus, the message of the beast with the mortally wounded head that was healed is not that Nero is coming back, but rather that Satan has a regular program of imitating God and puts up empty counterfeits such as profligate a ruler as Nero and as far-fetched a legend as his threatened return. Then the world chooses to believe him and worship him, but they resist Jesus and His genuine sacrifice for their souls. This is not a scene Satan has chosen to show us his work. The beasts are the symbols God has chosen in order to portray what the devil is doing daily.

The Work of the Beast (5-8)

Even though the dragon had given power and great authority to the beast, what he did is usually prefaced by the words "he was given to...." In other words, he is in a subservient role and receives his orders and permission from a higher power. The question still remains as to whether this is Satan, who gives him a mouth of arrogance and blasphemy, or whether it is God, who allows it. Here the answer includes a combination of both. The devil devises his schemes, but God sets His bounds. Since Satan's activity is coupled with a time restriction of forty-two months, this would indicate that God is in control, and neither the dragon nor the beasts are allowed unlimited license. The forty-two months is the regular three and a half years, whether literal or figurative (see the glossary above), that is frequently indicated for severe tribulation in the book of Revelation.

In this period, the antichrist is allowed to prevail over the saints. In Daniel's vision, the fourth kingdom (Roman), the nameless beast, "terrifying and frightening" (Daniel 7:7), had ten horns, and then another horn came up, "more imposing than the others and that had eyes and a mouth that spoke boastfully. As I watched, this horn was waging war against the saints and defeating them" (Daniel 7:20, 21). The seeming victory was cut short by the arrival of the Ancient of Days and the pronouncement of judgment; and the saints of the Most High possessed the kingdom for ever and ever.

In this time when evil was rampant, the authority of the beast was universal—"over every tribe, people, language and nation" (Revelation 13:7). This is the precise description of the universal recognition Christ will receive. But in this case, the usage is followed by a qualifying idiom. *All the inhabitants of the earth* is a description used to denote those of the world in contrast with citizens of God's kingdom, and it is all those of the world who are one in worshiping the beast. Then, as though John is anxious not to leave any misunderstanding, he adds—"all whose names have not been written in the book of life" (Revelation 13:8). Worship of the beast is universal among those of the world, but not from those truly in the church, whose names are in the book of life.

The phrase *from the creation of the world* (Revelation 13:8) has been taken two ways. Some maintain it should modify Jesus' being slain; others hold it should go with the names' not being written in the book of life. Although the Greek would grammatically allow either translation, the word order favors its going with the Lamb that was slain. The death of Christ was not an emergency measure that God thought up when the devil was winning for a time. "From the creation of the world," God had known that Christ, His Son, must die for the human beings He was creating. But the foreknowledge of God is complete. That His foreknowledge included a list of the redeemed, and also a realization of those not included there (and this is what it says in Revelation 17:8)—are equally true to His knowing about Christ's sacrifice, but since both are true, it is well to let each passage speak for itself. Here it seems to emphasize "belonging to the Lamb that was slain from the creation of the world."

Urgent Note to the Saints (9, 10)

In a time when evil is running rampant, what should the saints be doing? The temptation is to fight with the same tactics that are being used against them. Or worse still, to worship the beast and go along with the wicked, hoping the tide will turn and they can return to the Lord's ranks some time in the future. In answer, words are found in John's writing that are also found in Jeremiah, written when the prophet was delivering God's message in a time of destruction for Jerusalem and exile for Judah because of the manifold sins of Manasseh and Judah. The quotation in its full form follows:

> Then the Lord said to me: "Even if Moses and Samuel were to stand before me, my heart would not go out to this people. Send them away from my presence! Let them go! And if they ask you, 'Where shall we go?' tell them, 'This is what the Lord says:
> "'Those destined for death, to death;
> those for the sword, to the sword;
> those for starvation, to starvation;
> those for captivity, to captivity'" (Jeremiah 15:1, 2).

First, the observation should be made that the setting is different in John's Revelation. In Jeremiah, the suffering comes as a consequence of Judah's unfaithfulness to God. Not so in this passage found in Revelation 13. In fact, the words appear in other settings in Jeremiah. (See Jeremiah 43:11.) Although John's figures and terminology can be constantly paralleled by language from the Old Testament, the context and meaning must be sought from the book of Revelation itself. John himself is in exile for his testimony about Jesus. So be it, he is in exile. Paul was the same way. He had learned in whatever state he found himself to be content (Philippians 4:12). Even if it meant death ahead, far better to be a martyr and receive the blessings of Heaven than to worship the beast and suffer eternally in the second death. Accept the will of God and be confident that He will provide strength to endure and full blessings in the eternal age.

Another interpretation to this passage makes it a challenge to the assailants as well as a reminder to the Christians. Do they not realize the realistic principle of life that one reaps what he sows? If one sends others into captivity, he himself will end up in captivity. The one who kills with the sword must be killed by the sword. There is manuscript support for this last suggestion, and it is a principle enunciated by Jesus (Matthew 26:52), but the first interpretation is to be preferred in this context. The next sentence makes it clear that the Christians are being addressed and urged to patient endurance and faithfulness. Trust in God and let His will be done, no matter what comes. Even here, the other side of the coin is the warning not to take up the sword in furthering the gospel. This is spiritual warfare they are engaged in, and they must wait upon the Lord. How different from an admonition to take up the physical sword at this point!

The Beast From the Earth (13:11-18)

The Appearance of the Beast (11-13)

The second beast is made to resemble the Lamb also. He has two horns like him. But no one would confuse the two because he speaks like the dragon. In Revelation 19:20, he is identified as the false prophet.

The Deceitful Signs of the Beast (13, 14)

The pagans had to be impressed by the miracles associated with the life of Jesus. Some determined they would not accept Jesus, and in resisting Him, they tried to duplicate His works with their own stories. It would seem that Apollonius of Tyana was just such a creation developed to rival Jesus. The figure had lived and associated with Nero, Vespasian, and Titus, but it was Philostratus who had immortalized him with stories of a miraculous birth, attributing to him powers of healing, of driving out demons, and even claims of raising the dead. The same type of things surrounded the name of Simon Magus, as stories grew up about his rivalry with Peter in town after town and a finale in Rome. He was supposed to have brought statues to life.[56]

The Image of the Beast (14, 15)

This reference to an image is probably the reason so many commentators associate this beast with the propagation of

---

[56]*Clementine Recognitions,* 3.47; Justin, *Apologies,* I.26; see C. B. Caird, *Commentary on the Revelation,* p. 172.

Emperor worship in the first century. Many statues of the emperors were put up in the provinces, many temples were built in honor of the Emperors, and their deity was acclaimed all over the holdings of Rome. This lends itself in a natural way to the figures used in the work of the second beast as he erects an image and requires its worship or death for the individual.

The Mark of the Beast (16, 17)

Papyrus documents of the first and second centuries were frequently stamped with a seal known as *charagma,* the very word translated "mark" in this passage. These seals left the name of the ruling Emperor and the date inscribed on the document. Some may have included a likeness of the Emperor's features as well. They were used as part of the paperwork in buying and selling.[57] There is nothing here about the hand or the forehead.

The Number of the Beast (18)

Accepting a challenge, feeling futility, and expecting a reward, one joins the search for the meaning of the number 666. After all, John has warned us: "This calls for wisdom." You are not going to read this on the run and get the meaning in a hurry. It will take insight and deep thought to determine a helpful answer. But the very fact John puts it before us gives us the challenge to try. To say we're ignorant—we don't have an answer—and not even to try to understand what is involved is not enough. John challenges us to try.

We cannot escape, however, a sense of futility as we approach the subject because we recognize Christians for all the ages since the time of John have been making their suggestions to interpret this passage. Not one of them has been satisfactory for long for many. Perhaps the right answer is among the hundreds of suggestions, but what hope do we have to be sure, or much less to expect a new one that will be right? Why not admit we don't know and go on to more profitable studies? Or better still, you might say, accept the one most popular today and be satisfied. These are not good enough terms for deserting the quest.

---

[57]The first to have suggested a connection between the *charagma* and the mark of the beast was G. Adolph Deissmann in his *Bible Studies* (Winona Lake, IN: BMH Books, 1979), pp. 241ff.

We should approach a consideration of 666 expecting a reward. Not that we will fill the blank and have a man's name when we are finished, but we should know more about what we are looking for, both in John's day and in our own. We should know more about what the purpose is for John's telling us about these things. For that matter, we should profit by discerning where some of the suggestions made are wrong, and taking precautions lest we make the same mistakes. Unless we travel the whole tortuous route ourselves, we will never be able to come to the bottom line to the whole trip.

In as brief a summation as we will make here, we only give an example of different types of suggestions. The first type was pursued by those in the early church. They were accustomed to the fact that the Greek, Hebrew, and Latin used letters to denote numerical values. In the Greek language, the first letter of the alphabet, alpha (a) = 1, beta (b) = 2, gamma (g) = 3, and so on. Later, letters of the alphabet increase by tens, then by hundreds. For example, rho, (r) = 100, sigma (s) = 200, tau (t) = 300. To determine the numerical value of words and names was a common practice. In the first century, before erupting Vesuvius inundated the town of Pompeii, one day a man scrawled on a wall that he was in love with a woman having the number 545. Another shared in the graffiti, putting down 1045. In this way, the name was veiled, but the information was registered. In John's case in Revelation, he may have had several reasons to use this device to impart information. If this referred to a Roman Emperor, living or dead, or to any aspect of the Roman authority, it would not be wise to inflame further persecution by direct reference in written messages. Even if this was a direct reference to an individual in the distant future, only rarely were specific names given in prophecy. Intervening ages may lose the urgency of the message for their own times because they failed to associate the name with their time and place. But if the challenge is there to understand the meaning, the search continues in every generation. Or it may be that the name was of a person, but still a symbol for something significant in different ages, in different individuals, such as the antichrist. Even this may be one final individual at the last that will remain unidentified until the closing moments.

The solution in Greek letters. One of the early attempts to unravel the puzzle was made by Irenaeus (c. A.D. 180). He gave three solutions:

LATEINOS	TEITAN	EUANTHAS
L = 30		
A = 1		E = 5
T = 300	T = 300	U = 400
E = 5	E = 5	A = 1
I = 10	I = 10	N = 50
N = 50	T = 300	TH = 9
O = 70	A = 1	A = 1
S = 200	N = 50	S = 200
666	666	666

Observations:

(1) Irenaeus presents what to him are three possible solutions. The very fact that he presents more than one gives us a clue that he does not have one solid answer, but gives three uncertain ones.

(2) *Lateinos* denotes the Latin Kingdom (the Roman Empire). This has considerable to commend it because of coming descriptions (see chapter 17 especially) that link the beast with Rome. For both John and his earliest readers, the power and persecutions of Rome would be uppermost in their minds. It was a godless power that claimed the role of God. But this was not a man's name.

(3) *Lateinos* was later used following the beginnings of the Reformation movement to connote the Roman Catholic Church rather than pagan Rome. In rebuttal, Luther was made into 666—as have been Mohammed, Pope Benedict IX, and numerous others since.

(4) Irenaeus's suggestion of *Teitan* was on the basis of the role Teitan had as the mythical monster who assaulted the gods and matched somewhat the role of the beast as antichrist. But this, too, was not the number of a man.

(5) Evidently, the only basis of suggesting the name *Euanthas* was as a person's name, and its numerical value added up to 666.

(6) Irenaeus introduces another enigma. Even by his time, a manuscript difference had appeared that gave instead of 666 the number of 616. He decides in favor of 666, but later some manuscripts still follow the 616 reading. Did a careless scribe mistake the letter denoting 60 for the letter denoting 10 and therefore come up 50 short? Zahn thought not, and insisted it was a deliberate change. "Because of the desire to find here a reference to Caius Caesar, i.e. Caligula, ... before the time of Irenaeus, unknown persons residing in Rome or the West, not in Asia,

changed the number 666 to 616."[58] This would show an early interest in identifying the antichrist with a Roman Emperor. In fact, being so anxious to do so, they were prepared to change the number to *make* it fit Caius Caesar!

(7) The bottom line to all of Irenaeus's study of the subject of 666 is the most interesting conclusion of all. "Irenaeus has only uncertain guesses to offer, and he thinks the Apocalyptist intended the name to remain hidden till Antichrist should come."[59]

(8) As a postscript to Irenaeus's testimony, one should remember that Polycarp and Papias studied under the apostle John at Ephesus. Although Irenaeus became a bishop in Gaul, he had come originally from Asia Minor and had studied under Polycarp. Then, too, he had spent some time in Rome as well. He certainly had ample opportunity to receive traditional teaching on the book of Revelation. One wonders how many times John must have been questioned about solving the puzzle of 666. If he left any further clues, they are not evident at the end of the second century.

In the *Sibylline Oracles* (v. 12-42), there is a list of emperors with the numerical value of their initial letters. The list begins with Julius Caesar and ends with Otho (K = 20, S = 200, T = 300, G = 3, K = 20, N = 50, G = 3, O = 70). This adds up to 666.[60]

The solution in Hebrew letters. The earliest ones to suggest Nero as the answer to 666 lived in the early eighteen hundreds.[61] This is occasion for some surprise that an answer being sought in antiquity would wait so long for discovery. The surprise diminishes when one recognizes that the proposed solution is in the

---

[58]Theodor Zahn, *Introduction to the New Testament* (Grand Rapids: Kregel, 1953 reprint), vol. III, p. 448.

[59]Isbon T. Beckwith, *The Apocalypse of John* (Grand Rapids: Baker, 1979), p. 403. Swete concurs, stating: "Irenaeus's guesses (for they are obviously no more) are based on the hypothesis that the second Beast directly represented Antichrist" (*Commentary on Revelation,* p. 175).

[60]See C. B. Caird, *Commentary on the Revelation,* p. 175.

[61]I.T. Beckwith, *The Apocalypse of John,* p. 405. He lists four scholars as having reached the same conclusion independently (Fritzsche, Benary, Hitzig, Reuss). Proposed first in 1831 by Fritzsche. See T. Zahn, *Introduction to the New Testament,* III, p. 447.

wrong language, Hebrew instead of Greek, and fails to use the regular spelling (see the glossary above), and makes an application that is short of likely. Whereas Nero was certainly a likely candidate for the role of the antichrist, it seems he would be but one head on the beast and that the number of the beast would not be identified with only one of the emperors. Nor would it seem likely that a book preparing Christians for the future would look back upon a figure of the past to represent his prophecy.

All the objections above have received sufficient answer for some. After all, John was a Jew and knew Hebrew; so he could have used it. The spelling can be found in some cases, no matter how few, and Nero has been known down through history as the persecutor of the church. But there is no avoiding the forced treatment that is necessary at every turn in order to end up with the 666 answer. This is no different from all the other answers to the question, but this is no assurance that we have found the right answer yet.

Modern solutions to 666. Every century has had its crises. All Christians have sought help from the book of Revelation. Unfortunately, many have brought their own ideas and their own solutions they seek to superimpose on the book. Some have come to the 666 challenge and created their own system so they can arrive at the conclusion they desire. Only one example will be given, although there are as many systems as there are conclusions.

In our own century, Hitler excelled as without godly principles and insensitive to the value of human life. He was thought of as the beast with the number 666. Some worked it out.

If		then			
	A = 100	then	H	= 107	
	B = 101		I	= 108	
	C = 102		T	= 119	HITLER
	D = 103		L	= 111	
	E = 104		E	= 104	
	etc.		R	= 117	
				666	

Numerical solutions to 666. From especially Pythagoras on, the ancients were attracted to the magic that could be worked with numbers. Although no hope of enlightenment on the meaning of Revelation can be gained from this treatment of the text, this type of attempt at deciphering 666 is given as an example.

A Triangular Number: adding each consecutive number 1 through 36 yields 666 (1 + 2 + 3 + 4 + ...+ 35 + 36 = 666). This leaves 36 as the final number needed to reach 666 in the summation. Repeating the process, adding each consecutive number 1 through 8 gives 36 (1 + 2 + 3 + 4 + ...+ 8 = 36). This leaves 8 as the key number, agreeing with the eighth emperor, according to this triangular number. All this achieves is to lead us back to the eighth emperor of Rome, which is a doubtful solution in itself.

Symbolic interpretations of 666. Although some would follow numerology in order to find significance to every number found in Scripture, this is not a safe or sane way to exegete a passage. However, if Scripture points out the significance of a number or if it tells us a significance is there, then we know to look. Could these numbers be telling the reader something apart from what language he is using and what time he is living in? When one reads the book of Revelation, he cannot escape the importance of the number seven. It constantly appears throughout its pages. Those who have made studies of numbers rarely agree in their conclusions, but in the case of seven—although some variation is found in the way it is expressed—there is general agreement that seven denotes completeness. Could 666 be a symbol of someone or something—apart from numerical value or the letters of his name? If seven is complete, what is six? Of course, it is trite to say the number is one short of seven. It says this emphatically with the number repeated three times.

To this can be added another interesting fact. This is something that was pointed out in antiquity before Irenaeus was working on the problem of 666. This is the numerical value of a name that does not need to be put in another language or to be spelled in another way. It is a name that can be recognized in any language. The name is Jesus.

I	=	10
E	=	8
S	=	200
O	=	70
U	=	400
S	=	200
		888

The name equals 888.

The name of Jesus is a series of numbers one more than seven even as the number of the beast is one less than seven. This is symbolic of the antichrist. The beast is not only against Christ, opposing Him in every way, but he is the counterpart of Christ with God as the beast is to Satan. He is his helper who becomes man to do evil even as Christ became man to die in our stead. The beast even imitates Christ in order to deceive. The very death wound on one of the heads of the beast is only to emulate the One whom he seeks to displace. But every step of the way, the antichrist is 666, one less than 7, and Jesus is 888, one more than the completeness man knows.

Special Subject #8

Antichrist

The figure of "antichrist" is explicitly used in the Scripture. A number of other passages of Scripture describe character and behavior matching that expected of antichrist. In addition to this, the term became common in the early centuries to writings outside the canonical books. In fact, the title is used heavily in contemporary studies of the end times. Since the understanding of these uses is essential to an appreciation of what we are being told in the book of Revelation, we stop to review basic sources.

John is the only canonical writer who makes use of the term *antichrist,* and only then in his epistles. Four passages explicitly use the term: 1 John 2:18, 22; 4:3; 2 John 7. These passages emphasize the false belief, the false teaching of the antichrist. He denies that Jesus came in the flesh, that He is the Son of God. When Polycarp in Asia Minor was asked about the antichrist in the first half of the second century, it is sure he thought of the Docetists, of Marcion, and those who took their philosophy still further afield along those lines. But Polycarp, as he came to the point of death as a martyr and was asked to renounce Christ and accept the gods of the Romans, motioned to the crowds in the stands and indicated they were the actual atheists and he, Polycarp, believed in the true God and His Son, Jesus Christ. It is clear that by now Polycarp saw the power of Rome doing the work of Satan and opposing the work of God. This was the role of antichrist.

This interpretation of Scripture saw confirmation in other parts of Scripture. For centuries, the Jews had looked for the coming of the Messiah, but they also recognized there was prophesied one who would be the entire opposite of a Savior, a destroyer, who was also coming. This virtual antichrist was identified in the arrival of Antiochus Epiphanes as he set up the abomination of desolation in the temple area. This was in fulfillment to the prophecy of Daniel 8:9ff. So Antiochus became an archetype of antichrist before Jesus ever came. But he was not the only one. When Pompey took Jerusalem in 63 B.C., he, too, came into the temple area and desecrated the very Holy of Holies. He, too, was noted as a type of antichrist.

When Jesus taught of His return, He also combined with this warnings of the fall of Jerusalem. The word *antichrist* was not used, but He spoke of false Christs (Matthew 24:15ff; Mark 13:6, 21, 22; Luke 21:8, 9, 20-24). He also speaks of the prophet Daniel and again we read of the abomination that causes desolation in the holy place (Daniel 9:24ff). Jesus warned not to expect security in Jerusalem but to flee to the mountains. When the Romans marched on the city and destroyed it in A.D. 70, the Christians had heeded Jesus' prophecy and fled to the north across the Jordan to Pella and were not besieged in the city. Again the antichrist was Rome. In fact, some six years before, Nero had begun the first full-scale Roman persecution of the Christians following his own burning of Rome. Nero became a full-fledged candidate for the antichrist. Some in the church viewed the teaching of Paul as indicating that Rome was the power that was restraining the coming of the "man of lawlessness" ("man of sin"). As persecution continued, however, they altered their position completely and looked upon Rome as indeed the antichrist himself.

Another Scripture must be added to fill out the notes concerning antichrist. This is chapter 13 of Revelation, which is under study just now. Read all of the passages in Daniel, in Jesus' discourse cited above, in Paul, and in Revelation—all tell of a man with similar characteristics and aspirations. In Revelation, we must add the seventeenth chapter and the twentieth also for the outcome. We will return to the subject as we add the information given there.

One must keep the words of Paul in mind concerning the Lord's coming:

> Don't let anyone deceive you in any way, for that day will not come until the rebellion occurs and the man of lawlessness is revealed,

the man doomed to destruction. He will oppose and will exalt himself over everything that is called God or is worshiped, so that he sets himself up in God's temple, proclaiming himself to be God. . . .

And now you know what is holding him back, so that he may be revealed at the proper time. For the secret power of lawlessness is already at work; but the one who now holds it back will continue to do so till he is taken out of the way. And then the lawless one will be revealed, whom the Lord Jesus will overthrow with the breath of his mouth and destroy by the splendor of his coming. The coming of the lawless one will be in accordance with the work of Satan displayed in all kinds of counterfeit miracles, signs and wonders, and in every sort of evil that deceives those who are perishing. They perish because they refused to love the truth and so be saved. For this reason God sends them a powerful delusion so that they will believe the lie and so that all will be condemned who have not believed the truth but have delighted in wickedness (2 Thessalonians 2:3-12).

Note the clear indication that this antichrist is associated with the second coming of Christ. The revealing of his identification is joined with his being overthrown at the coming of the Lord. In Daniel, also, the last of the antichrists is overcome in the final throes of the age.[62] In our understanding of the antichrist, it is necessary that we allow for a number of antichrists along the way, but be forewarned of an archeantichrist at the end time. This is the reason we should not be too quick to see Nero as the full meaning of the beast. If he is simply a symbol of Rome and Rome a symbol of the antichrist, it may be. But this seems to be an unnecessary piling up of symbols unless it can be more certainly established. No doubt the earliest readers saw their own times reflected there. But we should not limit John's intent and

---

[62]Commentary on Daniel 11:45 (Edward J. Young, *The Prophecy of Daniel: A Commentary* [Grand Rapids: Eerdmans, 1949], p. 253): "At any rate, the great final enemy of the people of God, the Antichrist, will make his last stand and will come to his end in territory which is sacred and holy (peculiarly delighted in by the people of God—note the expression *mountain of holiness* —does this have reference to the church?). His end will be complete, apparently brought about by the glorious return of the Son of God from heaven."

especially God's revelation to the circumstances of the first century. The message is a bridge that begins in John's time and keeps extending over every succeeding age until the Lord returns to triumph over His counterpart, the antichrist. When John was writing, evil was running rampant and the Christians needed both endurance and faithfulness. Satan was using tactics in imitation of what he saw in God's plans. He works the same today in every deceit. But God will win. The message continues both timely and timeless in every time.

CHAPTER NINE

The Last Harvest

Revelation 14:1-20

An Indian tribe in the eastern part of the young United States had reached the point of desperation. They had tried valiantly to eke out a living in the face of the growing numbers of white civilization, but to no avail. The Indians had suffered losses in every way. Finally, they decided their only hope was to accept an allotment in the newly opened western Indian Territory. Their trek across the states was so filled with trials and disappointments that the saga describing it was called "the trail of tears."

Even when they arrived, their conditions were appalling. They decided they must get together and agree upon some plan of action to help one another or they would not be able to continue living. An appointed time and place were announced, under a certain tree at two on the next afternoon. When the time came, only two met there. The one Indian said to the other, "What can we do now? There are only two of us." But the other Indian replied, "Talequah (two are enough)." From that afternoon, plans were laid and efforts begun that led to a successful community. Today in the state of Oklahoma, one of the larger towns is named Talequah for the two that had the determination to persevere in the face of difficulty and in spite of their being only two.

In the thirteenth chapter of Revelation, we were appalled by the power of the beasts and the dominance they had over the inhabitants of the earth. In the fourteenth chapter, the scene changes and we are allowed to see our worries can be dispelled. Despite it all—two are enough: the Lamb and the redeemed.

Prelude

Overview

The two witnesses were killed in the streets. Satan is attacking the woman and her offspring. Two beasts have come from the sea and the land to aid the dragon in his assault on the people of God. How can all of this be taken as an encouragement to anyone who chooses to follow the Lamb?

But look at the other side of the coin each time. The two witnesses are resurrected and ascend to Heaven, where they are safe beyond the reach of any evil thought or action. Second, the attacks of Satan were thwarted each time—the woman was spared, the baby was safe, Heaven was secure. "Resist the devil, and he will flee from you" (James 4:7).

What of the beasts and their threats to kill anyone who will not worship the image of the beast? What if you cannot buy or sell if you do not have the mark of the beast? What do you do when evil runs rampant?

Again you look at the other side—to what is going on in Heaven. At the first glimpse, you see the Lamb, not being washed away, not being overwhelmed, but standing confidently on Mt Zion. With Him are the redeemed, the 144,000. They are not defeated, but they are singing a new song—one they have learned because of the trials they have lived through on earth. They would not be there today except for the Lamb and for their faithfulness.

Heaven is a tremendous answer that turns the picture around. But that is not all. Judgment is coming. This time it is not just another round of trials that causes some to repent but leaves most in the same company as before. This is at least the preliminary step in the final harvest of souls. Three angels announce the gospel, the fall of Babylon, and the fate of those who worship the beast compared with the blessings of those who die in the Lord.

This final judgment is pictured as a harvest, the ingathering of the wheat and the grapes. This is the resurrection, one to life and the other to eternal death. This is the encouragement to the followers of Jesus. Any suffering, any trial now is but small in light of the alternatives of sharing eternity with Satan or with God.

Key Message

"Take your sickle and reap, because the time to reap has come, for the harvest of the earth is ripe" (Revelation 14:15b).

Glossary

Read through Revelation 14. As you come to the terms listed below, note the explanation.

Lamb	Despite the evil raging on earth, the victorious Lamb, Jesus Christ, stands untouched in heaven. This is the same Lamb introduced in 5:6.
Mount Zion	In more ancient times, the stronghold and city of David. The site and another name for Jerusalem. The name used for the secure center of the Messianic reign (Psalm 2:6). In spiritual Zion, everlasting joy pervades (Isaiah 35:10). This seems to be in Heaven, but premillennialists hold this is the beginning of the millennium and is on earth.
144,000	Same as the redeemed group, sealed of God (Revelation 7:4). They represent in Heaven the redeemed still living on earth. They belong to God as those having the mark of the beast belong to the beast. (See below under Content Notes.)
Voice	From Heaven (earlier Revelation 10:4; another Revelation 18:4). It sounded as (1) waters—see Revelation 1:15, (2) thunder—see Revelation 6:1, and (3) a harpist—see Revelation 5:8.
New song	See Revelation 5:9. New songs were sung to celebrate acts of deliverance. The sacrificial death of Jesus is central in the theme in Revelation.
Another angel	The last angel designated was Michael (Revelation 12:7), but this is more likely a reference to the two coming angels—another and another and another (Revelation 14:8, 9).
Eternal gospel	In all of John's writings in the New Testament, this is his only use of the word for "gospel." Some question whether this would be "good news" to the whole of the world if a person was among the unsaved. But these are the everlasting facts that have saving power—the death, burial, and resurrection of Christ, as well as the sovereignty

	of God, the condemnation of the wicked, and the salvation of those faithful to God.
Hour of judgment	A part of the gospel, however, is the coming judgment. At that time, all will worship God who is the creator of the heavens and the earth.
Second angel	Another angel follows the flight of the first one into the height of the sky between the two horizons.
Babylon fallen	Rather than literal Babylon along the Euphrates, or even the specific, figurative application to ancient Rome, it probably is best viewed as a still more general application to the corrupt, evil opposition to God present continually among people of the world.
Third angel	Another angel in a loud voice announces the conclusion of the matter for those who worship the beast and his image.
Cup of God's wrath	The judgment of God with its consequences. In the Greek, two words are used for wrath, descriptive of God: *orge,* divine anger, and *thumos,* righteous indignation. Both are used in this verse (10).
White cloud	White denotes purity and holiness. Clouds are frequently associated with judgment or the approach of the consequences of judgment.[63]
Like a Son of Man	"Son of Man" is a Messianic title, Daniel 7:13f, applied to Jesus in Revelation 1:13. This one wears a crown and holds a sharp sickle, yet an angel instructs him to reap with the sickle. If this is the Christ, it is strange that He is told what to do by an angel and to perform a task that angels proceed to do in the coming scenes. Perhaps this is an angel designated to reap the victorious on behalf of the Christ.

---

[63]See Isaiah 19:1; Jeremiah 4:13; Matthew 24:30; 26:64.

Crown of gold	The symbol of victory *(stephanos),* like the one worn by the rider on the white horse of the first seal (Revelation 6:2), but the rider on the white horse in Revelation 19:12 is wearing many crowns *(diademata,* the ruler's crown).
Sharp sickle	The tool for harvesting. When reaping grain, it was a flint or iron blade secured to a handle of bone or wood. This word is used in the New Testament only in Mark 4:29 and seven times in this chapter.
Another angel	This angel was equipped with a sharp sickle also, but he followed the instructions given by the "fire" angel who came from the altar and commanded him to harvest the grapes.
Gather the grapes	The grape-knife used to cut clusters of grapes was different from the blade used to cut wheat, but each could be called a sickle.
Another angel	This is the angel who came to tell that the time had arrived to harvest the grapes because they were ripe.
Charge of the fire	The angel that came from the altar had power over the fire. Two altars have been introduced thus far in Revelation. One was the altar for burnt offerings located, in the earthly arrangement, outside the Holy Place. In Heaven, it was the place beneath which the martyrs were gathered (Revelation 6:9-11). The other was the altar of incense located, in the earthly tabernacle, in the Holy Place just in front of the Holy of Holies. The prayers of the saints were offered here in Heaven (Revelation 8:3-5). In response, fire was taken from the altar, cast on the earth, and judgment was the result. This latter altar is the reference here to an angel commissioned to command the beginning of the harvest of grapes.
Winepress of God's Wrath	The gathering of the grapes included tramping out the juice and saving the

resulting "fruit of the vine." This was a common figure in the Old Testament for God's execution of judgment.[64]

Outside the city Executions were regularly made outside the walls of a city so the city would not be defiled by the blood of the victim. Jesus, too, was crucified outside the city gate (Hebrews 13:12). As the figure changes here in Revelation from the winepress of grapes to the vat overflowing with blood of suffering, the site is moved outside the walls.

Sixteen hundred stadia A symbolic number either indicating the whole world or the length of Palestine (see below, p. 220). The toll of this suffering is depicted by the volume of blood portrayed. This is the result of the judgment of the wicked.

Content Notes

The Lamb and the Redeemed (14:1-5)

The contrast between chapters 13 and 14 is deeper than one can grasp. We leave the earth where all are following the instruction of the beasts and have been marked as worshiping the first beast. Now, however, John sees the Lamb, and everyone—the 144,000— is following Him. They are marked with the name of the Father and the Lamb on their foreheads. But where is this latter scene taking place?

The Scene on Mount Zion

You feel the contrast between Satan, the dragon, standing on the sands of the shore on earth (Revelation 13:1), and the Lamb standing on the rock of Zion. But is this in Heaven or on earth? Is this the old Jerusalem at its early site or is this associated with the Mount Zion of the Heavenly city? In Hebrews we read:

> But you have come to Mount Zion, to the heavenly Jerusalem, the city of the living God. You have come to thousands upon

---

[64]See Isaiah 63:3; Lamentations 1:15; Joel 3:13.

thousands of angels in joyful assembly, to the church of the first-born [ones], whose names are written in heaven. You have come to God, the judge of all men, to the spirits of righteous men made perfect, to Jesus the mediator of a new covenant, and to the sprinkled blood that speaks a better word than the blood of Abel (Hebrews 12:22-24).

That this is the Heavenly Mount Zion in the Revelation passage as well is borne out by the personnel we meet. Jesus is seen in the figure of a Lamb; the 144,000 are there, as well as the four living creatures and the elders. Even the throne is there. Little doubt can be left that Heaven is indicated.

Some, however, insist that this scene must be on earth because this is an opening scene to Christ's millennial reign on the throne of David in Jerusalem.[65] But rather than prove this must be situated on earth, this is an indication that the claims for a millennial reign on earth must be seriously questioned. (See pp. 289ff; pp. 294ff.)

The question of the identity of the 144,000 is a perennial debate. What seems to fit best is that these are the redeemed, but a representative number of the total redeemed (see pp. 109, 110). These represent those who are still living on earth but whose names are in the book of life, they are among the redeemed, but their spirits are represented in the 144,000 in Heaven. That is the reason they are the only ones who are learning the new song of deliverance. The only way to learn it is through the experience of tribulation, and they are just now living through such trials as pictured in the activity of the beasts in the chapter before. Even Jesus is described as having "learned obedience from what he suffered" (Hebrews 5:8). This understanding gives further point to the description, "They [the 144,000] follow the Lamb wherever He goes" (Revelation 14:4). When Jesus gathered His disciples, His summary word was, "Follow Me." This is a situation where a statement can be turned around and found to be true: "As it was on earth, so it will be in Heaven." For as they were following Him on earth and learning obedience, so the 144,000 were following Him in Heaven and learning a new song.

---

[65]John F. Walvoord, *The Revelation*, p. 214.

The Sounds of Heaven (2, 3)

Even the sounds described are those we have learned to expect in Heavenly scenes. Although the voice of Jesus was reported like the sound of rushing waters before John was taken to Heaven (Revelation 1:15), nevertheless in this passage it explicitly states the sound came from Heaven (Revelation 14:2). So also the loud peal of thunder accompanies pronouncements of judgment as well as seasons of rejoicing in Heaven (Revelation 11:19; 19:6). Likewise, we have met the new song and the harp in Heaven before (Revelation 5:8, 9). The "new songs," both of the Old Testament and of the book of Revelation, have to do particularly with deliverance from tribulation.

The Cast in Heaven (1, 3)

Who is doing the singing is not explicitly explained. The sound is pleasing, harmonious, but also loud. They sing in front of the living creatures and the elders; so this seems to exclude them from the chorus (although they were the singers in a former scene—Revelation 5:8, 9). Thus the 144,000 seem to be the singers. Note, however, the contrast between the Heavenly cast in this chapter compared with the earthly cast for the beasts in the chapter before.

Characteristics of the 144,000 (4, 5)

Another constant debate about the 144,000 concerns just how special is this group? Do they represent all of the redeemed or just one particular group? If just one group, which one: the Jews from the old dispensation who are redeemed, the redeemed who are still alive and on earth in person but represented by the 144,000 in Heaven, or all martyrs who have given their lives for their testimony for Jesus? This following passage should be helpful because it lists at least some of their characteristics.

(1) They kept themselves pure. The language used here, "They did not defile themselves with women," must certainly be taken metaphorically rather than any reflection on marriage as sinful or even the preference of celibacy over marriage. The words are a description of fornication or adultery—sexual immorality—rather than the relationship of husband and wife. But both in the Old Covenant and the New Covenant, spiritual adultery was the figure used to cover the whole gamut of loyalty and purity in vows to God. Time and again, Israel is accused of adultery because of

212

compromising with the heathen worship of idols and other gods. Paul used the figure when he wrote the Corinthians: "I am jealous for you with a godly jealousy. I promised you to one husband, to Christ, so that I might present you as a pure virgin to him" (2 Corinthians 11:2). This would include both men and women because the language is to be applied figuratively. Ignatius in his epistle to the Smyrnans could address the married as virgins because, as Lightfoot interprets it, "the widows whom I call virgins because of their purity and devotion."[66] They are chaste in their life-style. Especially because of the frequent use of the figurative in Revelation, one might expect purity to be expressed this way in describing an essential characteristic of the 144,000, both men and women. The masculine form of virgin is even used here to indicate an unusual type of application to his words.

(2) They followed the Lamb. "To follow" means to follow His leadership as a good soldier follows his commanding officer. But "to follow" also means to emulate His example. Since Jesus is the Son of God, none of His followers can duplicate what He has done. But His example challenges us in the right direction. He is the "author and perfecter" of our faith (Hebrews 12:2). This has been translated, He is our "trailblazer." We must be ready to follow wherever He leads. The soldiers of Alexander the Great were said to have loved and admired him so much that they were willing to "march off the map" in following him. How much more dedicated are the redeemed in their following the Lamb from this life on into the very throne room of God—and into eternity!

(3) They were purchased from men. From among all the men of all the world, the redeemed have been bought back. When the new song was sung in honor of the Lamb (Revelation 5:9), this purchase was described: "... because you were slain, and with your blood you purchased men for God from every tribe and language and people and nation." But now John learns of another purpose for the purchase.

(4) They were offered as firstfruits. These people were firstfruits in more than one way. Under the old law, the first sheaf of the harvest was brought to the priest and presented to the Lord. Besides this, a sacrifice of a lamb was given. This represented the

---

[66]See I.T. Beckwith, *The Apocalypse of John,* p. 650.

harvest that year. Other offerings were made in the year and at the close, but the firstfruits were special. This figure is used of the "first converts" in an area (Romans 16:5; 1 Corinthians 16:15). Epenetus was the firstfruits to Christ in the province of Asia, as was Stephanas in Achaia. In another way, Christ is the firstfruits in the resurrection, for He has been raised first, and He represents all who follow Him in the resurrection (1 Corinthians 15:20).

In what way, then, are the 144,000 firstfruits? They may be early, among the first to have entered Heaven; they may be representative of the whole of the redemption harvest that will follow until the Lord returns; or they may be representative in that they are the firstfruits standing in for the living redeemed until they join the ranks above at death; or they may be firstfruits in a special-offering way, in that their lives have been laid down in sacrifice or martyrdom as they fill up the special number of 144,000. The strongest likelihood is that they are representative in a special way.

(5) They do not lie. Basic honesty is essential to anyone who determines to follow Jesus. It was a rarity in antiquity, and it is a sad commentary on our society today to see the steady erosion of integrity in every level of the land. There is no indication that these characteristics of the redeemed are listed in the order of importance. In fact, one would have difficulty in listing the characteristics in such an order.

(6) They are blameless. Not only is this term all inclusive, but it also recalls the Old Testament sacrificial system. Each sacrificial animal was to be without blemish. Each of the redeemed is without fault, blameless. Does this mean he is offering himself in sacrificial service?

From this list of characteristics, the identification of the 144,000 has not been established as a special group. Their qualities are necessary to all the redeemed.

Three Angels of Judgment (14:6-13)

The second montage of the chapter is now introduced. An angel takes his position high in the sky so that he can be seen and heard from horizon to horizon most advantageously by the most people of the earth. The word used to describe this angel's position (*midair* in the NIV) is one sometimes used in classical Greek to denote the position of the sun at midday. The angel is about to make an announcement to every nation, tribe, language and people. His mission is to present the everlasting gospel. This poses a problem to some. They maintain that the way this universal audience of mankind is described is the usual way to designate the unbelieving mass. To them, the way of salvation is no "good news." This will only be bad news of judgment to them. But perhaps this brings out an essential element in the gospel *(euangelion)*. As long as an invitation is included to repent and receive the message, it is good news to the hearer. This is the case here. (See Mark 13:10.)

To God Be the Glory (7)

The message of the angel can be considered point one for the presentation of the gospel. This will be an alternate outline to Paul's summation (1 Corinthians 15:1ff). Give God the glory (not Satan, not the dragon or his beasts, not the world, not self). God is our Creator, He will be our Judge; worship Him. This is as they did under duress in Revelation 11:13. This is the way Paul approached his audience at Lystra:

> We are bringing you good news, telling you to turn from these worthless things to the living God, who made heaven and earth and sea and everything in them (Acts 14:15).

To Babylon Be Destruction (8)

Babylon is the notoriously sinful city in antiquity and could be used to refer to Rome in the time of John or any other sinful city since that time. This warning of the miserable destruction for the great city of Babylon, as it lay in ruins in John's day, was given as an essential part of the gospel. Truly, the gospel is good news with facts to be believed, but it also has commands to be obeyed along with the faith. The promises to be enjoyed are also a welcome part of the good news, but along with these are given warnings to be heeded. Babylon is presented as one of these grim reminders of the consequences of the maddening wine of her adulteries.[67] Two lessons are combined in the angel's brief message. Babylon has contributed to the corruption of others by providing a potion of sin, but God will bring judgment as they share His drink from the cup of wrath. This passage also prepares the reader for the coming fuller description of Babylon's fall (chapter 18).

---

[67]See Isaiah 21:9; Jeremiah 50:2; 51:7, 37.

To the Worshipers of the Beast Be Torment (9-12)

Psalm 75:8 provides a commentary for this: "In the hand of the Lord is a cup full of foaming wine mixed with spices; he pours it out, and all the wicked of the earth drink it down to its very dregs."

You may well ask, "Is there a difference between the second angel and the third angel in their messages?" To understand them with consistency would seem to demand a difference. If the message of the angels is the gospel and includes an invitation to repent and honor God, then there must be a place to say no to the final undiluted drink that seals a person's doom. This point comes in the third step. There are judgments that come both as punishment and warning. Many of these have been experienced through the ages and are anticipated in the present and in the future. Even the "day of the Lord" has an extended meaning. But there is the final judgment when the books are closed, the marks are acknowledged, whether of the beast or the seal of God and the Lamb.

After this, the condemned will suffer from fire and brimstone (sulphurous, relating to or dealing with the fire of Hell). Is it any wonder that the lost described in the sixth seal (Revelation 6:16) called for the rocks to fall upon them and destroy them, hiding them from the face of Him who sits on the throne and from the wrath of the Lamb? "For the great day of their wrath has come, and who can stand?" By now they knew the only alternatives. We shudder at the severity of the picture. We try to say eternity does not mean forever, we try to avoid such a word as *brimstone*. Who knows what brimstone is today? It becomes a faceless word used only with fire in a context seldom referred to in the Bible. What is a contemporary synonym? Sulphur? Yes, I know that word. The chemists use it regularly. It has a dreadful odor. But did you ever notice? The chemists spell it one way (sulfur) and the theologians another (sulphur) as though they are afraid to get the two confused. In fact, it is getting more and more difficult to find sulphur in the dictionary. Some emphasize this must be taken figuratively, not a literal fire and brimstone. Truly, we have not experienced this, so we could not have any impression of what this describes in a spiritual world except some materialistic words are used.

The same must be admitted of the golden streets and precious stones in Heaven. They may not be literal, but the literal words that are used leave as close an impression that can be reached to the spiritual truth that needs to be conveyed. Thus the description of Heaven leaves the understanding of something rich and beautiful, whereas the accompaniments of Hell are filled with horror and torment.

Immediately we think of the love and mercy of God. Where is this? But again we are confronted with the question of the martyrs, "What about justice? When will this be shown?" (Revelation 6:9, 10). Vengeance is not the ultimate goal, but the very exoneration of the justice of God. Besides love and mercy and grace, God answers the call of righteousness, holiness, and justice in His nature as well.

In a final attempt to escape the unpleasant thought of God's involvement in so grim a fate assigned to the worshipers of the beast, the thought is presented that at least Jesus is so kind and gentle, He will not be involved in such action. To the contrary, Jesus' teaching more than anyone else's emphasizes warnings of what lay ahead for the wicked.[68] To stop any such suggestion's being made that Jesus was not in agreement with the fate of the followers of Satan, a note is given here that the suffering was witnessed by the holy angels and in the presence of the Lamb.[69]

The language describing the suffering as eternal is consistent throughout the Scripture. "The smoke of their torment rises for ever and ever" (Revelation 14:11). This is reminiscent of the example of Sodom and Gomorrah cited by Jude, "those who suffer the punishment of eternal fire" (Jude 7) and of Edom's destruction, whose "smoke will rise forever" (Isaiah 34:10).

The saints are asked to be patient, and keep the faith. The faithful in the church in Philadelphia were promised: "Since you have kept my command to endure patiently, I will also keep you from the hour of trial that is going to come upon the whole world to test those who live on the earth" (Revelation 3:9, 10).

---

[68]See Matthew 18:8f; 25:41, 46; Luke 16:23, 28.

[69]"It is impossible to translate these words otherwise: they prove that the holy angels, and the Lamb himself, acquiesce or something more in the justice and necessity of God's awful judgements. This being so, we dare not give weight to sentimental or a priori arguments against their possibility, though to our present faculties God's future treatment of sin may be as hard to reconcile with His known attributes as His permission of its origin in the past. We are *forced* to pass over the one difficulty: faith and humility will pass over the other." W. H. Simcox, *The Revelation,* p. 87.

To Those Who Die in the Lord Be Blessings (13)

Three angels have given their messages. Although the first offered the gospel, the second announced the fall of the wicked, and the third described the consequences for the same ones who have worshiped the beast. But now a voice from Heaven (no angel is indicated) announces the blessings enjoyed by those who have remained true to the Lord.

(1) They will rest from their labors. Peace is the ultimate goal of all mankind. Both the Stoics and the Epicureans were striving after peace and tranquility, but they were trying to travel different roads. One said, "Satisfy the cravings of the flesh whatever they ask." The other said "Choke the cravings of the flesh, they will only lead to unrest." Neither found rest. Jesus said, "Follow me." He promised rest—not as the world gives. His is a peace of body, peace of mind, and a peace of soul.

(2) Furthermore, their deeds will follow them. This is not to say that they will be saved by meritorious works. No good works, no matter how many nor how great, will avail to take away a single sin and its consequences. But good deeds of those faithful in Christ have good results, both directly and indirectly, as a proof of their faith in Jesus, as a support for that which is right, and as an influence in the decision of others—goodness is contagious just as evil is contagious. Goodness has continuing value both in person and in deeds.

Reapers in Harvest (14:14-20)

The third montage of the chapter introduces a white cloud, one like the Son of Man, and two angels—one to harvest wheat and the other to gather the grapes. The general picture is clear, but some of the particulars are not. Harvest time is not some months away, the day of harvest is not approaching, this is the beginning of harvest right now. Thus far in the book of Revelation, the scenes have continually advanced to the time of judgment and then abruptly fallen back to retrace the steps of approach one time after another. But now the scene advances further than ever before. One must be forewarned, however, that this ground will be covered again in the chapters to come and in greater detail.

This scene poses some details difficult to explain. One question concerns the figure seated on the white cloud. He is described as like the (or rather "a") Son of Man. Who is he? Is He the Messiah as prophesied in the book of Daniel (7:13)? This is the title Jesus applied to himself and even referred to His own return in this language.[70] Furthermore, the descriptive words, "like a son of man," were used to designate Christ in Revelation 1:13. Then, too, this figure on the cloud is wearing a golden crown. What possible objection could be raised to this being Jesus?

There are several. The figure is holding in his hand a sharp sickle, showing he is ready to serve as the reaper. The next verse states that "another angel" came out of the temple and gave the order, "Take your sickle and reap." This seems unnatural for an angel to be telling God's Son what to do. The answer is given that the angel came from the temple where he had received instruction from God himself to pass on to the Christ. After all, Jesus had declared He did not know the day nor the hour of the end time (Mark 13:32). But one must recognize a vast difference between the Jesus at work on earth in His incarnate days and the exalted Lamb beside God on His throne with every opportunity for communication and no need of another angel to convey an order.

Another problem is to determine the number of harvests depicted here. The reaper on the cloud clearly swung his sickle, and the earth was harvested. The sharp sickle was used to harvest grain. Then another angel was used to harvest the clusters of grapes. Are these two figures to portray one harvest, or are these two different harvests? The problem is increased when one studies a similar passage in Joel (3:13). There it seems to say quite clearly the judgment is one and those who are judged are the wicked. This does not necessitate the same conclusion here in Revelation, but it causes us to take another look.

1. The Earth Is Ripe

When God promised Abram a land, He informed him that he could not have it then for himself, but his descendants would come back there, "for the sin of the Amorites has not yet reached its full measure" (Genesis 15:16). In other words, God was not ready to bring final judgment on the Amorites. They had more opportunities provided by the patience of God. In like manner, He answered the prayers of the martyrs beneath the altar. They wanted to know when God was going to stop the unjust slaughter of their brothers still suffering persecution. God answered, "Not

---

[70]Matthew 16:27, 28; 19:28; 24:30; 25:31.

yet" (Revelation 6:11). The full numbers of the martyrs had not yet been reached. Peter said: "The Lord is not slow in keeping his promise, as some understand slowness. He is patient with you, not wanting anyone to perish, but everyone to come to repentance" (2 Peter 3:9). But just as sure as the world looked for Jesus' first coming, and He came, there will come the time finally when the Lord will say, "The time to reap has come, for the harvest of the earth is ripe" (Revelation 14:15).

2. The Sickle Is Sharp

Not only will man have reached the fullness of his sins, but God will finally have run out of continued patience. And the sickle of His judgment will be sharp and prepared for use. If Jesus is the Son of Man sitting on the cloud, it may be that He did not perform the same tasks as the angels did. An angel came out from the temple with a sharp sickle, also. And the earth was harvested.

3. The Winepress Is Filled

Still another angel came who had charge of the fire at the altar. The reference to fire introduces the symbol for judgment. This passage introduces imagery so severe we must remember the language is figurative. This is a judgment pictured as a wine vat. It divided into two sections. The upper part received the clusters of grapes, and people in bare feet trampled on the grapes until the juice was wholly stamped out of the crushed grapes. The juice ran from the upper vat to a lower vat, which continued to fill until the juice was removed. If it became full, it would simply overflow so long as the trampling continued in the upper vat. The grim picture here is that God's judgment is so severe on the wicked that their lives become as grapes, and instead of vats filled with juice, it is blood mounting in such a flow as to cover a stretch of land about 180 miles (1600 stadia) in length and up to a horse's bridle in depth.

This is pictured as taking place outside the city. Which city is not specified, but Jerusalem is suggested because of the language in Hebrews—that Jesus suffered outside the city gate (Hebrews 13:12). This is an appropriate place for judgment to be held, within sight of the place where God's Son had been killed. The distance from Dan to Beersheba, a common way of speaking of the length of the land in Old Testament times, was 163 miles. Some think what is indicated here is the length of Palestine, but this is too literal a way to think of the passage. Others see the number 1600 as symbolic of the whole world. Four is considered significant as the world (the four corners of the world); when it is multiplied by itself, this assures the whole of its surface. When it is then multiplied by 100 again, it denotes still fuller completeness, and the whole of the earth would be signified in a thorough way. Rather than think of any particular terrain in the world or any specific capacity of blood, it is better to think of a full, complete, and awful judgment in the vintage judgment upon the wicked and possibly a different wheat judgment on the righteous. This calls for an examination of the manner and number of the resurrections at the end of time. This will help us in our understanding of this chapter of judgments.

Special Subject #9

Resurrection

A popular concept summarizes the book of Revelation as describing one event, the second coming of Christ. A single reading of this book will dispel such a notion. True, the book keeps building until it reaches the culmination of all history and the beginning of eternity, and Jesus' return is at the heart of that point; but the unfolding of this event involves far more than the description of one happening. The role of tribulation, the challenge for faithfulness, impending judgments—all are important markers along the course of our journey. The constant conflict of God and Satan, of good versus evil—this is pursued as well.

The last enemy to be overcome is death, and this is related to resurrection, and in turn this is related to the second coming of Christ. Questions immediately rise in our minds. Who will be resurrected? Just the good or the evil also? When will they be resurrected? What is the order of Christ's coming, the judgment, the new heaven and earth? The millennium is not introduced until the twentieth chapter, but how does it fit in? We will treat this last question at a later time. In order to understand some of the problems, we are interjecting at this stage a brief review of what we can conclude especially about the general resurrection and the likelihood of other resurrections. This relates to our study in this chapter—whether there is one harvest or two.

Resurrection in the Old Testament

Man's understanding of the resurrection has grown through the years according to the progressive revelation God has given concerning the subject. The Hebrew belief in life after death was in deep contrast to the gloomy outlook of some kind of immortality of the soul anticipated by the Greeks. Only a shadowy, feeble, dismal continuing life awaited the common man in the beliefs of the first-century Gentiles. According to their teachings, only the heroes enjoyed their days on the Isle of the Blessed with a more substantial normal human existence.

The Jews, however, leave evidence of belief in a bodily resurrection to life with full capacity of joy, activity, and peace. Abraham believed that, even if he took the life of his son Isaac, God could raise him up (Hebrews 11:19; Genesis 22:5). Job believed in a resurrection of the body (Job 19:25-27). David was confident that God would not allow the Holy One to remain in the grave nor David himself (Psalm 16:9, 10). Isaiah and Daniel give prophecies concerning future resurrection (Isaiah 26:19; Daniel 12:1-3). Besides the belief, there are three examples in the Old Testament of temporary resurrections; that is, individuals were raised from the dead, but they died later just as others close their earthly days. Elijah raised the son of the widow of Zarephath (1 Kings 17:17-24); Elisha raised the Shunamite's son (2 Kings 4:32-37); a man was raised from his burial when his body touched Elisha's bones (2 Kings 13:20, 21). But understanding and references to the resurrection are relatively limited in the Old Testament.

Resurrection in the New Testament

In the New Testament, records are given of Jesus' performing three temporary resurrections: Jairus's daughter (Matthew 9:23-25; Mark 5:38-42; Luke 8:51-55); the widow of Nain's son (Luke 7:11-15); and Lazarus (John 11:38-44). Peter and Paul have resurrections attributed to them: Peter raised Dorcas (Acts 9:40, 41) and Paul raised Eutychus (Acts 20:9, 10), and Paul himself rose up after being stoned at Lystra (Acts 14:19, 20).

Jesus' resurrection, however, was permanent. He did not die again. He was the firstfruits of those who have died and are raised for the final time. Since He is the firstfruits, this puts Him in a class of His own. (See 1 Corinthians 15:23-25.)

Other resurrections will follow. Throughout the New Testament different resurrections are indicated.

But when you give a banquet, invite the poor, the crippled, the lame, the blind, and you will be blessed. Although they cannot repay you, you will be repaid at the resurrection of the righteous (Luke 14:13, 14).

Do not be amazed at this, for a time is coming when all who are in their graves will hear his voice and come out—those who have done good will rise to live, and those who have done evil will rise to be condemned (John 5:28, 29).

Obviously, there are at least two kinds of resurrection: (1) a resurrection of the righteous, which is a "better resurrection" (Hebrews 11:35) to which Paul was striving to attain (Philippians 3:11), the resurrection of life, and (2) a resurrection of the wicked, which is the resurrection of condemnation. For this reason, it may well be that the harvest of Revelation 15 is given in two figures because the first is the harvest of the righteous and the second, the harvest of the evil. This does not mean that the righteous have earned salvation by their own works, but, through their faith and faithfulness to the Lamb and His sacrifice for them and their refusal to accept the mark of the beast, they will be gathered for the resurrection of the just. The resurrection of both the just and unjust together is referred to as the general resurrection. If the harvest is but one harvest and the figures are symbolic of the same thing, then the reference is to the coming general resurrection.

The questions concerning the first resurrection and the millennium will be treated in the comments on Revelation 20.

CHAPTER TEN

The Final Cup of Fury

Revelation 15:1—16:21

A famous evangelist was scheduled to leave for an overseas assignment far from home. Just before departing for the airport, he received a phone call from a close minister-friend. After last minute plans and words of encouragement, the minister made a request. "When you're settled on the plane and well on your way, I want you to read Joshua 1:5."

After the flight had begun, the evangelist looked up the passage. He knew the section followed the death of Moses and told of the words of the Lord to Joshua. He found the verse. It read, "As I was with Moses, so I will be with you; I will never leave you nor forsake you."

In the book of Revelation, God is continually making the promise to Christians of the first century—and to Christians down through the ages—"as I was with Moses and with the Lamb, so I will be with you." In the thirteenth chapter of Revelation, the picture is grim. All who refused to worship the image of the beast were to be killed. Even in death, God did not forsake them. The martyrs themselves were those who were now singing triumph in Heaven.

Here in the fifteenth chapter, preparation for the final series of judgments is under way. The song of Moses and the song of the Lamb are sung in triumph. Even though there were trials for God's people, He opened the Red Sea for Moses to deliver Israel and closed it again to destroy the oppressors. Even though Christ died on the cross, He was not defeated but gained His victory in the atonement and the resurrection. The judgments on those who worship the beast and serve him are seen in the sixteenth chapter and the next four chapters. The victory of all God's children is coming. As God was with Moses and the Lamb, so He will be with you.

Prelude

Overview

The conflict of Satan and the world against the community of Christ begun in Revelation 12 still continues in chapter 15. This introduces a new series of seven. One set of figures after another has approached the final judgment only to circle back and head in the same direction via a different route. But this one last cycle has the mark of finality.

The first series of seven portents was the seals. They introduced crises, sufferings, and panic, but the intensity of destruction was limited to a fourth of the earth—desperate futility was the reaction of the others. Then the trumpets had emphasized the destruction of one third—great agony, but no repentance.

Now with the pouring out of the contents of the bowls, the picture is final. This is the last time around. As in the case of the trumpets, the course is similar to the plagues of Egypt. Similar to the scene in the Old Testament, a song of celebration is sung to commemorate the occasion, but this one is sung in Heaven, and the action was initiated from the temple on high in the fullness of God's presence there.

The first four of the bowls follow the pattern of the trumpets and the plagues of Egypt, involving earth, sea, rivers, and sun. But there are differences between trumpets and bowls. The trumpets show the suffering of the faithful when spokesmen of God had been murdered for refusing to worship the beast. Now in the bowls, God's retributive justice is seen in the punishment of the worshipers of the beast (the first four bowls) and the demise of the beast's kingdom (the last three bowls). God's faithful followers have been vindicated.

This is the response to the pleas of the souls beneath the altar (Revelation 6:10), the ones who had been slain for their witness. The very altar cries out for a leveling of justice. God achieves His redemption, but retribution must have its place as well. The cycle will be final and complete in the end. But whether we live in the closing days or are far removed from the actual second coming, there is a message for us. Every day carries an urgent appeal to repent initially and to remain true to commitment to God while it is yet day, for the time will come when it will be too late. The final pouring out of judgment must eventually follow a rejection to repent or to remain faithful in the face of opposition.

Key Message
"I saw in heaven another great and marvelous sign: seven angels with the seven last plagues—last, because with them God's wrath is completed" (Revelation 15:1).

Glossary
Read through chapters 15 and 16 of Revelation. As you come to the terms listed below, note the explanation.

Chapter 15

Sign	Usually a miraculous event signifying the hand of God in a significant happening (for example, see Revelation 12:1). In this case (chapter 15), the portent of the judgments of God, but more specifically, the final series of judgments.
Seven plagues	After seven seals (Revelation 6, 7) and seven trumpets (Revelation 8—11), now seven plagues present their message. This is reminiscent of the plagues in the time of Moses. These are strokes of disaster, bringing suffering.
Sea of glass	This sea is like the sea of glass before the throne (Revelation 4:6), but was mingled with fire—perhaps related to the fire the martyrs had experienced or the coming judgment associated with the plagues.
Harps	Not the size of a modern harp, but the zither, an instrument held in one hand and played with the other. The elders had them (Revelation 5:8), and here the victorious ones accompany themselves as they sing.
Song of Moses	In Exodus 15, a song is given in celebration of Moses' triumph over Pharaoh at the crossing of the Red Sea. This is a new song, showing interrelation with the old.
Song of the Lamb	This song praised God for what He had done more than praising the victorious saints. The reference here may be to one song with a double title (Moses and the Lamb).

Temple	Not Solomon's temple, but the tabernacle in the wilderness; and not on earth, but now in Heaven. The tent of witness (martyr), designating the presence of God. Named for the two tablets of the Testimony kept in the ark (Exodus 32:15; 38:21).
Golden sashes	Angels clad in linen robes and golden sashes depict purity and concern for the good. They are symbolic of royalty and priestly functions, coming directly from the presence of God.
Seven golden bowls	Vials (see Revelation 5:8) formerly used for the container for the prayers of the saints, but here the container for the plagues of the final judgments. They are brought by one of the four living beings.

Chapter 16

First angel	This angel proceeded to pour out the contents of his bowl on the land. He did not return to his place, but disappeared from the scene. He caused everyone who had worshiped the beast to be plagued with sores.
Second angel	This angel poured out his bowl on the sea, and it turned into blood. Everything died in the sea.
Third angel	Like the third trumpet when the one third of the waters became bitter (Revelation 8:10, 11), but here all of the water is blood. All the water is affected; there is nothing to drink but blood. The angel of the waters affirmed the justice upon those who had shed the blood of the martyrs.
Fourth angel	This angel poured his bowl on the sun, and the people were scorched by the heat of the sun. But they did not repent.
Fifth angel	This angel poured out his bowl as an attack on the citadel of the beast. His throne and whole kingdom were plunged into darkness. But they refused to repent.

Sixth angel	The sixth angel poured his bowl on River Euphrates, which then dried up. This provided a highway for the kings to gather their soldiers and to march on Armageddon.
Three evil spirits	They looked like frogs (see the plague in Egypt, Exodus 8:6) and came from the mouth of the dragon, the beast, and the false prophet.
Battle of the great day	The evil spirits enticed the kings to prepare for an all-out battle against the forces of God.
Armageddon	Mount of Megiddo. The scene of many battles, this was a strategic site providing passage through the mountain ranges in Galilee. Some feel the phrase is figurative and the site should be Jerusalem. There are many interpretations: see below under Special Subject #10.
Seventh angel	When he poured out the bowl, a voice declared that it was completed. An earthquake split the city, mountains were leveled, islands disappeared, huge hailstones fell. But the people did not repent, they only cursed God because of the plague.
Earthquake	Symbol of divine judgment on the enemies of God in the sin and pride of men (see Isaiah 2:19ff). It accompanied the climax of each series of seven signs in the visions of Revelation (8:5; 11:13; 16:18).
City split	The identity of the city is disputed. Some say Jerusalem, some say Rome, some say Babylon, and some say a figurative city for the inhabitants of this earth rebellious against God (see under Content Notes, below).
Island fled	This event is symbolic of the destruction and the complete dissolution of the old order of things.
Hailstones	This is symbolic of judgment on the foes of God's people. The seventh Egyptian plague

(Exodus 9:24) and the battle along the Beth Horon road (Joshua 10:11) had hail storms. This was worse: each stone weighed a talent, probably between 100 to 130 pounds.

Content Notes

Seven Angels and the Victorious (15:1-4)

With each new series come preliminary remarks to introduce the main action. The introduction this time fitly focuses on the glory of God, but the scene is shared by seven angels and redeemed ones who had been victorious. The angels are to play an important part in the coming release of the seven last plagues, and the presence of the victorious is a part of what holds the book of Revelation together.

At the beginning of the book, in the letters to the churches, promises are made to "him who overcomes" (Revelation 2:7, 11, 17, 26; 3:5, 12, 21). Then, throughout the book, we have been following the path of the victorious ones. "They were purchased from among men and offered as firstfruits to God and the Lamb" (Revelation 14:4). They were "victorious over the beast and his image and over the number of his name" (Revelation 15:2). This does not mean they must have gained a military victory in life. In fact, their lives on earth may have ended in untimely physical death, but this did not mean defeat.

Truly, the day of the Christian martyr's death was as remembered as his day of birth. "They did not love their lives so much as to shrink from death" (Revelation 12:11b). Victory is not how successful you have been in evading trouble, but how strong a witness you have given in remaining faithful. Ultimately, however, the victory does not depend on the meritorious works of the individual but on the love and grace of God. Appropriately the song of victory that follows does not extol the feats of the Christians; only the marvelous works of God are praised. Though the theme includes those who are victorious, the occasion is used to acclaim the glory of God.

The victory song sung in Heaven included the names of both Moses and the Lamb. We should not be surprised at the combining of the two. In the vision given of the work of the two witnesses, certainly the power to turn the waters into blood and to strike the earth with every kind of plague points toward the person of Moses (in a figurative way) for one of the two witnesses. Likewise, in the plagues of the trumpet series, there is a similarity with the plagues of Moses: the hail, the locusts, the darkness, and the sea's becoming blood. And in the series introduced here (verses 1-4), the plagues of Egypt are again clearly related. The person of Moses cannot be ignored in the background. But this is the first explicit reference made to him. The associations are too numerous to count. The victory over Pharaoh was a foreshadowing of the victory over the beast. Moses' successful crossing out of Egypt was followed by a song of victory sung beside the Red Sea. This song in Revelation is sung beside a Heavenly sea, a sea of glass mixed with fire.

Paul used the scene of the crossing as a type of baptism: "that our forefathers were all under the cloud and that they all passed through the sea. They were all baptized into Moses in the cloud and in the sea" (1 Corinthians 10:1, 2). In turn, the baptismal act was joined with sharing in Christ's death, burial, and resurrection.

> Or don't you know that all of us who were baptized into Christ Jesus were baptized into his death? We were therefore buried with him through baptism into death in order that, just as Christ was raised from the dead through the glory of the Father, we too may live a new life (Romans 6:3, 4).

Jesus used the figure of baptism in reference to suffering also: "You will drink the cup I drink and be baptized with the baptism I am baptized with . . ." (Mark 10:39).

These victorious ones who sing the song of victory in Heaven could have told something of their sufferings and their endurance for God. Figures could have been used for the crossing of the sea or praises could have been sung for the sacrifices of the Lamb. But none of these is referred to in the words of the song. The praises are directed entirely to the glory, the justice, and the righteousness of God. His deeds are worthy of the highest awe and worship.

Seven Angels and the Temple (15:5-8)

Another montage unfolds before the eyes of John. This was not a Heavenly copy of Herod's temple with its seventy-foot-high doors standing open. Nor was it Solomon's temple with its stately columns, Jakin and Boaz, standing in front. But this was the old tabernacle of the wilderness, the Tent of Meeting, where the two tablets of Testimony, brought down from Mt. Sinai, were placed in the ark. Exodus 40:34 and 35 describes the scene when Moses had seen to the completion of its construction.

> Then the cloud covered the Tent of Meeting, and the glory of the Lord filled the tabernacle. Moses could not enter the Tent of Meeting because the cloud had settled upon it, and the glory of the Lord filled the tabernacle.

What John saw previously (Revelation 11:19) in the open temple was the ark of the covenant. This time he saw seven angels emerge from the temple. All of this is still tied to the throne room scene of the fourth chapter, for one of the four living creatures introduced at that time steps forward now to deliver seven bowls to the angels. Although the angels were striking in their crisp, clean, and pure appearance, the bowls were filled with plagues. Although the former view within the temple had emphasized the place of the ark, this scene focuses on the presence of God in all His glory. The smoke, like the cloud reported in Exodus and the smoke in Isaiah's vision (Isaiah 6:4), depicts the holiness of God. All others were forbidden entrance into the Tent of Witness until the seven plagues were loosed to accomplish their purposes.

The Bowls of God's Wrath (16:1-21)

The First Bowl (1, 2)

A loud voice from within the temple commanded that the wrath of God be poured out from the bowls upon the earth. Despite the use of the third person in the "wrath of God," it seems to be the very voice of God, or the angel of His presence, that speaks these words. No one else is allowed to enter until after the judgments are delivered.

A thread begins here that continues to the conclusion of the book. First, the judgments descend upon all those who have worshiped the beast. Then, the very throne of the beast is the target of attack and, finally, the whole of his kingdom is vanquished. A description of the fall continues with another figure, but the same forces of evil and the same defeat are being described. This time, the figure is Babylon as a harlot. The fall is complete, and her fate is terrible. On the other hand, the corridors of Heaven echo with hallelujahs and the word of God advances. He leads as a conquering commander on a white horse. Then comes the final judgment, and the ultimate destination of the devil and his followers is made clear. After this action, the focus turns to a new heaven and a new earth. Heaven is described. But the final long sweep of the world's course through the ages begins with this sixteenth chapter and the first bowl of plagues poured out by the angel who had just come from the presence of God.

The first plague is simple and brief in its description. Ugly and painful sores made miserable those who were marked with the beast and worshiped his image. No deaths are recorded, no further suggestions are given to help extend the application. These painful ulcers remind us of the distressing boils that plagued the people of Egypt (Exodus 9:10f).

The Second Bowl (3)

The second angel poured out plagues that turned the sea into blood. We think immediately of Moses' first plague in Egypt, given in order to influence Pharaoh to let the children of Israel leave his land. It also resembles the second trumpet and its results (Revelation 8:8f). However, there are differences. The results affected only one third of the living in the trumpets' series, but the consequences were universal from the bowls' plagues. Every living thing in the sea died. The blood is particularly loathsome in the bowl figure because it is described as from a dead man. The significance is not explained, but the obvious contrast between the trumpets and bowls is that the plagues of the bowls are complete and final.

The Third Bowl (4-7)

In similar manner, this third bowl resembles the third trumpet, but there are major differences. It is the same in affecting rivers and springs of water, but it is different in that the trumpets poisoned by Wormwood and the bowls by blood. Also, the trumpets affected a third, whereas the bowls' results were evidently complete.

Another voice is heard in the case of the third bowl. This comes from the angel in charge of the waters. Although we do not have such a designation elsewhere in Scripture, we have numerous examples of specific responsibilities given to angels. Four angels stood at the four corners of the earth, holding back the four winds (Revelation 7:1). Another angel was told, "Take your sickle and reap . . . and the earth was harvested" (Revelation 14:15, 16). It is particularly fitting that the angel managing the waters should voice his recognition of the justice of God in turning the water into blood so that those who had shed the blood of the saints (the Christians) and the prophets (Christian prophets of the early church) would have no other recourse but to drink blood to stay alive.

Still another voice adds his note of agreement. This time it comes from the altar. Of course, it is not the altar itself doing the talking, but either the angel of the altar or—more than likely—a spokesman for the souls beneath the altar (Revelation 6:9-11). These latter had asked how long things were going to continue like this—Christians losing their lives because of their testimony for Christ. This makes the admission of the altar all the more meaningful when the altar now affirms "Yes, Lord God Almighty, true and just are your judgments" (Revelation 16:7).

The Fourth Bowl (8, 9)

Once again, we find similarities with the series of the trumpets, but this time the differences are even greater. The sun plays a major role in both the fourth trumpet (Revelation 8:12) and the fourth bowl. But in the trumpet, the moon and stars were involved. This is not so with the bowl. Furthermore, in the trumpet's case, once again only a third was struck, true of the moon and stars as well as the sun. But with the bowl, the sun is totally involved. The greatest divergence is in the results: they are almost the opposite. The trumpet plague brought a degree of darkness, but the bowl plague brings an intense heat that scorches people alive. A further note is given in the bowl description: the pain is so severe from the fire and heat that men curse God, but refuse to repent.

Another observation should be made concerning this plague. The similarities with Moses' plagues should not be dropped. The second to the last plague upon Pharaoh and the Egyptians was one of darkness that lasted for three days (Exodus 10:21-23). This more nearly reflects the fourth trumpet. But the intricate pattern woven in this apocalyptic tapestry is not nearly finished. The next plague of the bowls is going to involve darkness. It is in a separate plague, but it is coming. This leads to more observations and questions. Where do these relationships come from—the plagues in Egypt, the judgments upon Israel and other nations throughout the Old Testament, the series of seals, trumpets, and bowls in Revelation? Not only is it difficult to discern the meaning, but how can they be so different and so similar at the same time?

To keep reminded of three different starting points used by different interpreters of Revelation is important. Beware of the person who starts with the assumption that every thought, every figure, every conclusion is limited to putting together former thoughts, figures, and conclusions available at the time. This person will begin searching for necessary sources for all figures and thoughts expressed in this book of Revelation. He must find it used somewhere else to justify its being used here.

Another starting point gives John himself a more important role. This start insists on the possibility the author could think new thoughts, invent new expressions, and introduce his own arrangement of material to get his points across. This does not mean that he does this work in a vacuum, unaware of Old Testament passages or the beliefs of people around him, or the figures of other apocalyptic works, but he himself is capable of being a fresh starting point for an independent narrative, aware of, but not copying whole cloth nor totally dependent upon, any one source or group of sources.

A third starting point accepts the claim made by the author himself—that the book of Revelation is indeed a revelation from God through Jesus Christ. God could introduce new thoughts and new figures, or He could use old ones if He chose to do so. In fact, He could use old ones in a new way. He could unfold the visions in the way He preferred. Even in this, He need not choose to work in a vacuum, but to employ the setting of the author who was doing the writing to provide the backdrop for the truths and principles He wanted to communicate. The exigencies of the time and the ingenuity of the author might be used in the writing, but the starting point is not the circumstances of the author, not the written sources and man's beliefs surrounding the author, but the visions God gave to him. If the Scripture is inspired of God, then ultimately the starting point is the infinite knowledge, wisdom, and understanding of God.

So when we ask, "What does the fourth bowl hold?" we do not expect to find a mechanical mixing of sources or John's clever integration of his former uses or others' uses of figures, but simply a report on what God shows him in his vision. Accepting this passage as being figurative in language and striving to interpret the significance in line with the context, we see the following points.

(1) Judgment is controlled by God and will ultimately be brought upon those who rebel in sin against Him (as for example, Revelation 9:20f; 14:9ff).

(2) The suffering is intense, but the judgment is just.

(3) Even then the opportunity to repent is still there; so the suffering is not simply punishment, but potentially reformative as well.

(4) In this scene, however, instead of repenting and glorifying God, the stricken curse Him.

The Fifth Bowl (10, 11)

Darkness is the fifth plague. One might feel that the severity of the former plights would make darkness seem a relief. But accumulation of the pains and sores continues and the darkness adds the unknown, the guilt, and further agony to the whole. The progression in this plague seems to focus as its target on the very seat of Satan's power, the throne of the beast, the center of his kingdom. With the descent of the darkness the activity of Satan's realm would be put on hold. "But they refused to repent of what they had done" (Revelation 16:11).

The Sixth Bowl (12-16)

The plagues are building to a climax. This sixth plague, making use of four different scenes, is described more fully than all the rest.

Scene 1. The Euphrates is a river reaching 1700 miles across western Asia. It was one of the names of the four headwaters for the river flowing from Eden (Genesis 2:10-14). This river formed the natural boundary between Israel and her constant enemies, Assyria and Babylon. The sixth angel poured out his bowl on the river, and it dried up. Strangely enough, this seemed to be helping to make a highway to facilitate the coming of a great army of the kings from the East. The Romans recognized the importance of good roads. One reason they were anxious to maintain their network of highways was to make one army do the work of three armies by enabling the soldiers to travel rapidly to where they were needed. What an easy way to provide a highway, simply by drying up the Euphrates and using the river bed. To dry up a path through the water was not beyond the power of God. He had done it with the Red Sea for the children of Israel (Exodus 14:21, 22). He did it again in stopping the Jordan so Israel could pass over (Joshua 3:15ff). It took Cyrus considerably longer to divert the waters of the Euphrates into another channel so he could enter Babylon along the drained bed of the river and conquer the city.

But why should God be preparing a way for the kings from the East? Who are they? Rome feared the Parthians; so those who tie Revelation to the setting of the first century can see no further than the Parthians. Perhaps this is a move to clear the way for whatever forces of evil may be gathered for the final conflict of Satan's hosts against the power of God in the end time. Actually, we hear no more about these kings, and we can only relate them to the action as it unfolds. Once again, the sixth bowl is paralleled by the sixth trumpet. Here also the Euphrates was specified. Here also a mighty army had been gathered and a third of mankind died (Revelation 9:13-21). How does the sixth bowl turn out in contrast to the sixth trumpet? The trumpet told more of the consequences of battle than the bowl; but the bowl continued to prepare for the final confrontation.

Scene 2. Satan and his two helpers, the beast and the false prophet, come to the forefront. The false prophet is evidently another name for the beast out of the earth (Revelation 13:11), for he is further identified at Revelation 19:20 with Revelation 13:14. From their mouths come forth frogs—at least they look like frogs (echoes of the Egyptian plagues again). They were demonic spirits who were able to perform miraculous signs and convince the kings of the whole world (no longer just the kings of the East) to gather for an all-out effort against the forces of God. This seems to fit well what Paul wrote in 2 Thessalonians about the end time:

> The coming of the lawless one will be in accordance with the work of Satan displayed in all kinds of counterfeit miracles, signs and wonders, and in every sort of evil that deceives those who are perishing. They perish because they refused to love the truth and so be saved. For this reason God sends them a powerful delusion so that they will believe the lie and so that all will be condemned who

have not believed the truth but have delighted in wickedness (2 Thessalonians 2:9-12).

"The great day of God Almighty" is at hand (Revelation 16:14). This is what the second scene is preparing for. We saw it coming back in Revelation 5:5-14; we have almost arrived again and again in Revelation. Is it about to break?

Scene 3. A voice breaks into the scene and introduces an urgent note. "Behold, I come like a thief!" It must be the Lord Jesus. The words are unmistakable. It identifies the day, it identifies the person. This must be the second coming of the Lord. "For you know very well that the day of the Lord will come like a thief in the night. While people are saying, 'Peace and safety,' destruction will come on them suddenly . . ." (1 Thessalonians 5:2, 3). Why does this appear at this time? Did a new written source just come to John's attention? Did John decide to put in his own beatitude at this point? Or was the voice actually heard and John put it down? The very fact that it is such a surprise to us shows how much we need to be reminded of this element. Just when we become smug in our watching for the battle of Armageddon and we feel assured we could never miss the time when all the kings of the whole earth are gathering for the worldwide conflict, then Jesus reminds us He is going to come suddenly when we least expect Him. But we will certainly be aware of the signs of such judgment and tribulation as described in this sixteenth chapter of Revelation. Certainly that will not be a time when we will be saying, "Peace and safety." Yet we need to be reminded of these other warnings about His coming. We need this word of suddenness and surprises to balance our sure interpretation that Jesus cannot come until things have been accomplished as we expect them. We need to be told that just at this moment when we feel the signs cannot be mistaken, He will come suddenly and unexpectedly. We do fairly well with the pieces one by one. But when we try to put them together for the total picture, we have our difficulties.

Have you ever seen how a fireman arranges his clothes when he goes to bed upstairs in a firehouse? He carefully leaves them in place so that when an alarm is sounded, he can with one bound be out of bed, into his clothes, and on his way at a moment's notice. In a figurative way, this is how we must live. Not bound to the things of this life, but when He is ready to call us, we are ready to go with Him. To gain an appreciation of the picture as a whole, this is a piece of the puzzle we must not neglect. Jesus will come again at an unexpected time.

Scene 4. The last scene from the contents of the sixth bowl comes back to the gathering of the armies for the last final conflict when the evil are determined to go for all. The place is specified, Armageddon. (See Special Subject #10 below.)

The Seventh Bowl (17-21)

Both the series of the seals and the trumpets have an interlude of considerable material between the sixth and seventh acts (Revelation 7 between the sixth and seventh seals, and Revelation 10:1—11:14 between the sixth and seventh trumpets). But the bowls take us immediately from the sixth to the seventh without a break. Nor is this the introduction to another series. This is not a preparation for a coming battle. No more offers of repentance are expected. *"Finis"* is declared (Revelation 16:17). We see the lightning, hear the thunder, and feel the earthquake. We have experienced this before in the book, but never to the extent given at this point. The cities of the world crumble into nothing, there is no foundation on earth, no source of strength at the command of man, that can sustain them. The city of Babylon, representative of everything man in his pride and avarice can achieve as he pits himself against God and pledges his services to Satan, that great city is split asunder, and God "gave her the cup filled with the wine of the fury of his wrath" (Revelation 16:19). The mountains melted into the plains, and the islands disappeared beneath the waves. Huge hailstones pulverized people who were struck. At the end of the shock, still there were voices that cursed God.

Special Subject #10

Armageddon and Gog and Magog

Armageddon

Armageddon is a word used in Revelation 16:16 describing the gathering place for the kings of the whole world. A tremendous battle is anticipated. This much is clear, but difficulties surround the passage.

Mageddo, in the Greek, is the way of writing the Hebrew town of Megiddo, and there are factors that support this identification. This was a site of tremendous military importance. It had figured greatly in the past history of Israel. A glance at its geographical location would convince anyone of its importance. The Mediterranean Sea and the Lake of Galilee are separated by hills and plains. To the north, Mt. Carmel blocks the plains along the shores of the sea. But to the south, the maritime flats extend for miles along the Mediterranean, providing a thoroughfare in and out of Egypt. Through the centuries, armies have marched over this route, whether soldiers from Egypt bent on conquest or forces going the other direction determined to invade the land of the Pharaohs. To the east are hills, then the upper plains of the Shephelah, and finally the long range of mountains that make slow and tortuous any north-south travel. This is the reason Megiddo was so important. It was the only opening at the north end of the maritime route. This was the gateway through the land of Palestine.

When Josiah wanted to stop Pharaoh Necho from going to the assistance of the last of the Assyrian kings, Ashur-Ubbalit, he made a stand where he could do so most advantageously, at the bottleneck of the north-south route. But Josiah was killed in battle—at Megiddo (2 Kings 23:29). Saul had suffered death four hundred years earlier in the same locale. He was killed by the invading Philistines on the slopes of Mt. Gilboa, just southeast of Megiddo (1 Samuel 31:8) with Beth Shan further to the east. All was not defeat in this area, however. Almost two hundred years before Saul, Barak had stopped the Canaanites near here. In the song of victory, Deborah and Barak included these words:

> Kings came, they fought;
> > the kings of Canaan fought
> at Taanach by the waters of Megiddo,
> > but they carried off no silver, no plunder.
> From the heavens the stars fought,
> > from their courses they fought against Sisera.
> The river Kishon swept them away,
> > the age-old river, the river Kishon.
> > March on, my soul; be strong!
> Then thundered the horses' hoofs—
> > galloping, galloping go his mighty steeds (Judges 5:19-22).

Another great victory for Israel was Gideon's triumph over the Midianites (Judges 7). This, too, was near the hill of Moreh, just north of Megiddo. So when Armageddon is related to Megiddo, the site is associated with an important military location and one that is rich in Old Testament significance.

Although Zechariah relates final scenes with the city of Jerusalem (Zechariah 14:2, 4), he also makes a comparison to the weeping of Hadad Rimmon in the plain of Megiddo (Zechariah 12:11).

As compelling as the application of the passage in Revelation 16:16 is to Megiddo, there are difficulties as well. The word *Armageddon* seems to come from two Hebrew words, *Har-Magedon,* meaning the "mount of Megiddo." But nowhere else in extant earlier literature do we have any reference to the Mount Megiddo, nor is Megiddo on a mountain. It is in the Plain of Esdraelon. Because of this and the uncertainty of the text itself, many conjectures have been made in a rewording—perhaps the original was "mount of plagues" or "city of Megiddo" or "land of Megiddo," or perhaps "Mount Megiddo" is correct, but it was meant to designate a portion of Mt. Carmel extending nearby.

Others, however, feel that passages from Revelation indicating the battle of the end time (Revelation 9:13—11:14; 14:14-20; 16:12-16) should be coordinated with Zechariah (12:2-9; 14:2), Joel (2:32; 3:16, 17), and Isaiah (29:1-8). From this it is concluded that Jerusalem, Mt. Zion, is indicated for the final struggle. Thus the text is amended by some to read "city of desire," i.e. Jerusalem, or "His fruitful mountain," i.e. Mt. Zion.

Gog and Magog

Another passage from Revelation must also be coordinated: Revelation 20:8. There a description is given of a final conflict that will build up when Satan is released from the Abyss after the millennial period. His forces of evil will be gathered from the four corners of the earth and will converge on "the city God loves." The word *Armageddon* does not appear in this passage, but in its place a pair of words is used, *Gog and Magog.* These words, too, have an Old Testament history.

From the line of Reuben, a Gog is listed as the son of Shemaiah in 1 Chronicles 5:4. Also, in the Samaritan Codex and the Septuagint of the Old Testament, Gog is substituted for Agag in Numbers 24:7. But in Ezekiel 38 and 39, both these words are used together, *Gog* and *Magog.* In Ezekiel 38:1, Gog is addressed as the chief prince (or prince of Rosh) of Meshech and Tubal. In that passage, a prophecy is given of the coming of nations from the north in an attack on Israel. In the time of Ezekiel, this would have been the Scythians. Some maintain they were the inventors of the bow and arrow. Certainly they were famous as archers and also as expert in use of cavalry in warfare. The prophecy proceeded, however, to assure Ezekiel that divine judgment was to interrupt this campaign and an earthquake would result in the soldiers' turning upon one another. Rain, hailstones, and burning sulphur would descend on the troops and the nations. Then, in chapter 39, Ezekiel is told how this will be fulfilled. The slaughter will be so great that it will take seven months to bury the bodies, and Israel will be seven years using up the weapons as firewood. They will bury Gog and all his hordes in a place called the Valley of Hamon Gog.

But how does Magog figure in Old Testament usage? In Genesis 10:2 the word is used to designate a person, the second son of Japheth. But in the Ezekiel passage (38, 39), it designates a place. Gog is from the land of Magog (38:2). In fact, it would appear that *ma* is simply a prefix denoting the land belonging to or associated with the name that follows—the country of Gog or possibly the people of Gog. But in the book of Revelation, it seems to have reverted to its personal use and that two individuals, Gog and Magog, are indicated. In any event, there are great similarities that are evident. The enemies of God's people come in a mass attack against the citadel of God, only to be wiped out in catastrophic blows before the battle is begun. The age-long battle of the good and the evil will end in complete victory from the hand of God.

Conclusion

As to the difficulties of *Armageddon,* probably the translation, "mountain of Megiddo," should stand with an understanding that it is a combination deliberately used for an apocalyptic figure. It may not be the geographical place, but indicate the crossroads of the world, the very gateway through the mountains where the final confrontation will take place.

The basic message is clear from all of these plagues: an end is coming. God will be just. The evil ones will suffer and be defeated. Wherever and whenever the last conflicts take place, the God who was with Moses and with His own Son will also be with each of His followers.

CHAPTER ELEVEN

When Babylon Falls

Revelation 17:1—18:24

Every coin has its front side and its back side—the obverse and the reverse. In the same way, every papyrus sheet has its recto and verso. The message of the book of Revelation has a definite positive side and then a negative side as well. Each side is equally true. More often than not, the sheets used in making a papyrus scroll are written on only one side; the outside of the scroll is left blank. In John's Revelation, however, this was one of the remarkable characteristics of the scroll with seven seals—it was written on both sides (Revelation 5:1).

In a sense, the whole book of Revelation is written on both sides, for it unfolds in parallels: it tells of God, His qualities and His work; but it tells also of Satan, his characteristics and his evil deeds. It tells on one side of the Lamb, His sacrifice for sins, His continuing love, and His coming again. On the other side, it tells of the work of the beast, Satan's helper, the antichrist—of his deceit and sinister actions, of his final defeat and doom.

Jesus informed the Sadducees explicitly there will be no male and female in eternity—but at the resurrection, we will be as the angels in Heaven. "People will neither marry nor be given in marriage" (Matthew 22:30). But almost as if to pay respect to the role of women, God chose the figure of a glorious woman to represent the people of God and the community of Christ after His first coming (Revelation 12:1ff). Also as New Jerusalem comes down from Heaven in the dramatic conclusion to all earthly existence, she comes as a radiant bride (Revelation 21:2). But then to give a parallel even in the choice of figures, the other side of the coin is represented by a woman, also. Whereas the church and its faithful saints can be portrayed by a glorious woman, the reverse of the coin has the image of a woman, too: a sensuous, gaudy, provocative harlot.

The community of Christ, the bride of the Lamb, characterized by chastity, truthfulness and endurance (14:4,5), is paralleled by the community of the beast, the great harlot, characterized by murder, fornication, sorcery and falsehood (21:8).[71]

In another look at both sides of the coin, we see the blessed salvation of the redeemed versus the horrible fate of the condemned. The plight of the lost is not pleasant to behold. It would be easier just to leave that side blank and to look only at the pleasing, the beautiful, and the good. This would not be true to the facts; it would not carry the warning that is needed. It would leave the good only half told if the bad were not recognized on the other side.

When a person is asked, "Why do you want to go to Heaven?" he may impulsively reply, "Because I don't want to go to Hell." True, this does not reflect the deepest or most noble of motives, yet it cannot be dismissed as irrelevant. But in addition to a desire to avoid Hell, one should establish that his motive is not a selfish one, looking out for his own salvation alone. His anxiety extends further than self and is demonstrated by efforts to win others to Christ. He wants them to respond to the grace of God and come to the joy of salvation, too. The desire to go to Heaven is not selfish of the Christian as long as it is accompanied by the desire to take as many to Heaven with him as he possibly can. This spirit of evangelism is seen in Revelation as well, for the preliminary judgments are given not simply in retribution, but as a persuasive urge to repent. Repeatedly, however, the results are factually given with great concern, "but they did not repent" (with the possible exception of Revelation 11:13).

At this scene of the fall of Babylon, another point needs clarification. The suffering of those who have rebelled against God is not welcomed as an occasion for rejoicing because God is getting even and someone else is suffering now—namely, those who committed much evil and brought hardship, even death, upon the people of God. The rejoicing that comes in Heaven when the beast and his followers suffer defeat is rather that God's judgment

---

[71]Paul Barnett, "Polemical Parallelism: Some Further Reflections on the Apocalypse," paper for the Ancient History Documentary Research Centre, Macquarie University, June 30, 1988, p. 2.

is vindicated fully in His victory, His justice is completely established, and His righteousness is fully maintained. This final judgment is necessary for God to remain God.

Prelude

Overview

Twice before in the book of Revelation, the doom of Babylon has drawn attention, but nothing more than announcements have been given (Revelation 14:8; 16:19). The next two chapters (Revelation 17 and 18) are a window, providing a view of scenes depicting her fall. While this is happening, other action may be taking place on the larger screen of other visions. They are not to be taken as action chronologically following the series of messages given earlier.

Some of the actors are the same. The scarlet beast is the helper of Satan who came out of the sea in chapter 13. The seven heads and seven horns are still there. The peoples, multitudes, nations, and languages still provide the broad background to the action. Kings of the earth still give their power and authority to the beast.

The message, however, is not in the figures themselves, but in what they speak to each generation. The first lesson for John's readers in the initial flash of the scene is surprising and puzzling. The woman wears purple and scarlet, expensive material, indicating importance, royalty, or even priestly function. She is decked out with glittering gold and precious stones, and she carries a golden cup. But inside the cup is disgusting filth. It introduces a realization of immorality under the surface, a violation of faithfulness to God, a corruption of self and enticement to destruction for others. She is drunk from the blood of those she has killed—those who had stood up to be counted for Christ.

Why is John surprised? Is he amazed at the harlot's attraction or her lavish taste or the dregs of her behavior? For whatever cause, an angel comes to give explanation. One gets the feeling that his words are sobering but do not exhaust the explicit significance of all the figures. In fact, the symbols are described with still other figures. For example, the horns are identified as kings who do not have kingdoms, and one becomes unsure whether or not the kings may be symbolic of something further (Revelation 17:12). One thing is clear. The Lamb and His faithful followers will win out in the war against the beast and his kings. This leads to another surprise. The beast and the kings who have shared the sins of the prostitute are the very ones who turn upon the woman and destroy her.

The third scene, given in chapter 18, is a dirge sung over the doom of the harlot, who is a figure representing the fallen city of Babylon. She in turn may be a figure of ancient Rome, contemporary with John, which in turn becomes a continuing lesson warning every nation of people joined to the sinful practices and standards of Babylon and Rome. In addition, these may well be figures for the eschatological city of the end-time, when the final defeat will be complete and everlasting. Here, too, the ultimate lesson is clear. Just as a victory song was sung for Moses and the Lamb, so a dirge is sung for the demise of Babylon. The fall involves all those who have sought gain following the beast and the dragon. The kings huddle together in terror. The merchants are ruined in one hour. Even the sea captains cry out in despair. The lament over the doomed as chapter 18 closes is in direct contrast with the rejoicing of the redeemed in Heaven as chapter 19 opens. Here are the two sides of the book of Revelation, as clear as the difference between the darkness of night and the light of day.

Key Passage

"Therefore in one day her plagues will overtake her: death, mourning and famine. She will be consumed by fire, for mighty is the Lord God who judges her" (Revelation 18:8).

Glossary

Read through chapters 17 and 18 of Revelation. As you come to the terms listed below, note the explanation.

Chapter 17

Great prostitute "The woman you saw is the great city that rules over the kings of the earth" (Revelation 17:18). She is "Babylon the Great" (Revelation 17:5), the opposite of the glorious woman of Revelation 12:1ff and the bride of chapters 21 and 22. Babylon represents the world with all its godless lust and evil ways as a direct counterpart to the church.

Kings	May not refer to specific kings, but instead allude to kingdoms and nations influenced by Babylon's example or at least following a similar course.
Scarlet beast	To be identified with the beast that came out of the sea (Revelation 13:1, the antichrist). Scarlet color, similar to the red of the dragon (Revelation 12:3, Satan).
Seven heads and ten horns	This terminology was used in the former description of the beast (see Revelation 13:1) and is explained below in more than one way. (See also under Content Notes, comments on Revelation 17:9ff.) It may not refer to specific kings, but to world powers and completeness.
Blasphemous names	The obscenities and blasphemy used in advertising the barter of sin—all reflect a deliberate defiance of God and the righteousness He represents. On the person of the beast, the names may well reflect the claims of self-deification blaspheming the true God. (See below under Content Notes.)
Golden cup	The cup was beautiful on the outside, but inside it was full of filthy, detestable abominations. "Babylon was a gold cup in the Lord's hand; she made the whole earth drunk. The nations drank her wine; therefore they have now gone mad" (Jeremiah 51:7).
Woman and the beast	John was surprised. He expected to see a judgment. Instead, he saw grandeur and excitement and an air of victory. The beast even had a sense of power and authority. Specifically, he is an eighth king and going to destruction. She is a city and doomed to fall.
Seven heads	An example of a figure used with more than one meaning. The seven heads are seven hills, yet they are also seven kings (see below). But the hills may indicate Rome and the kings may indicate

kingdoms. Together, they may indicate a type that extends to the end-time. (See also seven kings under Content Notes, comments on Revelation 17:9, 10.)

Ten horns

The ten horns indicate ten kings (or kingdoms). It is doubtful they represent any particular individuals. Their type is characterized by:

(1) They do not yet possess a kingdom.

(2) For a short hour, they will have power along with the beast.

(3) They will relinquish their power to the beast.

(4) They will war against the Lamb.

(5) They will be defeated.

Seven hills

To characterize Rome as built on seven hills was common.[72] Since the seven heads are explained as seven hills, one concludes that the meaning has a reference to Rome. However, some hold that the allusion is to the Old Testament usage denoting power (Daniel 2:35; Jeremiah 51:25).[73]

Seven kings

Some maintain these must be Roman emperors. In the first century, the emperors were Augustus (31 B.C.-A.D. 14), Tiberius (14-37), Caligula (37-41), Claudius (41-54), Nero (54-68), Galbo (68), Otho (69), Vitellius (69), Vespasian (69-79), Titus (79-81), Domitian (81-96), Nerva (96-98), Trajan (98-117). Since it is evident there are more than seven in the span of time indicated, a great variety of selections are made trying to determine the proper seven.

Others say it must be kingdoms rather than kings: Old Babylonian, Assyrian,

---

[72]For a convenient list of references from Virgil, Horace, Ovid, and Cicero, see C. B. Caird, *Commentary on the Revelation,* p. 216.

[73]Joseph A. Seiss, *The Apocalypse* (New York: Cook, 1913), pp. 391-394. See also George Ladd, *Commentary on the Revelation,* p. 227.

New Babylonian, Medo-Persian, Graeco-Macedonian, Roman (the one that now is—as John writes), and the seventh is all the rest of the godless kingdoms between Rome and the end—the eighth kingdom, identified with the beast,[74] the final oppression of the antichrist preceding Christ's second coming. (See below, pp. 255, 256.)

Eighth king   The beast is the eighth king. In a special way, he belongs to all seven of the others. Whether this is a specific ruler or a whole kingdom, or the embodiment of the antichrist, two points are clear—he is the helper of Satan, and he is going to his destruction. He is identical to the beast that came out of the sea (Revelation 13:1).

Chapter 18

Another angel—great authority One of the angels who had delivered plagues from his bowl had introduced the harlot on the scarlet beast and explained the meaning of the scene. Now to describe the Fall of Babylon itself, another angel descends from the very presence of God, reflecting His glory and authority.

Babylon the Great   The symbol of power and glory in the ancient world, famous for its luxury and wealth, known for its military might and success in commerce, the enemy of God's people and Judah's captor in exile, the representative of a godless nation flouting its seeming achievements in defiance against the ways of God. (See Special Subject #11 below.)

Kings   See above.

Merchants   Those who buy and sell will mourn Babylon's fall, not out of sympathy for the fate of that city, but because they themselves

---

[74]W. Hendriksen, *More than Conquerors*, pp. 204, 205.

	will now lose all their trade. They will fall with Babylon.
Sea captains	Likewise, the shipmasters, the travelers, the sailors, and the profiteers will mourn their losses. They stand afar off and lament the fall of Babylon, but do not offer to help.
Musicians	An appreciation of the arts accompanies a prosperous city's growth. But in the collapse of a declining metropolis, the sounds of joy and music are the first to disappear.
Millstone	When the millstones have stopped going around, no grain is being ground; and bread, the staff of life, is no longer available.
Bridegroom and bride	If the glad, excited voices of couples in marriage are no longer heard, there will be no families; and if no families, no babies; and if there are no more children, there is no hope to renew a desolate site.
Magic spell	By the very sorcery of her ways, Babylon had bewitched the world into living by her standards of selfish lust, luxury, and idolatry to the extent of oppressing men and defying God.
Prophets and saints	The people of God who died in persecution witnessing for the truth. Babylon is held accountable for their deaths because Babylon is representative of that way of life that seeks to crush anyone who interferes with the satisfaction of their desires or would stand up for the one true God.

Content Notes

The Woman on the Scarlet Beast (17:1-6)

A new episode is being introduced, related to the last scene of the seventh bowl. The tie is made by an announcement from one of the angels of the seven bowls. He informs John of the coming vision. John will see the punishment of "the great prostitute who sits on many waters" (Revelation 17:1). The fact that this follows the action of the seventh bowl, and is also linked to it, does not necessarily mean it follows in chronological order. Rather, the new picture zooms in, giving a close-up of particular phases of the last plagues. This episode includes a description of the woman and the beast, then an explanation of the figures, and only after that the final judgment.

The fact that John is carried away into the desert in the Spirit for the unfolding of this panorama may have no more significance than to remove him—and us, the readers—from the crowds on earth and the hosts in Heaven. The angel wants us to concentrate on the participants in this particular scene.

Do not be troubled that one moment the woman is sitting on many waters, and the next she is sitting on a beast. This does not necessitate the beast's swimming through the water. You could not find a better example of why you must be ready to take these as individual snapshots, montages, rather than rigid, literal, chronological, or concurrent descriptions. George Ladd, in his commentary on Revelation, continually resorts to the phrase "the fluidity of apocalyptic language."[75]

One is still baffled, however, in trying to explain the significance of "seated on many waters" until the answer is seen on the woman's forehead, "Babylon the Great" (Revelation 17:5). This clears it up. Babylon was situated on the Euphrates, with the river flowing through the middle of the city and a grid of canals passing through its precincts. The woman represented Babylon, situated on the waters (Jeremiah 51:13).

Besides being seated on many waters and on the beast, she was also seated on seven hills (Revelation 17:9). Some leap at this and say, "Oh, this means Rome." This does seem likely, but remember, when we say that the woman stands for Babylon, invariably we mean both Babylon and a good deal more beyond Babylon. The city of Babylon becomes a figure for all of the godless attempts of nations to rise to power and dominance following the ways of the beast in conflict with God and His course. This includes attacks upon the very people who are determined to walk with Jesus as Lord.

What happens next is surprising. Many interpreters of Revelation drop the name of Babylon and start using the name of Rome

---

[75]George Ladd, *Commentary on the Revelation,* p. 223.

as though this is the city intended. Revelation does not designate the city of Rome explicitly as it does Babylon. Then the answer may properly continue, "Oh, but John could not use the name Rome, for this would lead immediately to more persecutions if the writing fell into the hands of Roman officials—which it would be sure to do. So, for this reason, he used Babylon as a cryptogram, a word with a hidden meaning standing for something else, and that something else is Rome."

This interpretation seems to be on the right track, but some reminders have to go along with it. Whereas the woman is explicitly identified as Babylon, the seven hills are taken to be an almost explicit identification of Rome. On the other hand, not only is the name of Rome missing, but the seven hills are explicitly labeled, not as a city, but as seven kings (Revelation 17:9, 10). At this point, all that is being urged is that one does not use the name of Rome as though he has arrived at the full significance of the depths of Revelation. Even if the application to Rome is intended in this passage, the same can be said of Babylon. Babylon has great significance as a choice to represent the lesson, but more than the city of Babylon is indicated in the application, and the same can be said of Rome. This city is not simply an application, but it becomes a figure for further application. It is more than Babylon and more than Rome. Although Henry Swete in his monumental commentary on Revelation finds much material in Revelation to relate to Rome and vice versa, he nevertheless concludes with this reminder:

> But Rome does not, of course, exhaust St John's perception of Babylon. His vision sounds a note of warning which may well be taken to heart by any great metropolis which prostitutes its wealth and influence to base or self-seeking ends. The city of the Caesars was the contemporary representative of Babylon; other ages may witness the rise and fall of other mistresses of the world not less magnificent and depraved.[76]

The beast is covered with blasphemous names. Those who emphasize the role of Rome in identifying the beast insist these must

---

[76]Henry Swete, *The Apocalypse of St John* (London: Macmillan, 1906), p. 223.

be the titles used by the Emperors in their growing bids for deity (such titles as Divine, Savior, and Lord). Perhaps the names are not designated because it would too clearly identify the beast with contemporary Rome and put the circulators of the writing in jeopardy. Or it may well be that the intent of the figure was to have numerous applications through the years or have a specific application at the last that would sound strange to the ears of those contemporary with succeeding ages before the end time. At any rate, the names would probably indicate not as much the beast's direct railing against God as an attempt to set up his own self-deification (such as the claims of Paul's "man of lawlessness" as he was "proclaiming himself to be God," 2 Thessalonians 2:4). To be insistent upon a literal application to a specific individual in John's lifetime, such as Nero for the beast, or Messalina, Claudius's profligate wife,[77] for the harlot, reduces the significance of the figure. They serve as possible examples, but not as the overall fulfillment, or as necessarily intended by John.

The prostitute—arrogant, confident, and amicable—sits on top of the monstrous beast. The two are fully compatible. She blatantly announces her immoral intentions, and she is drunk, intoxicated with the blood of Christians who sacrificed their lives for the testimony of Jesus. This is an accurate picture of any godless people who strive for power, wealth, pleasure, and luxury at the cost of fidelity to God and regard for justice and the needs of fellow man.

An Angel Explains (17:7-18)

John is amazed. He had expected to witness the punishment of the harlot, and here she was in all her glory. The angel who accompanied John proceeds to make explanation:

(1) The beast—the one who was and who is not; he will come out of the Abyss and be destroyed.
(2) The inhabitants of the earth—those whose names have not been written in the book of life.
(3) The seven heads—seven hills on which the woman sits; also seven kings (five were, one is, one will remain for a little while). The eighth king is the beast, and belongs to the seven, going to destruction.

---

[77]See Juvenal, *Satires* 6.114-132.

(4) The ten horns—ten kings who do not yet have a kingdom, for one hour will have authority.

(5) The Lamb—victorious King of kings and Lord of lords and with him His faithful followers.

(6) The waters—where the prostitute sits; also peoples, multitudes, nations, and languages.

(7) The woman—the great city that rules over the kings of the earth. The beast and the ten horns bring her to ruin.

The Beast Who Was and Is Not (7, 8)

The description of the beast is a parody.[78] It parodies (a) the Lamb who had the death wound but came back to life and is alive forever (Revelation 1:18; 2:8) and (b) the Lord, who is, who was, and who is to come (Revelation 1:4, 8; 4:8). In contrast, the beast "was" (he came out of the Abyss in Revelation 11:7 and came out of the sea in Revelation 13:1), and "is not" (he suffered a death wound in one of his heads—Revelation 13:3). Afterward, he astonished the world—that is, those whose names were not in the book of life—in his recovery (Revelation 13:3, 12, 14). He will later come out of the Abyss, only to go to his destruction. This was a characteristic of the beast throughout the history of man—the continual rise and fall of evil powers.

The Seven Heads (9-11)

The interpretation of the "seven heads" is most crucial. Whatever interpretation one chooses here indicates what overall school of interpretation one has decided to pursue. Or if one suspends judgment here, this would reflect a tendency to follow that practice along the whole of the book. One thing is certain, however; nothing is so sure here to cause a person to found his whole interpretation of Revelation upon it. In fact, the danger is in the opposite direction. Everyone comes to this passage having already determined what it has to mean in order to agree with his predetermined notion as to its significance.

For example, those who see Rome as the final fulfillment of what John is intending to record will naturally insist that the emperors leading up to the time of writing must be indicated by

---

[78]See Robert H. Mounce, *The Book of Revelation* (Grand Rapids: Eerdmans, 1977), p. 312.

the seven heads. The best evidence that this is wrong is clearly seen in the incredible variety of solutions offered by the advocates of the Roman emperor interpretation themselves. They agree it must be Roman emperors, but no one has come up with a way to work it out that is acceptable to the different ones in their own school of thought. They have difficulty determining where to begin count-ing—Julius Caesar or Augustus Caesar. They have difficulty de-ciding whether to count the quick succession of emperors: Galbo, Otho, and Vitellius. Some want them, and they count them; some do not want them, and they arbitrarily leave them out. Since John indicates that the sixth is in power as he is writing, this creates another difficulty. Most believe that John wrote as Domitian was ruling or soon after. But Vespasian, not Domitian, is the sixth emperor according to one popular calculation. Refusing to be thwarted, they suggest that John wrote down some of his visions years before the exile on Patmos, and although he completed it in the time of Domitian, he really wrote this part during the reign of Vespasian. Still others maintain John wrote in the time of Domi-tian, but he projected himself back to the time of Vespasian in his imagination for the writing. All of this is stretching a figure be-yond its limits when there are so many incongruities. Several con-venient charts are available showing the way various scholars have worked out the details of this theory.[79] Eight different views are displayed with as many as six varying explanations in the details in each. This is the best indication that it is looking for a solution in the wrong direction.

Other explanations leave the number seven as symbolic of the Roman empire as a whole and seven as an indication of complete-ness.[80]

The solution that seems to fit best is to understand the word *kings* to indicate "kingdoms."[81] Daniel reported the meaning of

[79]For example: Thomas Kepler, *The Book of Revelation* (New York: Oxford, 1957) p. 177. See also J. Massyngberde Ford, *Revelation* (New York: Doubleday, 1975), p. 289.

[80]See I.T. Beckwith, *The Apocalypse of John,* pp. 704-708.

[81]See Henry Alford (vol. IV, pp. 710, 711). W. Hendriksen, *More Than Conquerors,* p. 204. George Ladd, *Commentary on the Revelation,* p. 229.

the four great beasts as four kingdoms (Daniel 7:17). Although John uses the word *king* here, he describes the five as "fallen." This word describes better the end of a kingdom than the death of a king. This would mean that five empires had already fallen in the past, and one was present at that time (when John was writing), and another was to come. Five likely candidates for the past include Old Babylonian, Assyrian, New Babylonian, Medo-Persian, and Graeco-Macedonian. This, in fact, covers the history of Babylon and its final fall (see below under Special Subject #11: Babylon). The Roman was in power as John wrote, and the seventh could represent in one the ephemeral succession of empires that had the same characteristics of Babylon, extending from Rome to the return of Christ in the end time. This succession of kings "must remain for a little while." When an emphasis is placed on "remain," an extended, temporary period is indicated, but the shortness of the "while" is left relative (see Revelation 12:12).[82] The eighth king was different from the rest in kind. He is the beast who came out of the Abyss (Revelation 11:7). His work is intermittent as he is allowed. He came out of the sea to aid Satan (Revelation 13:1), but, as John writes, "now [he] is not" (Revelation 17:11). But he will be coming out of the Abyss again (Revelation 17:8). One thing is sure: he is going to his destruction (Revelation 17:11).

The Ten Horns (12-14)

Many suggestions are made to identify specifically the "ten kings who have not yet received a kingdom." They are not likely to be Roman rulers; they are in the future to John's writing. They do not yet rule.

They "for one hour will receive authority" (Revelation 17:12). The length of one hour is figurative and need not be restricted even to one year.

Some try to list Roman provincial governors for these "kings," but there is no necessity to chain these rulers to the first or second century. And there is nothing but pure conjecture to indicate the Parthians are needed to fill the description.

What is indicated is a direct allegiance to the beast. They have but one purpose—to give all power and authority to the

---

[82]See W. Hendriksen, *More than Conquerors,* pp. 204, 205.

antichrist. They make war on the Lamb and are defeated. As we watch for references to Armageddon in these closing chapters, this may be one. The ten kings may refer to the number of completeness and not expect literal identification.[83]

The Fate of the Woman (15-18)

Besides locating the site of Babylon on the waters of the Euphrates and canals, the identification of the waters indicates the universality of the prostitute's characteristics permeating the beast's followers all over the world. They are "peoples, multitudes, nations, and languages" (Revelation 17:15).

In spite of her universal influence, the very beast on which she rides will turn on her and destroy her, just as evil invariably turns upon evil and destroys its own kind.

The Destruction of Babylon (18:1-24)

Babylon's Doom Announced (1-3)

When another angel with particular authority comes down from Heaven, one expects a climax. Chapter 10 began with just such a description, and announcement was made that all delay was over and fulfillment had come. Now, in chapter 18, the announcement we have been expecting is definitely made: Babylon has fallen. In the last chapter, John had been toggling back and forth between two figures, Babylon and the prostitute. He continues to do so in this chapter as each figure adds dimension to the same truth. The evil of an individual or of a nation of individuals arises from a Satanic source and leads to gross unfaithfulness and insatiable lust for selfish pleasure and material gain whatever the cost.

Warning of Destruction (4-8)

As in chapter 10, another voice speaks forth from Heaven to corroborate the message of this crucial moment. The sins of the prostitute, or this godless city, are piled up to Heaven. And now all the evil is going to be poured back into the lives of those who

---

[83]"The number ten is symbolic and indicates completeness. It does not point to ten specific kings nor to ten European kingdoms of a revived Roman empire." R.H. Mounce, *The Book of Revelation*, p. 317.

have indulged in them. How ironic at the moment the individual is saying to himself or herself, "Nothing can happen to me. I will never regret anything I have done nor suffer any setback in my ways. I am not a widow." (In other words, my husband has not been killed in battle and left me without support.) And then, "In one day her plagues will overtake her: death, mourning and famine." The judgment of God includes the words, "consumed by fire" (Revelation 18:8).

The plea of the angel was to leave the city of Babylon and its sins so that one will not be a partner in its sins nor suffer its resultant plagues.

The Terror of Her Fate (9-13)

The kings who had lived like Babylon, who had shared in her sins and corruption, were now lamenting what was happening. But they stood far away. Their concern was not for the dreadful suffering of Babylon, but that their own position was diminished and a like fate was threatening them in the coming hour.

The merchants of the earth, pursuing the sin and practices of Babylon, will lament because their own business is ruined (see the extended list of losses at the fall of Tyre in Ezekiel 27). They have even trafficked in the lives of people—both in slave trade and the sacrifice of lives to gain material profit.

The Splendor Has Vanished (14-20)

In one hour, their riches and splendor have vanished. They are gone forever. The sea captain who is responsible for directing the course of the owner's ship will lament the fate of Babylon because he, too, will sink when the city and its merchandising are no longer there. Whereas he had been living by her godless, sinful principles, now—in one hour—he, too, looks forward to the same fate as the fallen city.

The rejoicing of the saints and apostles and prophets will come, not over the suffering of the wicked, but over the justice that has been fulfilled as the righteous God levels the accounts in judgment.

A Mighty Angel Declares Her End (21-24)

A boulder was found. It was as large as a heavy millstone that would need a donkey to turn it. The mighty angel lifted the stone with his great strength and threw it into the sea. Thus, a tremendous mark of punctuation was put after the sentence that has just been declared. It was punctuated with strength and violence to emphasize its finality and gravity. The magic spell of the deceiver has been broken, and the blood of the saints and suffering of the oppressed have been requited.

Special Subject #11

Babylon

Why was Babylon chosen to represent the spread of evil, the persecution of the good, and blasphemy against God? Babylon was an old and famous city. It had been great in men's eyes, but it lay in miserable ruins in John's day. It had a history of opposing God and His people. It was a natural example of insolent disregard for right and wrong. Success was its story for a time, but then complete destruction descended in the end. This sounds like the course of Satan's community of followers, and Babylon becomes its symbol.

Arrogance and Defiance

Our first glimpse of a Mesopotamian town related to Babylon in name and spirit is found in Genesis 11:4-9.

> Then they said, "Come, let us build ourselves a city, with a tower that reaches to the heavens, so that we may make a name to ourselves and not be scattered over the face of the whole earth." . . . it was called Babel (Genesis 11:4, 9).

Babylon is associated with Erech, Akkad, and Calneh, in Shinar (Genesis 10:10). Akkadian scribes thought the name came from "babilim" (gate of god); but Genesis 11:9 explains a connection with the root of *balal,* which is the Hebrew for confusion, because the confusion of tongues had its beginning there. The earliest records from the vicinity of Babylon date from about 2500 B.C. and commemorate the building of temples to the god Aba and the goddess Anunity. In the third dynasty of Ur, Babylon emerged as the provincial capital. Under Hammurabi, the sixth ruler of the dynasty, Babylon governed most of Southern Mesopotamia. In this period, Babylon reached a new high in its power and prestige. This was the Old Babylonian period lasting from

1800-1600 B.C. The Hittites overran the country in 1600 B.C. In the following periods, the middle Casside and Babylonian period, the city again became a capital. Next the Assyrians from the north captured and controlled the city (1235-1198 B.C.). In the eighth century B.C., under Sargon II (722-705), Babylon regained control in Southern Mesopotamia. But the Assyrian Sennacherib came from Nineveh in 689 B.C. and nearly wiped out the ancient center on the Euphrates. In time, however, his son had the city rebuilt. But when the Assyrian Empire fell in 608 B.C., Babylon entered its most prosperous period as capital of the Neo-Babylonian Empire. So the Old Babylonian Empire had long since been eclipsed by the centuries of Assyrian dominance, but now in 600 B.C., Nebuchadnezzar carried out a tremendous building program and sweeping conquests on all sides. This included Jerusalem. The holy city and its temple were destroyed, and the people of Judah were brought to Babylon in exile.

> I am raising up the Babylonians, that ruthless and impetuous people, who sweep across the whole earth to seize dwelling places not their own.... guilty men, whose strength is their god (Habakkuk 1:6, 11).

Quest for Other Gods and Magical Powers

Apparently, the early urge to reach to the gates of Heaven is reflected in the type of temples later built in the region. The ziggurat was a temple-tower with a large square base and sloping, stepped sides reaching up to a top extensive enough to support a shrine to the gods. One of these, dating to the Neo-Babylonian period, is still seen at Babylon with the designation, "The House of the Foundation-Platform of Heaven and Earth." Babylonian texts indicate at least fifty other temples were known by name as well.

Marduk was a younger deity among the gods of Babylon, but, once arrived, he came to overshadow the other pagan deities in all of Babylonia. The "lofty house" (the temple-tower referred to above) was a temple to him. Besides the important temples and a powerful priesthood in the city, soothsaying and exorcism were important to the religion of the Babylonians. This included reading the omens from the heavens, particularly solar, lunar, and planetary phenomena, and gaining supposed conclusions from the shape and conditions of livers, often of the sheep offered in sacrifice. Much astrological superstition today still follows their ways.

> Day after day, my Lord, I stand on the watchtower;
>   every night I stay at my post.
> Look, here comes a man in a chariot
>   with a team of horses.
> And he gives back the answer:
>   "Babylon has fallen, has fallen!
> All the images of its gods
>   lie shattered on the ground!" (Isaiah 21:8, 9).

Lust for Rule and Might

Babylon was situated in the heart of Mesopotamia along the Euphrates and close to the Tigris. It served as a crossroads for armies and merchants. Geographically it was important. Time and again politically it became the capital of vast territories surrounding the city. Religiously it was a powerful influence through its strong priesthood. Each year in its most influential period, the image of Marduk (Bel was another name for the same god) was taken in a gorgeously adorned ship-cart along the festal street from his temple, Esagila, to the house of the New Year Festival and then back to his temple. It was the grand occasion of the year. Towns for miles around sent their gods and goddesses to be included in the procession. All this added power and glory to Babylon.

Babylon of the Neo-Babylonian Empire resembled a tight rectangle in its layout, an area of approximately one thousand acres. Herodotus reported it was fourteen miles long on each of its sides, but excavators have their doubts about this unless walls running to nearby towns were included. Main temples with the royal palace, and the older part of the city were on the east side of the Euphrates. Two imposing walls enclosed the rectangular city. The innermost wall was twenty feet wide on the top and the outermost part of the double wall was eleven feet wide. Included in the outer wall were towers extending beyond the outside surface of the rampart and spaced every sixty-five feet.

The might of Babylon was evident in many ways, but the Lord gave His warning:

> This is the word the Lord spoke through Jeremiah the prophet concerning Babylon and the land of the Babylonians:

"Announce and proclaim among the nations,
    lift up a banner and proclaim it;
    keep nothing back, but say,
'Babylon will be captured;
    Bel will be put to shame,
    Marduk filled with terror.
Her images will be put to shame
    and her idols filled with terror.'
A nation from the north will attack her
    and lay waste her land.
No one will live in it;
    both men and animals will flee away" (Jeremiah 50:1-3).

Ambition for Wealth and Glory

Jesus said: "Where your treasure is, there your heart will be also" (Matthew 6:21). Based upon the remains left from the written records of the people from that part of the world where Babylon was its hub, we have little doubt about where their hearts were. Ninety percent of the cuneiform (an early language written in Babylon's part of the world) texts available today "are economic in content."[84] They have to do with trade and international commerce; the sale of property and the rate of interest charged for loans occupied much attention. If one charged more than 100% interest, it was considered too much! In the Old Babylonian period, an important class was known as *tamkarum,* commonly translated "merchant." He was often more than simply a salesman. He might be a traveler selling goods, but he also might be a money-lender, a broker, a banker, or a government agent. Dishonesty was a problem: "delivering by small measure, receiving by great measure, delivering by a small shekel, receiving by a great shekel."

Another class of people who drew attention was the shipmasters. Considerable correspondence tells of the difficulties they had in keeping time schedules and making promised deliveries. Their boats sailed in the rivers and on the sea. The glory of Babylon was not only in battles and in buildings but in barter and boats. They had a heart for material riches, the pride of life, and the lust of the flesh. Isaiah had warned them:

---

[84]H.W.F. Saggs, *The Greatness That Was Babylon* (London: Sidgwick & Jackson, 1962), p. 287.

Babylon, the jewel of kingdoms,
   the glory of the Babylonians' pride,
will be overthrown by God
   like Sodom and Gomorrah.
She will never be inhabited
   or lived in through all generations;
no Arab will pitch his tent there,
   no shepherd will rest his flocks there.
But desert creatures will lie there,
   jackals will fill her houses;
there the owls will dwell,
   and there the wild goats will leap about.
Hyenas will howl in her strongholds,
   jackals in her luxurious palaces.
Her time is at hand,
   and her days will not be prolonged (Isaiah 13:19-22).

Patroness of Beauty and Arts

Babylon was famous for its appreciation of the arts, its music, its architecture and buildings, its statues, and its terrain of beauty. One could stand on a main street and look to the south down a straight street for the extent of the city in that direction, then turn to view toward the center of the metropolis in the other direction. A temple to the goddess Nimmakh was on the left. To the right was the largest of the palaces. There were three units to this palace alone. The throne room was in one. Another had unusually heavy walls, supposed by some to have supported the famous "Hanging Gardens of Babylon." The walls of another palace facing the street were decorated with processions of lions in colored relief made of enameled bricks. The Ishtar Gate to the city was an arched entry fifteen feet wide and thirty feet high. It, with the towers flanking it, was faced with blue tile decorated with rows of bulls and dragons in colored relief. The report has come down that a queen had longed for the mountainous scenery characteristic of the surroundings where she grew up and that Nebuchadnezzar had provided it for her. It was recognized as one of the wonders of the ancient world.

Still the Lord God of Israel sent his prophets to cry warning:

The Lord will carry out his purpose,
   his decree against the people of Babylon.

You who live by many waters
    and are rich in treasures,
your end has come,
    the time for you to be cut off (Jeremiah 51:12, 13).

Enemies of God and His People

When Ahaz, king of Judah, invited the Assyrians to come help against Pekah of Israel and Rezin of the Syrians, they gladly responded because they wanted territory giving access to the Mediterranean Sea. The Assyrians took Damascus, capital of the Syrians, in 732 B.C. and proceeded to take Samaria, capital of Israel, in 722/21. But when they tried to take Judah, God turned Sennacherib back. Jerusalem was spared. Then, in 689 B.C., Sennacherib almost destroyed Babylon as well. But by 612 B.C., the Neo-Babylonians had begun to roll. In that year, they took Nineveh and proceeded to crush one nation after another. This time God did not spare Jerusalem because Judah insisted on disregarding Him. But neither did He approve of the tactics of Babylon and their oppression, sin, and idolatry. After previous defeats, finally, in 586 B.C., Jerusalem was taken for Nebuchadnezzar and the king, Zedekiah, fled, but he did not escape.

> All his soldiers were separated from him and scattered, and he was captured. He was taken to the king of Babylon at Riblah, where sentence was pronounced on him. They killed the sons of Zedekiah before his eyes. Then they put out his eyes, bound him with bronze shackles and took him to Babylon.... Nebuzaradan the commander of the guard carried into exile the people who remained in the city, along with the rest of the populace and those who had gone over to the king of Babylon (2 Kings 25:5-7, 11).

Despite the victories and power of Nebuchadnezzar, God's warnings had been given by Jeremiah.

> "Summon archers against Babylon
>   all those who draw the bow.
> Encamp all around her;
>   let no one escape.
> Repay her for her deeds;
>   do to her as she has done.

For she has defied the Lord,
   the Holy One of Israel.
Therefore, her young men will fall in the streets;
   all her soldiers will be silenced in that day,"

declares the Lord.

. . . .

This is what the Lord Almighty says:
"The people of Israel are oppressed,
   and the people of Judah as well.
All their captors hold them fast,
   refusing to let them go.
Yet their Redeemer is strong;
   the Lord Almighty is his name.
He will vigorously defend their cause
   so that he may bring rest to their land,
   but unrest to those who live in Babylon"

(Jeremiah 50:29, 30, 33, 34).

Engulfed in Sin and Debauchery

Double significance can be seen in the book of Revelation when the prostitute is chosen to represent Babylon. The figure of unfaithfulness is used time and again to call Israel to repentance for deserting God and going into the idolatry of false gods as a kind of spiritual adultery, and the pagan nations are likewise condemned for their rejecting God as they have opportunity to know right from wrong and to see God in the nature of His creation. Five principal passages in the Old Testament apply this theme to Jerusalem as a harlot,[85] but two others refer to two non-Israelite cities, Tyre and Nineveh.[86] Because of the Old Testament passages plus several references from Qumran commentaries, J. M. Ford maintains that "the harlot in Rev 17 is Jerusalem, not Rome."[87] Her arguments, however, are not sufficient to rule out Rome nor to make the fulfillment refer exclusively to Jerusalem. It does

---

[85]Hosea 2:5; 3:3; 4:15; Isaiah 1:21; Jeremiah 2:20; 3:1, 6, 8-10; 5:7; Micah 1:7; Ezekiel 16 and 23.

[86]Tyre: Isaiah 23:15-18; Nineveh: Nahum 3:4.

[87]J.M. Ford, *Revelation,* p. 285.

strengthen the conclusion that the lesson of Babylon can be applied to more than one setting. It should be heard and heeded in every succeeding generation. It carries truths both continuing and final. The city of Babylon stands as a symbol, accused of both figurative prostitution and literal drunkenness, immorality, selfish materialism, and general defiance against God.

On the eve of the fall of the Neo-Babylonian kingdom, Belshazzar was giving a great banquet for a thousand of his nobles, and they were drinking their wine from goblets that had been taken from the temple in Jerusalem. This speaks volumes for the life-style of these people. That night Belshazzar was killed and his kingdom lost.

God sent message after message to warn about the doom of Babylon.

> Flee from Babylon!
>> Run for your lives!
>> Do not be destroyed because of her sins.
> It is time for the Lord's vengeance;
>> he will pay her what she deserves. . . .
>> The Lord has vindicated us; come,
>> let us tell in Zion
>> what the Lord our God has done.
> Sharpen the arrows,
>> take up the shields!
> The Lord has stirred up the kings of the Medes,
>> because his purpose is to destroy Babylon.
> The Lord will take vengeance,
>> vengeance for his temple.
> Lift up a banner against the walls of Babylon!
>> (Jeremiah 51:6, 10, 11).

Weighed and Found Wanting

On that very night when Belshazzar gave his drinking feast, and the Medes were preparing to enter the city, the final warning was issued.

> As they drank the wine, they praised the gods of gold and silver, of bronze, iron, wood and stone. Suddenly the fingers of a human hand appeared and wrote on the plaster of the wall, near the lamp-stand in the royal palace. The king watched the hand as it wrote.

His face turned pale and he was so frightened that his knees knocked together and his legs gave way.

The king called out for the enchanters, astrologers and diviners to be brought and said to these men of Babylon, "Whoever reads this writing and tells me what it means will be clothed in purple and have a gold chain placed around his neck, and he will be made the third highest ruler in the kingdom."

Not until Daniel was found and brought to the banquet hall were they given the answer to the writing. Daniel told them:

You praised the gods of silver and gold, of bronze, iron, wood and stone, which cannot see or hear or understand. But you did not honor the God who holds in his hand your life and all your ways. Therefore he sent the hand that wrote the inscription. . . .

This is what these words mean:
Mene: God has numbered the days of your reign and brought it to an end.
Tekel: You have been weighed on the scales and found wanting.
Peres: Your kingdom is divided and given to the Medes and Persians (Daniel 5:4-7, 23-28).

A Tragic Example

Cyrus and the Medes and Persians took over that night and, although Babylon did not occupy as single a role of prominence as it had known before, it still had a place. This introduced the period of the Persian empire in the history of Babylon. Furthermore, it seems significant that just over two hundred years later, after Alexander had replaced the Persians, he was taking steps to make Babylon the capital of his whole empire. These were the opening years of the Graeco-Macedonian period.

What happened? Alexander died while he was occupying the palace of Nebuchadnezzar. Think about it. Alexander could endure a decade of campaigns and battles, but he did not die fighting in the field. He died at thirty-three while he was enjoying life in the ancient capital at the hub of the Mesopotamian land.

Babylon was the logical choice for the capital of Alexander's new empire. But when Alexander died, his successor in this area,

Seleucus, founded Seleucia on the Tigris a short distance away, but put his capital at the new site of Antioch on the Mediterranean. Little by little, people moved from Babylon to Seleucia; so by the time John was writing, only small groups of astronomers and mathematicians still continued to live among the ruins of the ancient queen city on many waters.

> "I will rise up against them,"
> declares the Lord Almighty.
> "I will cut off from Babylon her name and survivors,
> her offspring and descendants," declares the Lord.
> "I will turn her into a place for owls
> and into swampland;
> I will sweep her with the broom of destruction,"
> declares the Lord Almighty (Isaiah 14:22, 23).

Thus Babylon was preeminently qualified to serve as the example for the lesson that God wanted to teach. This presents a tragic side of the coin, but the awareness is necessary. Notice again, not the literal city in location and the literal battles that were fought and the precise way destruction came—these are not the ultimate truths to see. Rather the truths that run alongside carry the message:

(1) Babylon attained fame, fortune, and power, but they were bought at the cost of service to the beast and evil. So they were only temporary, for a while, and the final cost was judgment and destruction.

(2) The Prostitute was a figure added to emphasize the presence of the sin, unfaithfulness, and idolatry that ran rampant and drew condemnation. She was destroyed by the very ones who had shared in her sins.

(3) The People of God suffered persecution at the hands of those following the program of the beast.

(4) Prophecy was given to warn the supporters of the beast and to encourage the people of God.

(5) Rome stood in the shadow of Babylon's ruin. Her lesson was not as convincing as Babylon's in John's day, for she was at the height of her power and glory; but she was following the same course as Babylon, and the ruins of Babylon could be viewed as the consequences. She becomes a second example to us, like Babylon.

(6) The application was appropriate to Babylon and timely to Rome, and points to the continuing application that follows in every generation. (See below in Concluding Notes, p. 328) "The waters you saw, where the prostitute sits, are peoples, multitudes, nations and languages." Babylon will be the continuing symbol of all man's effort to resist God and take Satan's side until the last desperate eschatological combat.

(7) Judgment will be complete. God will be victorious. The fall of Babylon is inevitable.

Arnold J. Toynbee was a renowned historian and an avowed agnostic who wrote a world history for the middle of this century. His approach was different in that he made a special study of the rise and decline of successive civilizations. This took him ten volumes—then he added three more—to analyze the conditions that accompany the birth of a civilization and the causes that bring about its breakdown and eventual death. He concluded that twenty-six civilizations can be identified in the history of man, and that sixteen have had their day but are now dead and buried. Of the ten that remain, he felt that "two are now in their last agonies," and that seven of the eight others are in varying degrees of breaking down or being assimilated into our own civilization of the West.[88] He left doubtful whether Western civilization is still climbing or is heading for decline. Both the Babylonic and the Hellenic (including Roman) were among the sixteen fallen civilizations.

In 1955, Toynbee wrote an essay, "A Study of History: What I Am Trying to Do." He began this explanation by telling that he was engaged in two major writing assignments at the same time. One was *A Study of History* and the other, *Survey of International Affairs.* He went on to observe:

> I could not, I believe, have done either piece of work if I had not been doing the other at the same time. A survey of current affairs on a worldwide scale can be made only against a background of world-history; and a study of world-history would have no life in it if it left out the history of the writer's own lifetime, for

---

[88]Arnold J. Toynbee, *A Study of History* vol. IV (London: Oxford, 1939), pp. 1, 2.

one's contemporaries are the only people whom one can ever catch alive.[89]

Mention is made here of Toynbee's work, not to give a review, commending or condemning, but for two reasons: (1) to show that lessons are still being found in the rise and fall of empires (civilizations), and (2) to indicate that the study of the past can be locked into the application of contemporary events as well.

Objection must be raised even in the quotation used above. John most certainly would deny, at least in his case, that his contemporaries were the only people whom he could "ever catch alive." John has spoken in his book of Revelation to every generation from his to ours, and he will continue to speak until Jesus comes again. This does not diminish, however, the way that John spoke to his generation and at the same time mingled this with a message meaningful for all the ages.

In John's inspired writing, he can tell us with assurance of the past and the present, and the future, also. His message has a divine source. The figure of Babylon was chosen for him. The contemporary scene of Rome was woven in for him as part of the divine vision. The future was included in a way that transcends the wisdom of man. A sad distortion of Scripture occurs, however, when interpreters carry the application of Rome to the extent that Rome becomes the final fulfillment, and all generations after her day are left with only unintended messages. Some would make it appear that John was wrong in allegedly indicating that the fall of Rome would be immediate, when it actually endured for centuries after John wrote; or that Nero would return with Parthian soldiers as it had been rumored, which never happened. Let us not misinterpret Revelation and then blame John for being wrong when the mistakes belong to the interpreters.

Messages from both Babylon and Rome must be applied to the people of our day. The lessons are not reserved for the end days, but indicate the struggles through which nations must live in each age until the cry is heard: "The final Babylon has fallen. The Lord is here!"

---

[89]Ashley Montagu, ed., *Toynbee and History: Critical Essays and Reviews* (Boston: Porter Sargent, 1956), p. 3.

CHAPTER TWELVE

Conquest and Judgment

Revelation 19:1—20:15

God forgives and never remembers the sins of His children; but He does not forget His promises. Jesus made promises, too. He told His disciples: "If I go and prepare a place for you, I will come back and take you to be with me that you also may be where I am" (John 14:3). God promised through His prophets that the Messiah would come. As they delivered these prophecies, they surely did not realize the span of hundreds or even a thousand years that would lie between the prophecies and the Messiah's first coming, let alone the long span between the first coming and His second coming. But God did not forget. Time does not dim the promises of God.

A father was walking home with his little daughter late one night. They were following a country road, and it was very dark. As they were nearing the last turn before reaching their own home, they passed the neighbor's house. The father suddenly remembered a message he wanted to leave there and turned in at the gate. He told his daughter, "You wait here at the gate, and I'll be back in a minute to take you home. I just have to tell them something." The little girl stood obediently at the front gate and waited in the dark.

Then two unforeseen things happened. When the father was in the neighbor's house, he talked longer than he had anticipated, and when he left, he went out the back door and took his usual short cut home. The first thing he wanted to know after he greeted his wife was where the daughter was. Then it dawned on him—he had left her at the neighbor's front gate. Instantly, he took off on the run to get back to her as fast as he could. All the way, he was grimacing to think of how terrified she must be in the dark, and of how many things might have happened in the time that had passed.

271

Finally, as he approached, he could make out the little figure still standing in the dark, waiting at the gate just as he had left her. As he gathered her in his arms, he saw the tears streaming down her cheeks. He gave her words of assurance, told her how much he loved her, and how sorry he was he had forgotten her. Then as they walked the rest of the way home, the father asked her, "Were you afraid?" Dodging a direct answer, the little girl went to the heart of the matter, "You said you would come back, and I knew you would." If a child can trust a forgetful father like that, how much more should Christians have confidence in their Heavenly Father. He never forgets His promises.

Jesus promised not only His return, but promised crowns as well.[90] Before His followers can reign, however, He warns them of suffering. In fact, when James and John were seeking the chief seats in the kingdom, Jesus did not promise the seats to them, but neither did He say there were no such things as chief seats. He made clear that the Father would see to it that the proper ones would occupy those seats. They would be the ones who had suffered most, those who had drunk of the same cup of suffering as Jesus had experienced (Matthew 20:20-28).

Preparation for suffering was given throughout Jesus' ministry, and, in fact, throughout the ministries of Peter and Paul as well. Certainly, suffering or tribulation is a theme throughout the book of Revelation, also. The need for strength, faithfulness, and endurance is an emphasis. This is accompanied by the necessity of hope and the assurance of fulfillment of promises. Here at the close of Revelation, the fulfillments are made specific. They have been anticipated in one cycle after another, in a succession of mounting events moving toward a climax. Instead of reaching the culmination, however, a withdrawal has been made each time for another buildup. But now, at last, the climax is actually reached. The nineteenth and twentieth chapters prepare for the finale. They unfold the second coming, the millennium, and the judgment.

Where should one focus his attention when he approaches these chapters? So much interest has been engendered by debates about the time and place of the millennium that the awaited coming of Christ is eclipsed by this surprising puzzle of the thousand years.

---

[90]See 2 Timothy 4:8; James 1:12; 1 Peter 5:4; Revelation 2:10.

In fact, the title used to head this chapter in the commentary has been renamed three times.

"The Millennium" was the original choice for the title because of the interest and the curiosity aroused by the mere mention of the word. Unfortunately, while John is introducing his readers to the bright picture of victory in the end, many interpreters of the book are more interested in drawing up their lines for defending a position than for viewing what is said. So instead of a brighter picture of encouragement and assurance, an impression filled with cloud and smoke results.

Tragic division and uncertainty enter in. So the title was changed from "The Millennium" to "Jesus Reigns." This is more appropriate as it puts Jesus' reign as the highlight of the chapters and does not confine it to a particular millennial period, whether before or after His second coming. But the reign of Christ alone is not what makes the millennium significant. Two factors set this period apart from other eras: (1) Satan was bound for this period, and (2) there were saints who reigned *with* Christ. So more than the reign of Christ should be included in the title.

But what about the title, "The Second Coming"? This book is reputedly devoted to the second coming, so now that we have arrived at its description, why not call it that? But more than the second coming is presented in the details given and less than the full Scriptural picture of His coming. Since, then, the aspect of His coming is pictured as conquest, and the millennium is both conquest and judgment, followed by more judgment, it was decided that the title "Conquest and Judgment" would cover all the important subjects. A special study on the millennium concludes this chapter and one on the second coming follows in the next chapter.

Prelude

Overview

In chapter nineteen, you turn from the growing destruction on earth to songs of praise in Heaven. The hallelujah chorus rings out, acclaiming the justice of God in avenging the blood of His servants. The scene is the same throne room John introduced in the fourth chapter. The twenty-four elders and the four living creatures are there, and God is seated on His throne. Further rejoicing proclaims the wedding of the Lamb and His bride, the church. The angel with John pronounces a beatitude over all those invited to the wedding supper of the Lamb.

Another montage appears before John's eyes when he sees Heaven open, and lo, a rider on a white horse advances to judge and make war. This is the second coming of Christ. The very armies of Heaven follow Him as He leads with complete control and brings full justice. The rider's name is King of kings and Lord of lords.

Another angel sends out word to the birds in the skies to come to "the great supper of God" for they are going to feed on defeated kings and horses and the remains of all the invading people, small and great.

Then another montage spreads before John's eyes. He sees how the beast that came out of the sea earlier and kings with their armies gather to confront the rider and His army of followers. No battle is recorded, only the capture of the beast and the false prophet, his companion. They are thrown into the fiery lake of burning sulfur. The rest are killed, not by fire, not by sword of steel, but by the sword of the rider's mouth, the Word of God. And they are eaten by the birds gathered for the occasion.

Another angel now inaugurates a new action, unheard of elsewhere in the Scripture. This scene informs us of the fate of Satan. He is bound with an extra large chain and put into an Abyss and confined there for a thousand years (figuratively meaning at least a considerable period of time). He cannot deceive the nations for the duration of the period. After that, he is set free for a little time. While he remains bound in the Abyss, the picture in Heaven is a deep contrast. Thrones are set up for the very souls who have been slain for resisting Satan and his representatives. Some of these have been seen before when the fifth seal showed them beneath the altar pleading for vengeance of their blood and a halt to more lives' being taken in martyrdom (Revelation 6:9-11). But they have been told to wait, for the number of martyrs was not yet full. Now those who had suffered are honored on thrones, and they are reigning and judging with Christ in Heaven. They have nothing to fear in the death of Hell (the second death); they only serve God and share the rule of Christ. They are granted the special privilege of the first resurrection that the rest will experience later.

After the period designated as a thousand years is over, Satan is released. He immediately resumes his desperate program of deception. The nations of the world follow him. Gog and Magog are gathered from the four corners of the earth to besiege the city of God. Fire stops the attack in its tracks. The devil is thrown into the lake of burning sulfur, where the beast and the false prophet have been thrown. Scripture affirms, "They will be tormented day and night for ever and ever" (Revelation 20:10).

Another scene unfolds. A great white throne comes into view, and someone is occupying the seat. Whether this is God or Christ is not made explicit, but they are both One, and this is the Divine One. All who have lived are resurrected; they must stand before the throne and be judged. The books are opened that tell all about the lives of the individuals standing there. Another book containing the names of those included in eternal life is opened. After the resurrection and the judgment, Death and Hades are thrown into the lake of fire. Since all have died of the first death who were going to die, and all have been judged, there is no more occasion for death and the temporary holding place between death and the eternal destination of each individual. Therefore physical death and Hades are thrown into the place of eternal destruction, the lake of fire. There were only two places for continuing existence, eternal life or the lake of eternal death. Those whose names were not found in the book of life were thrown into the lake of fire.

Key Message

"... There before me was a white horse, whose rider is called Faithful and True" (Revelation 19:11).

Glossary

Read through chapters 19 and 20 of Revelation. As you come to the terms listed below, note the explanation.

Chapter 19

Hallelujah   This word occurs four times in Revelation 19:1-6, but nowhere else in New Testament. It is derived from two Hebrew words meaning "Praise the Lord" (See Psalm 135:1), and is used particularly in the Hallel Psalms (113-118) at the religious festivals, especially the Passover.

Judgments   The reign of God has two sides: positive (the vindication of the saints—portrayed in

	the marriage of the Lamb with God's people) and negative (judgment—administration of justice—upon the evil).
Prostitute	The figure used to personify the community of those who follow the beast and oppose God, His ways, and His people. Her activity has been corrupting, enticing, and murderous.
Amen	An expression claiming the truthfulness of an affirmation, the authority with which it is stated, a denunciation upon any attempted denial, and, in the church, associated with worship.
Fine linen	In contrast with the linen of the harlot, purple and scarlet, this linen is bright and clean (Revelation 19:8). It was *given* to her, but it stood for the righteous acts of the saints.
Testimony of Jesus	This could be an objective Greek genitive (meaning testimony *about* Jesus or *for* Jesus) or a subjective genitive (coming *from* Jesus as the source of the testimony). It depends on the context for its best meaning. This passage could be taken either way. If the former is preferred, then the next statement would mean, "This is the spirit (the essence or heart) of prophecy, the testimony about Jesus the Messiah."
White horse	White—associated with the righteous and conquering (see Revelation 6:2; 7:9-14), and riding on a horse—appropriate to the general leading his forces into battle.
Faithful and True	(See Revelation 3:14.) The whole being of the rider, Jesus Christ, exudes faithfulness to God's word and the truthfulness of His testimony. His name is what He is.
Word of God	Here is the only place in Scripture where this full expression is used referring to Jesus Christ. See also John 1:1 and 14, and 1 John 1:1, where the same application of the personified "Word" is made to Jesus.

Sharp sword	This should not be understood as the literal weapon of physical battle but the word that issues from His mouth. This is the message of the gospel, which converts the believer and judges the wicked. (See also Isaiah 11:3ff.)
Iron scepter	This is the sign of the authority of the ruler. In this context, it is not so much the indication of a severe reign as the administration of absolute justice (Psalm 2:9; Revelation 2:27; 12:5).
Winepress	This is not the cup of the fury of God's wrath (Revelation 18:6) but the very winepress where the trampling of the grapes occurs and, in the figure, where the judgment is meted out (Isaiah 63:1ff; Revelation 14:19).
King of kings	The King over all kings of all times in every place. Moses declared, "The Lord your God is God of gods and Lord of lords" (Deuteronomy 10:17). In the same way, Jesus is the superlative King.
Angel in the sun	This angel takes a most important vantage point from which to make a most important announcement. The vultures are called to feed upon the carrion of the defeated who have defied God.
Great supper	This is not the wedding feast. Quite the contrary, this is a supper provided by God, and the invited are not asked to come but required to be there, and they are not there to eat, but they are there to be consumed. They are from all walks of life, but are only those who have accepted the mark of the beast in rebelling against God. The defeat of the wicked is complete and horrible to behold.
Beast and kings	Strikingly, the outcome of the battle has been anticipated before the battle as the birds are summoned to consume the remains. The forces of the beast and the

kings have been introduced before (Revelation 16:13, 14; 18:3). No battle is described, only the outcome.

Beast and false prophet This is the same beast introduced as he slew the two witnesses (Revelation 11:7), then he came out of the sea (Revelation 13:1), whose image was put up for people to worship as the antichrist (Revelation 13:14), whom the prostitute rode in the last vision (Revelation 17:3), and finally led in the battle of Armageddon; who now is seized and thrown into the fiery lake of burning sulfur. The false prophet must be the second beast who came out of the earth to assist the first (Revelation 13:11). He, too, is thrown into the lake of burning sulfur.

Chapter 20

Abyss The abode of demons and the beast, and the prison for the dragon (Satan). See the notes on Revelation 9:1. Of the nine times the term is used in the New Testament, seven are in Revelation. The other two are Luke 8:31 and Romans 10:7. (In the latter passage, the NIV translates the word, "the deep.")

Great chain This must be symbolic, for a spirit is neither chained with physical bonds nor locked up with a physical key. But to carry the figure further, it is a particularly heavy chain to bind a specially powerful individual.

Dragon The dragon is fully identified here as the ancient serpent (see Genesis 3:1ff), the devil (see Luke 4:2ff), Satan (see Luke 22:3, 31). The figure was introduced earlier as the one "who leads the whole world astray" (Revelation 12:9).

Thousand years Millennium (*mille* is the Latin word for thousand, *annus* is for year). This is the only place in Scripture that tells of the binding of Satan for a thousand years and of Christ's millennial reign with the saints (martyrs?). Since other numbers in Revelation appear to be regularly figurative, it is assumed this is not necessarily to be taken literally but might indicate a complete, definite period of time, more likely longer rather than shorter.

Souls of the beheaded The martyrs who had died in giving their testimony for Jesus. This seems to be a direct reference to those introduced beneath the altar (Revelation 6:9ff). These are to reign with Christ in the millennium. (See below under Content Notes.)

Mark of the beast Those who worshiped the beast and followed him received a mark on the forehead or the right hand (see Revelation 13:16). If anyone refused to do so, he did not receive the mark, but the beast gave command that he be killed. Some consider this a continued description of the martyrs just referred to. Others consider this a reference to all the rest of the saints as well. (See the discussion below, p. 290.)

First resurrection These people referred to as martyrs and ones who did not have the mark of the beast received a special privilege. They came to life in the same way that all the rest would come to life after the millennium was completed. This was called the first resurrection. There was no doubt about their salvation. They had no fear about the second death. (See below, p. 290.)

Second death The first death is physical death, which everyone must experience who comes to the end of life before the second coming of the Lord. The second death is the doom described in Revelation 20:14, 15 (Hell).

Priests of God The special privileges of those reigning with Jesus in the millennium will also include

	ministering with Him. The priest had a role of service, and they will continue to serve as Jesus serves.
Gog and Magog	(See Special Subject #10, pp. 239ff). Ezekiel speaks of a prince, Gog, who came from the land of Magog in an invasion from the north. (See Ezekiel 38:1; 39:6.) In this instance, however, the two words seem to be representative of two individuals or people bringing a worldwide attack by evil forces against the powers of God.
Great white throne	This is the final, general judgment at the end of time. (See Special Subject #5, pp. 129ff).
Book of life	From the context (see Revelation 20:15), this contained the names of all the redeemed. The other "books" would be records of the deeds in the life of each individual person.
Hades	Death is the common experience that comes to every individual and Hades is its inseparable companion. Sometimes it designates the place where the wicked are waiting for their final fate (Luke 16:23). At other times, it includes the place of the righteous dead (Acts 2:27 [grave]).
Lake of fire	Hell, the eternal place of existence for Satan, his helpers, the beast, the false prophets, and all who have chosen to follow them. Even Death and Hades are included because they are the consequences of sin.

Content Notes

Praise and Worship (19:1-10)

Hallelujah! Praise the Lord! (1-8)

While death and destruction reign on earth (Revelation 18:21-24), an entirely different picture is unveiled in Heaven. The first clue to the difference is the sound of a tremendous number of voices raised in a hallelujah chorus. This is probably the same angelic choirs we heard in the fifth chapter when we were first introduced to the Heavenly scene: "the voice of many angels, numbering thousands upon thousands, and ten thousand times ten thousand. They encircled the throne and ... in a loud voice they sang: 'Worthy is the Lamb ...'" (Revelation 5:9-14). Words of the former song of praise are not repeated here, but these are directed to God for the truth and justice of His judgments. The great prostitute has been condemned, and the blood of God's servants has been avenged. This answers the question of the martyrs under the altar in the sixth seal (Revelation 6:10). The rejoicing is not over the suffering of one's enemies, but because right is vindicated, justice is met, God is supreme. Praise the Lord!

Then another shout of hallelujah is heard. This time the message is the awesome negative side of the truth. In contrast with the joy and praise in Heaven, they recognize that the smoke and haze of smoldering destruction continues to rise from the remains of the corrupted earth. Shades of Sodom and Gomorrah (Genesis 19:28) continue to blight the place of destruction.

Quickly, a third hallelujah rings forth. This time, the worship comes from the twenty-four elders and the four living creatures. They were found in the same positions described in the opening scene in Heaven (Revelation 4:6-11). As they bow down to worship the one on the throne, they put a solemn emphasis to all that has been sung, "Amen [of a truth!], Hallelujah [praise the Lord]!" (Revelation 19:4).

A voice speaks from the throne. This does not seem to be the voice of God himself, but probably an angel acting as His spokesman. Frequently in John's visions, a voice has spoken representing God (Revelation 14:15; 16:1). Here, the voice admonishes all who fear God to praise Him. This includes both small and great. This terminology, "small and great," has been used in describing both the community of those following the beast as well as of those in the body of God's people. It does not matter whether a person is low on the social ladder or on the top. Whether he is rich in worldly goods or a pauper is not the deciding factor. What his height is does not count. But whether small or great or anywhere in between, it takes all there is of him, no more no less, to serve God and to praise His Holy Name.

A fourth hallelujah sounds. This reaches such a crescendo that the voices are like the roar of a waterfall and loud claps of thunder: "Let us rejoice and be glad and give him glory!" (Revelation 19:7). Since the first great throng may have been the angels, and the elders with the four living creatures are specifically named for the third, this last multitude may well be the redeemed through all the ages. This would make appropriate the announcement they have to make. "For the wedding of the Lamb has come" (Revelation 19:7). One woman has represented the community of God's people on earth (Revelation 12:1ff), another has represented the community of followers of the beast (Revelation 17:1ff), and now a third woman will represent all of the redeemed, the community of God's people in Heaven. The bride is ready to make her appearance.

A special garment is given for her to wear. It is made of linen, fit for royalty. The gown is bright and clean, morally pure, made righteous with the blood of Christ, sanctified. Many commentators emphasize that the clothing was given to her; she did not make it herself. We are made righteous through the righteousness of Jesus Christ. We cannot be saved by our own goodness. This is true, we cannot earn salvation. But see the editorial note that John puts in. "Fine linen stands for the righteous acts of the saints" (Revelation 19:8). Just when we feel we can anticipate all of the lessons on our own, we are handed a surprise package like this. We never would have guessed there was a relationship between the good works of the Christian and the fine linen she wore. This does not mean the righteousness of the believers was ever sufficient to save them. It does mean, however, that their goodness does not go unnoticed and is not inconsequential.

All the way through the book of Revelation, from the letters to the churches at the beginning to the final judgment when the books will be opened, the works of the saints have been counted. This is a vital part of remaining faithful, of enduring whatever comes. In the battle with Satan, the Christian wins out because of a combination: "by the blood of the Lamb and by the word of their testimony; they did not love their lives so much as to shrink from death" (Revelation 12:11). The *combination* of Christ and the believer wins out. This is seen especially in these chapters in Revelation.

When James and John, with their mother, asked for the chief seats in the coming kingdom, Jesus did not reply that there were no chief seats. He warned that the Father would make the selection, and the judgment would be decided on the basis of who had served the most and had drunk of Jesus' cup of suffering (Matthew 20:20-28). So the community of God's people are represented by a bride dressed in a garment both given to her and reflecting the righteous deeds of the believers.

Beatitude and Prophecy (9, 10)

Although we are not conscious of an angel accompanying John, periodically we are reminded of his presence. Now he speaks up and delivers the fourth of the seven beatitudes recorded in the book of Revelation.

"Blessed are those who are invited to the wedding supper of the Lamb" (9). Perhaps if we are not familiar with the customs reflected here, we will fail to appreciate the importance of this announcement. The wedding day is a time that cannot be climaxed by anything that has happened before or afterwards in a person's whole life. The wedding feast was an integral part of the wedding. This was a time when the bride and groom shared their own joy and happiness with their friends. To be invited to a wedding feast was a great honor for a most important occasion. Then, to contemplate the wedding of Christ—the Lamb—with the community of all His believers—the bride—is momentous in itself. But to receive a personal invitation to the wedding supper is overwhelming. Even then the angel does not want the occasion to be slighted. He adds, "These are the true words of God." The invitation has come from God himself. This is the meeting of time and eternity. This is the union between God and His people. This is the climax of all that has been before and all to come afterwards.

"I fell at his feet" (10). In this awesome moment, John wants to express himself somehow. He cannot attempt an audacious dash forward to the throne of God. He cannot make his way through the crowd to the Lamb or the bride. All he can do is throw himself at the feet of the angel. This would be a natural move to make. Peter did this after a miraculous catch of fish. "When Simon Peter saw this, he fell at Jesus' knees and said, 'Go away from me, Lord; I am a sinful man!'" (Luke 5:8). John is simply carried away by his feelings and makes the mistake of worshiping the nearest object, the one who has delivered the good news. Some commentators suggest John deliberately devised the scene so he could insert a lesson against angel worship (cf. Colossians 2:18). However, the situation seems rather to have arisen naturally and deserves the rebuke the angel gave.

"Do not do it." The angel and John have a common duty in life—to serve the will of God. They are both created beings: one, an angel, messenger; the other, a man, evangelist. John shares this duty with the other brothers "who hold to the testimony of Jesus." They worship Jesus and not one another.

Is this the testimony *about* Jesus (Jesus is the object of the testimony) or is this the testimony that Jesus *gives* (Jesus is the subject from whom the testimony comes)? Since John said that he was on the island of Patmos because of the testimony of Jesus—this would seem to mean because of the testimony John had given about Jesus (Revelation 1:9). John and his brothers are witnesses (martyrs) in their testimony about Jesus. The phrase is repeated in a coming sentence. Does it mean the same thing there? "For the testimony of Jesus is the spirit of prophecy." It could well be the same. John is saying that the heart of the message of the prophets is to give testimony concerning Jesus. Some maintain that John is alluding to his own role as prophet and in this writing of prophecy, his testimony about Jesus is the very spirit of his work. Others make a strong case for these passages' referring to the testimony Jesus made concerning himself (cf. Revelation 1:2). This is one of the many passages we want to check out with John when we have opportunity to ask him.

The Victor and the Vanquished (19:11-21)

The Victorious Rider (11-16)

The screens used for the scenes shown in Revelation become increasingly large as the book progresses. We began on a small island in the Mediterranean where John first saw his vision of Jesus (Revelation 1:12ff). Later, John saw a door opening into Heaven (Revelation 4:1), and he entered to catch his first glimpse of Heaven. By the twelfth chapter, our screen has grown to include the whole sky with the sun, moon, and stars. How could the screen get any larger than that? We can be given a view into Heaven and see still more. Besides the throne room of God, the whole temple opens before us (Revelation 15:5). But now in Revelation 19:11, we see "heaven standing open." We have come from a door into Heaven to the whole of Heaven before us. We began with just a small screen, then went to a large screen, then to a mammoth one, and after that to cinerama, and finally a 360-degree sweep all around us with no horizons.

The victorious rider comes into view on such a panoramic screen as this.

"Called Faithful and True" (11). This is one of the rare occasions where interpreters of the book of Revelation are in comparative agreement. The figure is Jesus Christ. He is called "Faithful and True." What more appropriate title could be applied to Jesus? He has proven himself faithful in every trial of life from the temptations in the wilderness to His death on the cross. He was faithful to the will of His Father and to the mission He was sent to accomplish. But His life was not measured by faithfulness alone. His life was the very personification of truth. What a tragedy when a life remains unshaken in loyalty to a cause, only to find the cause in itself was unworthy, mistaken, or outright wrong. Not so with Jesus. He is indeed, "the Way, the Truth, and the Life." Yet this is only part of the reason for the appropriateness of the title, "Faithful and True." Not only is the title fitting for Jesus, but this is what He urges His disciples to be. The whole book of Revelation was written to urge all Christians to be faithful and true. A beautiful scene in Heaven describes the 144,000 as "following the Lamb wherever He goes" (Revelation 14:4). In similar language here at the second coming of the Lord, "The armies of heaven were following Him" (Revelation 19:14). Whether these are the redeemed or angels is not declared. (See below under Special Study #13, pp. 319, 322). If actual combat is to ensue, certainly this would be the angels, but no actual force seems to have been needed from the followers in this confrontation. Nevertheless, that this army is made up of angels remains the more likely choice.[91]

The description of the rider is the most striking in Revelation:

"Eyes . . . like blazing fire" (12). This description leaves no doubt that His gaze penetrates the deepest corner of each individual's life and "with justice he judges and makes war."

"On his head are many crowns" (12). In the Hellenistic period, the Ptolemy at one time wore two crowns symbolic of his authority in Egypt and Asia.[92] The Pharaohs of Egypt wore a double

---

[91]See Ladd, *Commentary on the Revelation,* p. 255. "As the Lamb, Christ is followed by the saints (17:14); as the heavenly Warrior, Christ is followed by the angels."

[92]1 Maccabees 11:13.

crown if they ruled both upper and lower Egypt. The dragon representing Satan had seven crowns (Revelation 12:3), and the beast out of the sea had ten crowns on his ten horns (Revelation 13:1). But the conquering rider has "many crowns" denoting kingdoms beyond number. The crown is the royal diadem (*diadema,* see also Revelation 12:3; 13:1), not the winner's wreath (*stephanos*) worn by the first horseman of the seven seals (Revelation 6:2) or the harvester seated on the cloud (Revelation 14:14).[93]

"A name . . . no one knows." Some object that John proceeds to give us this name, "the Word of God." But, in fact, John gives us still more titles in the same paragraph, but these do not divulge this name that remains unknown. This should remind us that all of the future cannot be bared, and all of the depths cannot be plumbed by our finite minds. The person of Jesus is beyond the comprehension of man, and this name remains a secret except to Jesus himself.

"Dressed in a robe dipped in blood" (13). The question immediately arises, "Whose blood?" The interpreters of the earliest times pointed to the blood of the Lamb shed for redemption.[94] But in this scene, Jesus comes as judge to make war (Revelation 19:11). Caird maintains that it is the blood of the martyrs whose blood Jesus has come to avenge.[95] This is possible, but a third suggestion is still more likely. The blood of the enemy is on the robes of Jesus. Yet another question remains. Is this blood from battle or is it from the trampling of the winepress of judgment? From Isaiah 63, one finds language so fitting that he sees a commentary on the scene in the prophet's words:

> Why are your garments red,
>   like those of one treading the winepress? . . .
> I trampled them in my anger
>   and trod them down in my wrath;
> their blood splattered my garments,
>   and I stained all my clothing (Isaiah 63:2, 3).

---

[93]For the winner's crown, see also Revelation 2:10; 3:11; 4:4, 10; 9:7; 12:1.

[94]See Revelation 1:5, 5:9; 7:14; 12:11.

[95]C.B. Caird, *Commentary on the Revelation,* p. 224.

"His name is the Word of God." In the opening of John's Gospel, the logos (Word) was in the beginning and, from the start, was the instrument of God's creation. In the book of Revelation, the Word of God has already proven himself faithful and true. He deserves the name that denotes the wisdom and reason of God, the power of His commands, the continuing revelation of God himself. He looks forward to the fulfillment of all promises and the establishment of all justice. He is the divine Word.

"Armies of heaven . . . following him" (14). The scene described in Revelation 12:7 assures us that Heaven has its armies. Michael led them on that occasion, but Jesus leads them in this great finale to the earthly existence of man. The Heavenly hosts are clad in white and are mounted on white horses—emphasizing both righteousness and victory.

The alternate suggestion, that these may be the redeemed in Heaven rather than the angels, does not fit the picture as well. In this portion of the action, the saved are the bride of the Lamb, but the celestial forces of God are better suited to follow the victorious Commander in His final, irresistible advance against the troops of evil.

"Out of his mouth comes a sharp sword" (15). This sword is not to be imagined in a way that can be put down in a drawing, but to be felt in a realization that brings awe and a desire to pledge your life. This is not a physical blade extended from a lifeless figure, but all that is indicated by the name "Word of God" now issues from the mouth of Christ. It has the perception to penetrate to the finest lines of discernment. It has the authority to demand full obedience in response. It has the power to exercise full enforcement of God's decrees. This sword is ready and able to bring whole nations to submission.

"He will rule . . . with an iron scepter." As Jesus had said that John the Baptist was no reed shaken by the wind, so the iron scepter indicates the character of Christ's reign. He does not have a club in His hand to beat into subjection, but He does have a rigid symbol of power showing He cannot be intimidated. He is the dauntless Christ, without compromise and confident of victory. He is just and wise in all His judgments, and rules in a decisive way.

"Treads the winepress of the . . . wrath of God." The justice of God requires Him to bring judgment in order to be faithful to His divine nature. His wrath is nothing more than what is demanded

by righteous judgment. This results in necessary consequences on those who have defied the rightful ways of God.

"King of kings and Lord of lords" (16). This name was written "on his robe and on his thigh." Some explain this by suggesting that the writing was on the robe where it covered the thigh. This would be the most prominent place on the person riding a horse. Others emphasize this would be the spot covered by the sword in its usual sheath, but that the sword was not in its regular place on this rider. Others point out that the contrast cannot be missed between the scarlet beast and the victorious rider. The beast was covered with blasphemous names, but the rider's name indicated the greatest of Kings, the Ruler of all; the Lord above all lords, the Master of all powers.

The Vanquished (17-21)

A bird was heard in the eighth chapter flying at the high point in the noon sky and screeching a warning of woes. Two woes were delivered, and then the third woe seemed included in the last trumpet when the kingdom of the world becomes the kingdom of our Lord and the eternal reign begins (Revelation 11:15). Now, at a closing scene in another montage of the concluding frames in the drama of life, an angel calls an invitation to the birds (vultures, eagles) in midair to come to a supper. This occasion is planted in deep contrast to the joyous wedding celebration in Heaven as the multitudes sang their praises to the union of the Lamb and His bride (Revelation 19:6ff). But here the birds are summoned to an entirely different type of feast. They were to clear away the total devastation of rebellious men who gathered to attack the forces of God.

We read of the preparations made to fight at Armageddon (Revelation 16:12ff), but no battle is described. Now the conflict is to be pursued to the end. But even here, no combat is described. Only the outcome is given. The beast and the false prophet are captured and thrown alive into the fiery lake of burning sulfur. All the rest, the faceless, unidentified "kings of the earth" and "their armies" (mighty men and all kinds of people, free and slave, small and great) are killed by the sword that comes out of the mouth of the rider on the horse. The hosts of Heaven who followed Jesus did not need to lift a finger. The Word from His mouth spelled the conclusion of the conflict. The vultures did their work and the remains are cleared away. The same type of scene is the background for Matthew 24:28 and Ezekiel 39:17. For those who had been deluded by the beast, worshiped him, and received his mark, their final judgment still remains for the future after death. For the beast and the false prophet, their final fate has now begun in the lake of fire.

The Millennium (20:1-6)

Satan Bound (1-3)

Again, the unexpected is brought into view. In the former chapter, John informs us of the final fate of the beast and the false prophet. But where was Satan, the dragon? What happened to him? As though to answer our question, John tells us that Satan was bound for a thousand years. This is the unexpected. We can understand something of Satan's being hurled out of Heaven (Revelation 12:9), and we puzzle over numbers, such as 1,260 days (Revelation 11:3) or even three and a half days (Revelation 11:9), but here is a thousand years, and Satan is bound—put in an Abyss, closed, locked, sealed! This is more startling. We read nothing about this in either the Old Testament or the rest of the New Testament.

Then another surprise—after the thousand years, he must be set free for a little while. Why is this necessary? God is in control. Is it a compulsion God has because He is God? Or is it simply a plan that makes it necessary? We stand amazed and must be ready to admit man cannot plumb all the depths and see reasons for everything. We could not understand fully even if we had the details.

The reason that is given for the binding was so Satan could not deceive the nations until the thousand years ended. To say, however, that this means Satan could still deceive individuals but not nations is unrealistic. You cannot deceive a nation without deceiving individuals, and you cannot deceive enough individuals without deceiving a nation. Plato said the state is simply the individual writ at large.[96] Jesus sent His followers "to make disciples of all nations" (Matthew 28:19), baptizing them (but the pronoun *them* is in the masculine, showing it refers to individuals, rather than

---

[96]But along this line, some maintain that Satan could mislead individuals, but not on a great scale. See H.B. Swete, *Commentary on Revelation,* p. 257.

neuter, referring to baptizing nations). So when Satan's activity against nations is curtailed, his activity in relationship with individuals must be limited as well.

Martyrs Reign (4-6)

Then we learn there is more meaning to the thousand years than the binding of Satan. A special reward is given to those who sit on thrones and judge. But who are these people? They are carefully described. They are the souls of those who have been beheaded because of their testimony for Jesus. The description continues by specifying those who have "not worshiped the beast or his image and had not received his mark on their forehead or on their hands." A problem rises, however, since the Greek would allow this further description to refer to those who had been beheaded or it might indicate a separate, larger group. In fact, no one among the redeemed would be so marked by the beast. Thus, in that case, it would mean all of the redeemed would have thrones and crowns, reigning and judging. Of course, this is not impossible, and crowns are promised to all who suffer; but since the description so nearly fits the group who have given their lives in their testimony, this is the select group. So even though grammatically it is possible for two groups, it probably is the one smaller group of Christian martyrs that is indicated.

The same language of the description is found earlier (Revelation 13:14ff) when Satan's emissary gave the order that all who would not worship the image of the beast were to be killed. Then, too, we were introduced still earlier to those who had been slain because of the Word of God and the testimony they maintained (Revelation 6:9-12). They were given white robes and told to wait a little longer until the number would be complete who had suffered in the same way they had. So it seems that we have been told all along about this group, and now we see the special blessing they are to have. They will sit on thrones, reign with Jesus, judge with Him, serve, and be His priests for a thousand years while Satan is bound and in the Abyss. Furthermore, during that time, they will be enjoying a form of life that the rest will not know until the thousand-year period is over. Whatever "they came to life" means (Revelation 20:4), this is the same as others experienced later (Revelation 20:5). For the Christian martyrs, this was called the "first resurrection." They had no fear of the second death that must be suffered by the worshipers of the beast.

Satan's Fate (7-10)

Why Satan must be released after his confinement cannot be answered from the information given. It may be that Satan is due one more trial. A more likely reason is that man is due one more trial to resist the deceit of the evil one. What is noteworthy is that Satan immediately goes back to his regular program of deceiving man into a rebellion against God and His ways, and that just as quickly, man succumbs to his wiles, and the forces are gathered from the four corners of the earth for the final conflict.

A change of tense is made here. John has been telling us what he saw in the past tense. In the last of the nineteenth chapter, he saw the beast and the false prophet make their attack, they were captured, and thrown alive into the lake of fire. Then he saw the death of the kings and their armies, and the birds came and gorged themselves on their flesh. Obviously, this is something that will take place in the future, but proleptically he saw it as something of the past. Then John saw an angel coming out of Heaven and the imprisonment of Satan (past tense). At this same time, he saw the thrones and the ruling of the martyr-redeemed in Heaven (past tense). Then suddenly we come to the future tense: "When the thousand years are over, Satan *will* be released . . . and *will* go out to deceive the nations." This may, at least, be a clue as to where John has positioned himself in time to view the visions he is describing. He is at the end of the thousand years and the release is about to take place.

Another striking aspect of the order of presentation here is that all of this follows the second coming of Christ if one recognizes Revelation 19:11-16 as a description of Christ's *parousia*. This would put Armageddon and the demise of the beast and the false prophet in close relationship to the second coming, and Satan's release and Gog and Magog would be following sometime after. This would agree with the chronology reflected in the observation that when the dragon was thrown into the lake of fire, the beast and the false prophet were already there.[97]

One must be reminded, however, this is an apocalyptic work, and we have emphasized the presence of cyclical presentations

---

[97]Mounce notes that, in both Ezekiel and Revelation, the assault follows the period of the Messianic kingdom (*The Book of Revelation*, p. 361).

going back and forth in the passage of time. One certainly cannot establish chronology by insisting the events must be consecutive. Although nothing can be proved by the change in tense, it is worthy of note. The position of this commentary is that John is standing at the same point in time viewing the second coming of Christ, Armageddon, the end of the beast and the false prophet, near the end of Satan's thousand years in the Abyss, with the release in the immediate future. Then John projects himself to a new stance in time beyond the campaign of Satan and his siege of God's city where once again he reverts to the past tense.

The reference to the camp of God's people (Revelation 19:9) introduces a reminder of Israel's years in the wilderness joined with the thought of an army on the march,[98] plus the picture of God's people knowing nothing but a temporary residence on this earth. The city he loves could have no more likely earthly, geographical site than Jerusalem. The association with God's people is not simply the old Israel of the Old Covenant, but the new Israel[99] including both the remnant from the old and those from all people who remain faithful to the Lord of lords and King of kings. Fire came down from Heaven to stop the final assault of Satan and his forces, whose number were like the sand on the seashore. But their resistance amounted to nothing in the face of God's power.

When the devil was thrown into the lake of fire, the beast and the false prophet were already there. This is a time note that links the last chapter with this one.

Judgment (11-15)

The next scene introduces another throne. Who is seated on the great white throne? Since God has consistently occupied the chief throne in Revelation, our presumption would be that He is on the throne here as well. The only hesitation in the answer comes because Jesus is often described as being the judge on Judgment Day.[100] Since both God and Jesus are reported in that role, God

---

[98]See H.B. Swete, p. 266.

[99]Romans 9:25ff; Galatians 3:6ff.

[100]Jesus as judge: Matthew 25:31; Acts 17:31; 2 Corinthians 5:10; 2 Timothy 4:1. God as judge: Hebrews 12:23; James 4:12.

would be favored in this instance with the reminder that the two are one.[101]

This is a universal judgment of all, both great and small, good and bad.[102]

The good were judged by what they had done. This does not say they will be saved because of their deeds. All will already know whether their names are there or not. This is the public recognition, the official declaration. No doubt, evidence shown at this time will give basis for degrees of reward and degrees of punishment.[103] The parables of Jesus give every indication of degrees, as does Jesus' reply to James and John (Mark 10:35ff).

"The sea gave up the dead" (13). All the dead, even those lost at sea, with no physical remains, will be resurrected.

"Death and Hades." What had they done wrong to deserve punishment or what actual personal existence did they have? They did not have to have personal existence. It is the association of death as the penalty of sin that makes death such an enemy of man. Hades is the constant companion of death because it is the place for all souls during the intermediate state between earthly life and the final destination of either eternal Heaven or Hell.[104] Hades is used to translate the Hebrew *Sheol,* the grave. Its New Testament usage is more often than not employed to describe the intermediate place of the wicked, but it is used on occasion of the righteous as well (Acts 2:27, 31). The final irrevocable sign of the end of probation and trial for man is the conclusion of physical death itself. God "will swallow up death forever" (Isaiah 25:8). Both the threat of physical death and the memory of its association as the consequence of sin will be gone. But Hell is the second, spiritual death that is eternal. All with no name in the Book of Life were assigned to Hell.

---

[101]See John 5:19 ff. See Special Study #5 above (pp. 129ff).

[102]See Daniel 12:2. Cf. John 5:29.

[103]The Scripture gives indication of degrees of reward and punishment (for example, rewards to the good: ruler of ten cities, ruler of five cities, Luke 19:17, 19; 1 Corinthians 3:8, 14; punishment: many blows and few blows, Luke 12:47, 48; Jeremiah 21:14; 25:14).

[104]See R. H. Mounce, *The Book of Revelation,* p. 366.

All of existence is a matter of life and death. The surface view is taken with the appearance that life ends where death begins, but Revelation teaches us not only of God's victory, but at death's end, true life begins. Tragically, for those who have spurned the grace of God, death continues for eternity.

Special Subject #12

The Millennium

The book of Revelation is written in a different style from the rest of the books of the New Testament. Visions, figurative language, and lessons drawn from the past, true in the present, and significant for the future fill its pages. Both Heaven and earth are used for settings. The unveiling comes more often in cycles than in chronological sequence. Information is given in a new way. Yet the ground covered is also traversed in other parts of the Old and New Testaments. In fact, of its 404 verses, Revelation is purported to have 276 bearing in some way on a theme found in the Old Testament. In the New Testament, the second coming of Christ is referred to time and again, the resurrection of the dead, the judgment of all, salvation in Heaven, and the fate of the lost—all have been taught in the words of Jesus and in the apostolic teaching. In no other place in Scripture, however, do we find the designation of a thousand years' reign of Christ and the saints or of the binding and loosing of Satan. This makes the interpretation doubly difficult; the passage stands alone. Despite its singular nature, it must be correlated with material found elsewhere in Scripture. Even if the details are not identified with items described elsewhere, how does the millennium fit into the pattern of Jesus' return?

In the brief treatment of the millennial subject that follows, selected major questions are considered. Variant positions have already been summarized above (pp. 17-20). Some of the problems left dangling by the popular approaches are noted, and a possible resolution is offered.

Is the Thousand Years Literal or Figurative?

Numbers given in the book of Revelation are regularly used in a figurative way. Since there is no reason given to make an exception for this round figure of 1000, one is safe in concluding it was intended to be taken in a figurative manner. Thus, its use would not designate a specific thousand years, but it would indicate a definite period with a beginning and an end, the probable indication of completeness emphasized by ten multiplied three times ($10 \times 10 \times 10$), and the probability of a considerable length of time rather than short.

Where Is the Reign of Christ, on Earth or in Heaven?

Using the immediate context as indication, one concludes the scene is in Heaven:

(a) The furniture is Heavenly. Thrones for the righteous are used regularly for those in Heaven, about forty times for God or others in Heaven. (The only other uses are for Satan and the beast, three times [one of these is for Satan in Pergamum, but obviously not literal]).

(b) The personnel is Heavenly. "The souls of those who had been beheaded" (Revelation 20:4) have completed their witness on earth and are now safe in Heaven. Some were introduced in the fifth seal (Revelation 6:9); then they were under the altar, now they are on thrones. Also Jesus is regularly found in Heaven doing His work before the end.

(c) The work is commensurate with Heavenly tasks. Ruling and judging is what God and the Lamb have been doing all along; now the honored saints are given a share in the authority to judge and to reign. This would be fitting as a Heavenly task, in deep contrast to their prior suffering on earth.

When Will the Millennial Period Occur?

The time indicated is toward the end of the earthly age. Satan has suffered a succession of defeats. Jesus won out over Satan's temptations at the beginning of His ministry. Jesus saw Satan fall as lightning from the sky, as He reported when His disciples returned from an evangelistic campaign (Luke 10:18). Certainly in His death, burial, and resurrection, Jesus dealt the crucial blow to Satan's program to lead all mankind to destruction (Colossians 2:15). But Satan refused to stop his activity. The resilience of the evil one is an apt phrase. His role is pictured in the book of Revelation. Satan as the dragon took his place before the glorious woman and determined he would destroy her offspring before the baby gained maturity (Revelation 12:4). Satan was thwarted, however, as the child was taken to Heaven. Satan pressed his attack into the very Heavens, but suffered another defeat as

295

Michael drove him out of the Heavens he had dared to enter. He returned to earth and redoubled his efforts to destroy the woman and her offspring—those who obey God's commandments and hold to the testimony of Jesus (Revelation 12:17). Certainly this does not sound like the activity of a Satan who is bound and sealed in the Abyss; so the millennium had not started as yet. If a leash is long enough to allow the activity described, it counts for nothing more than the restraint he already knew. After this period of desperate activity, Satan realized his time was short. As he had been cast out of Heaven, now he is cast from the earth and held in the Abyss for a millennial period before the last days of time.

This would explain the subsequent absence of the dragon throughout so many chapters in Revelation. The beast, rather than the dragon (Satan), comes to dominate as a representative of evil. How does this happen? The beast was introduced in the account of the two witnesses who had been prophesying for 1,260 days. At the end of their testimony "the beast that comes up from the Abyss will attack them, and overpower and kill them" (Revelation 11:7). Next, but not necessarily in chronological order, we read that the dragon was standing on the shore when the beast came out of the sea. This was the same beast, and the "dragon gave the beast his power and his throne and great authority. . . . Men worshiped the dragon because he had given authority to the beast, and they also worshiped the beast and asked, 'Who is like the beast? Who can make war against him?'" (Revelation 13:2-4). Later, the figure of the great prostitute, Babylon, is seen sitting on a scarlet beast, which is described as one who "once was, now is not, and will come up out of the Abyss and go to his destruction" (Revelation 17:8). But where is Satan; why is she not riding the dragon? The "fifth angel poured out his bowl on the throne of the beast, and his kingdom was plunged into darkness" (Revelation 16:10). But why does he concentrate on the throne of the beast? Where is Satan? Why does the beast possess Satan's throne? Could it be that we are now in the period when Satan is in chains in the depths of the Abyss? Anticipating his time was short (Revelation 12:12), he had passed his program on to others for the time being. The beast is front stage now because Satan is bound.[105]

---

[105]Others have reached similar conclusions. "Gaechter suggests that the chaining took place a thousand years before the end of the beast; because

When Jesus, Faithful and True, came on His white horse, and the armies of Heaven were following Him, He was prepared to do battle with the nations. His enemies were the beast and the kings of the earth and their armies (Revelation 19:19). But where was Satan? At the conclusion of this conflict (no physical combat is recorded, only death for the followers of the beast from the sword that came out of the rider's mouth), both the beast and the false prophet were captured and thrown into the fiery lake of burning sulfur. But where was Satan?

This battle that occurs at the time of Jesus' second coming may well be the same battle that had been building up at Armageddon (Revelation 16:16). In the setting of this scene, at last, Satan has a part. "Then I saw three evil spirits that looked like frogs; they came out of the mouth of the dragon, out of the mouth of the beast and out of the mouth of the false prophet. They are spirits of demons performing miraculous signs, and they go out to the kings of the whole world to gather them for the battle on the great day of God Almighty" (Revelation 16:13, 14). But if this is the same battle as in Revelation 19:19-21, and Satan had a hand in instigating it, where was he when the battle action took place? Why was he not thrown into the lake of fire along with the beast and the false prophet? If Satan is at this time incarcerated in the Abyss, the beast and the false prophet may have had access to confer with him. After all, the locusts came out of the smoke of the Abyss at the sounding of the fifth trumpet (Revelation 9:3), so why could not the frogs—or the evil spirits that looked like frogs—have come from there? More serious objections might be raised: the star had a key to the Abyss or the smoke would not have been released. Who had the key to let the frogs out of the Abyss—or to let the beast and the false prophet in? Or is this simply making too much demand on figurative language? But, after all, was not the dragon forbidden to deceive the nations while he was bound? This would be doing just what he was bound not to do. Another explanation may be nearer the answer at this point. This battle was toward the end. Could this be in the period following the loosing of Satan? Perhaps he sent the beast and

---

he (Satan) was chained he sent his agents the beast and the false prophet into the world." J.M. Ford, *Revelation,* p. 329. P. Gaechter "The Original Sequence of Apocalypse 20-22," *Theological Studies* 10 (1949), pp. 485-521.

false prophet, but stayed away himself to escape the feared results.

The position taken here is that the millennium is introduced to trace the final defeats of Satan and his ultimate fate. The time fits best as a period that closed in the end days of the second coming, the resurrection, and the judgment.

The "End-Millennial" Interpretation

The position held here is similar to the amillennialist except for three main objections. Stretching the millennium from the resurrection of Christ to His second coming, as most amillennialists do, contradicts the presentation of Satan as persecuting the church (for example, Revelation 12:17). This leads to the second objection as to the extent Satan was bound for the millennial period. The Scriptural figures of "bound," "locked," and "sealed" (Revelation 20:2, 3) do not allow for Satan's activity advocated by the amillennial position in the period he was supposed to be in the Abyss. The third objection has to do with the name, amillennial. Such a word formation indicates a denial of the millennium rather than the denial of an earthly reign of Christ as is intended. Important agreements are found with the amillennialists, however: the thousand years is a figurative number denoting a period rather than a literal thousand years, the reign of Jesus is in Heaven rather than a Davidic rule in literal Jerusalem, and the timing at the end of the millennium: the second coming, the resurrection, and the judgment.

The position favored here likewise finds agreement and disagreement with the postmillennial approach. "On Postmillennial principles the Second Coming of Christ will be followed immediately by the general resurrection, the general judgment and the introduction of Heaven and Hell in their fullness."[106] This succession of events follows on the heels of the millennium. This timing seems commensurate with the Scriptural details, but the main tenets of the postmillennial approach pose serious problems. Advocates of this interpretation maintain that the kingdom of God is now being extended through the preaching of the gospel until the world eventually will be Christianized and that the return of Christ will occur at the close of a long period of righteousness and

---

[106]Loraine Boettner, *The Millennium,* p. 117

peace commonly called the millennium. Although the power of the gospel has not diminished through the ages, such expectation of an ideal kingdom on this earth at the close of time seems incompatible with Paul's warning that there will be terrible times in the last days and that evil men and impostors will go from bad to worse (2 Timothy 3:1-13). The picture indicated in Scripture is that things on earth are getting worse as the second coming approaches. This leaves the postmillennialists at fault on two counts: they favor a millennial reign on earth, and they picture conditions as being ideal toward the end, rather than getting worse as Jesus comes again.

The premillennialists and the dispensationalists[107] do well to see the element of tribulation as the coming of the Lord approaches. This has solid basis, but the question rises as to whether or not one can be certain of a "Great Tribulation"—with a capital G and a capital T—meaning one event to the exclusion of a series of tribulations growing more intense as the end comes.[108] Serious objection then must be raised for the next step in seeking a place for the millennium. These two schools, premillennial and dispensational, put the coming of Christ before the millennium, and insist on a literal thousand years before Satan is loosed. Then this leaves the final Gog and Magog and after that Christ comes again for a third return, this time in judgment after His earlier second coming a thousand years before. A third coming is nowhere taught in Scripture. An extended existence with Heavenly figures occupying earthly cities goes beyond anything indicated.

But when all is said, a person must wait to see how God will work together the details of the final days. In the meantime, each must be patient with the other and strive to come to as confident a conclusion as he can for himself. When he cannot find a school that represents his conclusions adequately, the best he can do is

---

[107]See above in the Introduction, pp. 19, 20.

[108]A concise comparison of the four main views on the millennium is given by four who each presents his own position and responds to the other three: Robert G. Clouse, ed. *The Meaning of the Millennium: Four Views* (Downers Grove, Illinois: InterVarsity Press, 1977). Contributors: George Ladd (Historic Premillennialism), Herman A. Hoyt (Dispensational Premillennialism), Loraine Boettner (Postmillennialism), Anthony A. Hoekema (Amillennialism).

Theories on the Period of the Millennium in Revelation

Amillennial	End-millennial	Postmillennial	Premillennial
a. Thousand is figurative number.	a. Thousand is figurative number.	a. Figurative depending on when the right conditions come on earth.	a. Thousand is taken literally.
b. It designates the period between the resurrection of Christ and His second coming.	b. Ends with loosing of Satan and the soon coming of Christ.	b. It will begin when the Gospel acceptance on earth will bring ideal response to the reign of Christ.	b. The second coming of Christ precedes the period.
c. The reign will be in Heaven.	c. Reign will be in Heaven.	c. The reign will be on earth.	c. Reign will be on earth [following seven dispensations, Dispensationalists].
d. Satan is bound and loosed but his activity continues though limited.	d. Satan is bound marking the beginning of the period, but his work will be carried on by the beasts as indicated in the latter part of Revelation.	d. Satan will be bound and Heavenly conditions will prevail on earth.	d. Premillennialists (historic) and Dispensationalists disagree about Rapture and Tribulation, but Satan will be bound and Heavenly conditions will prevail on earth.
e. The second coming, resurrection, and judgment will follow in immediate succession after the millennium.	e. The second coming, resurrection and judgment follow upon the close of the period.	e. Following the close of the period, the second coming, resurrection, and judgment will follow immediately.	e. After a thousand years the Lord will return a third time for judgment.

find a descriptive term to indicate what he sees. In order not to be confused with pre-, post-, or amillennial views—although something has been used from each—a designation must be found to suggest pertinent aspects of this present view. An apt phrase to label the position taken in this commentary is the end-millennial approach. This signifies the following:

1. The end of the millennium is crucial. Although its beginning may be uncertain, its end introduces the end days of all. This triggers the final series of events, which follows in rapid succession. It includes the loosing of Satan, the second coming of the Lord (see Special Subject #13 at the end of the next chapter), and the final conflict with the beast and the false prophet at Armageddon.

2. After the end of the millennium comes the defeat of Satan, Gog and Magog, the resurrection, the judgment. This means victory for God and the end of tribulation and of death for the people of God.

3. With the end of the millennium comes the end of the old order on earth, the end of time, and the beginning of the new order of life eternal.

Thus the millennium will be the reign of Christ with the martyr-saints in Heaven while Satan is bound in the Abyss in the last major period of earth's existence. Earth will not know when the millennium begins. It may be in effect now, it may still be future. If Satan is bound now, his emissaries, represented by the beast and the false prophet, are doing his work for him. Since we do not know what the schedule is, the Lord may come at any time "as a thief in the night." Tribulation will continue to the end, but also hope and assurance in God's promises for the millennium and all eternity remain secure. The greatest danger in anyone's interpretation of the millennium and the second coming of Christ is to conclude that we are living in a time when Jesus could not come just at this time. A complacency results and takes the edge off the urgency of preparing for His imminent return. We can be sure something is wrong with our interpretation if we are saying to ourselves, "He cannot come because the times are not bad enough," or "not good enough," or "not full enough," or, "He has just forgotten."

Not to be anxious. Jesus said He will come again, and we know He will.

CHAPTER THIRTEEN

New Jerusalem

Revelation 21:1—22:21

Late one night, a lone figure made his way along the deserted streets of Sydney, Australia. He came to a likely place in front of a store and settled down to do his work. With careful, beautiful strokes, in expert script of copperplate quality, he left one word on the cement walkway. He used chalk to inscribe his message and, having finished, he stood back to view with approval what he had done. Hundreds, even thousands, of people would see that word tomorrow morning as they went to work or to do their shopping. They couldn't miss it. The writing would remain there until worn away by countless pedestrians or by the downpour of rains. By then, however, the man would have repeated his work in scores of other places.

Even now he was several blocks away leaving the word in front of a school, a place of amusement, a factory, and a large office building. Always the same word was put down. He was never hurried, never crude in his lettering. Always it breathed with hope and assurance, with love and concern.

He had come into Sydney that evening on the last local train before the line stopped running for the night, and after his night's work, he would take the earliest morning train out of Sydney. He would return to his home in a suburban senior citizen's flat.

For years, the identity of this person remained undetected, but finally he was observed, and his story became known. Formerly, his life had been a disappointment—to say the least. He was a wreck, an alcoholic, and all his skills and ambitions had faded to nothing. He himself described his plight in this way when he heard the gospel one night in a mission meeting in Sydney. Then came a period of repentance and obedience to Jesus as Lord. In the years that followed, he was concerned because he lacked gifts to do more for the Lord and to let others know of the hope and encouragement the Christians have. But he decided he had one gift, the ability to produce beautiful, copperplate lettering. He could use this to witness to others of the hope that Jesus brought. The simple but profound word he immortalized in the streets of Sydney was "ETERNITY."

People did not resent his reminder. When the man died, his passing was noted in the headlines of the Sydney newspaper. Not long after, Sydney decided to inscribe the word more permanently both in memory of Arthur Stace and of the emphasis he wanted to instill in people's lives. In concrete pavement, they imbedded stainless steel letters of the same size and the same copperplate script of Stace's word, "ETERNITY."

Don't be discouraged if you find it difficult to locate the word in downtown Sydney. A man selling newspapers not a hundred yards away from it had no idea where the word could be found in Sydney. A security officer in the neighboring Town Hall Station could give no clue as to its location. Shopkeepers in the Queen Victoria Building remembered seeing the chalk word years ago, but had heard nothing about its existence now. Finally, a man taking down a flag between the Town Hall Station and St. Andrew's Church could give directions for finding it. Nearby was a cascade of water flowing continuously across the face of a wall. "Look to the right hand side, just in front of the water." There it is imbedded in the pavement, "ETERNITY."

Ironic that people should live so close to eternity and not recognize its presence or give little thought for preparation. The book of Revelation closes with a view into eternity.

Prelude

Overview

How can you describe eternity—especially when you have never been there? Or is it a condition rather than a place? Or is it first a condition and then a place? How can you tell about one day in eternity when there is no longer such a thing as one day? How can you talk about the coming of the new Jerusalem from Heaven to earth? Does this mean it will become earthly, just like the old order of things? Probably not. The old terms are used simply because we could not understand a new condition without using the language we know. When we speak of the coming of the Holy

City, it is not so much moving from one place to another in space, but the arrival of a new, continuing existence.

The first step in setting up a Roman military camp, whether for one night or a long period, was to lay out the pomerium, the boundaries that surrounded the site. This is what John does in describing new Jerusalem. He told about what would be kept out: death, mourning, suffering. He told about who would be kept out: the cowardly, the wicked, the deceivers.

Then John told about the walls that surrounded the City of God, the gates that stood open all the time and the foundations that could not be moved. Certain missing items are noticed: no sea, no temple, no sunshine, no night. All the inhabitants of the city had one thing in common: their names were written in the Lamb's book of life.

Certain landmarks characterized the city: one main street; one river of the water of life flowing down the middle of the city; one kind of tree, the tree of life. And what is the most important aspect of all about this city? The presence of God eclipses everything else. There is no need for a temple or the sun.

The whole book of Revelation and, for that matter, the entire Bible with all its parts, is concluded with a postlude. In this scene, Jesus speaks again as He did in the beginning, giving another beatitude (Revelation 1:8, cf. 22:14): "Blessed is he who keeps the words of the prophecy in this book" (Revelation 22:7).

Then John adds a note of testimony about his own role and the overwhelming impression from the awesome scenes. Almost losing his senses, he was ready to worship the angel who was showing him the visions, but the apostle was abruptly stopped from giving divine honor to a created angel. He was told to publish the prophecy of the book and emphasize the emergency of the message.

Jesus added His word of assurance, once again enumerating sins that will keep individuals from entering the city. The Spirit and the bride (the community of the believers) added their admonition, "Come." Then John gives warning to anyone who would attempt to add or subtract from God's Word.

The whole of the book of Revelation and the whole of the Bible, end as a note from Jesus, "I am coming soon."

Key Message

"Then I saw a new heaven and a new earth, for the first heaven and the first earth had passed away" (Revelation 21:1).

Glossary

Read through chapters 21 and 22 of Revelation. As you come to the terms listed below, note the explanation.

Chapter 21

New heaven and new earth Although described in material ways, these do not comprise a new model of the old earth. Not that it has two parts—Heaven and earth—but it will be a new universe, a new existence, a new order of things.

Holy city No longer separated in a Heaven, where God dwells, and an earth, where man lives, Heaven and earth come together in the new existence, symbolized by God's holy city, new Jerusalem, having descended to represent the new order. No sea is described, for none is there—only the holy city.

Bride This is the arrival of the bride adorned for her husband (Revelation 19:7, 8). She is identified with the new Jerusalem. The wedding of the Lamb and the people of God is about to take place. The Lord God will not be separated from the community of His believers but will live among them.

Old order The new existence will not be a new development from the old. It will be entirely new. Do not presume there must be oxygen to breathe or gravity to hold us in place, it will be different. None of the unpleasant features of the old order will be carried over into the new kind of existence.

Wife of the Lamb A description of new Jerusalem follows. This is the bride, the wife of the Lamb. The betrothed in Hebrew custom can be referred to as wife, and in New Testament usage Christ and the church are frequently indicated by this figure.[109]

---

[109]Mark 2:19f; Matthew 22:1ff; 25:1ff; John 3:29; 2 Corinthians 11:2; and Ephesians 5:25ff.

Jasper	Either a stone of transparent brilliance or of dark green hue. See the note on its use in Revelation 4:3. Whether it can be identified by a particular stone today or not, we can be sure of the precious quality, the brilliance in reflecting light, and the association with the very glory of God.
Twelve angels	The twelve gates of the city had names of the tribes of Israel, associating them with the old Israel; the wall of the city had twelve foundations with the names of the apostles, associating them with the new dispensation; but the twelve angels at the twelve gates carried the Heavenly representation.
Twelve tribes of Israel	On the twelve gates of the city are inscribed the names of the tribes of Israel. See also Ezekiel 48:30-34 for his vision of Jerusalem with the gates named for the tribes. John has already named the tribes (Revelation 7:5-8).
Twelve apostles	To portray the continuity of God's people through the ages, the old dispensation is represented by the tribes, but the new is noted by the apostles' names in the twelve sections of the foundation. See Ephesians 2:20, where Paul describes the household of God as built on the foundation of the apostles and the prophets.
Golden measuring rod	This measuring rod was provided for the angel who was to measure the holy city. In chapter 11, John measured the temple for the purpose of security. Here the extraordinary size and symmetry of the city are important.
Holy city — 12,000 stadia	A cube, same length, width, and height. A figurative number, drawing the round thousand number from something large and complete. The twelve could be associated with the tribes and the apostles, or perhaps $3 \times 4 = 12$. The miles for 12,000

stadia would be about 1,400 (2,200 kilometers), but translated into miles (or kilometers), the figurative number given is lost.

City walls—144 Cubits Here is another figurative number. This time 12 × 12 = 144. (See also Revelation 7:4; 14:1.) The Greek does not make clear whether this is the height of the wall or the thickness. Babylon's walls were said to be 200 feet high and 50 feet thick.[110] Such dimensions for the figurative size of the Heavenly city could be understood for either the height or the width. If it is for the height, it would be very short in comparison to the figure used for the literal number values (wall = 216 feet high; city dimension = 7,000,000 feet high).[111] But the walls were not meant to provide protection, only to mark boundaries.

Golden street The description of the gates and foundations of pearls and precious stones are climaxed with the street of gold. All of this description may be figurative because it is a new order of things and may not be the jasper or pearl or gold we know. But if it is not literal gold, at least this is as close as it can be described to us in a way to give us some impression as to how precious it appears. The gold has all the quality of pure gold and yet is as transparent as crystal glass, conveying the light and glory of God's presence.

Kings of the earth Kings whose names are in the Lamb's book of life will be able to enter because of the sacrifice of the Lamb. They will be able to bring with them the splendor that endures (see 1 Corinthians 3:10-15), but this will be

---

[110]Herodotus, 1.178.

[111]Henry Swete, *The Apocalypse of St. John,* p. 286.

entirely eclipsed by God's glory and the appointments of Heaven.

Honor of the nations The people of God include individuals from all nations. One need not lose his national heritage nor his individuality to enter the city of God. But nothing impure or anyone shameful or deceitful will enter it. On the other hand, all that endures the trial by fire, that which contributes glory and honor, can be brought in.

Lamb's book of life The book that lists all those who have a place in Heaven and have nothing to fear in the second death (see Revelation 20:12, 15).

Chapter 22

Water of life Its source is from the throne of God. It forms a river that flows through the middle of the city of God. It provides free drink to all (verse 17), and brings life (see John 4:10).

Tree of life John was instructed to write to the church at Ephesus, "To him who overcomes, I will give the right to eat from the tree of life, which is in the paradise of God." (2:7). When Adam and Eve sinned, they were separated from the fruit of this tree in the garden (Genesis 2:9; 3:22-24). Now, in the Heavenly city, the redeemed have access to the tree of life forever.

Twelve crops The crop of the tree is associated with everlasting life. (See the Adam passages cited above). Ezekiel associates such trees with food and healing (Ezekiel 47:12). John's description assures that the fruit will be fresh, abundant, regular, and without end.

Root of David Jesus identifies himself by His human ancestry. He was the Son of David. This was more than a simple genealogy, however. Prophecy affirmed that the Messiah would come from the stock of David: "a shoot from the stump of Jesse" (Isaiah 11:1, 10;

53:2; cf. Romans 1:3). Thus, Jesus is pointing out His fulfillment of the prophecy.

Morning star   Another Messianic prophecy was given by Balaam that "a star will come out of Jacob" (Numbers 24:17). Perhaps some association is indicated here, but this is the morning star that heralds a new day. Peter used the figure (2 Peter 1:19) indicating the dawning of a new day. The book of Revelation closes with the opening of the new and final, eternal day. No sun is seen. It is no longer needed. The very presence of God and the Lamb is abundant source of light, but Jesus is the herald of that new day, the bright Morning Star.

Spirit and the bride   The Spirit is the Holy Spirit who inspires the message, and the bride is the church who delivers the message. The ones who hear the message are (1) members of the body who are expected to repeat the invitation, (2) the thirsty in the world are invited to come, and (3) whoever chooses to drink of the water of life is free to come.

Content Notes

The New Order (21:1-8)

New Heaven and New Earth (1-4)

In the opening scene of the Scriptures, "God created the heavens and the earth" (Genesis 1:1). Now, in the closing scene of the Scripture, God creates a new Heaven and a new earth. Before the first heavens and earth were brought into being, God existed from eternity. After the end of the first Heaven and earth, God will also continue on, eternal; and with Him will live for eternity all of God's people and all His Heavenly hosts in the new Heaven and new earth.

The end has now come. The voice on the throne announces to John, "It is done. I am the Alpha and the Omega, the Beginning and the End." "I am making everything new" (Revelation 21:5, 6). Then follows a glimpse of eternity. If God had given this vision to John earlier, and John had recorded this in the middle of his book, we would not have been able to pay attention to the many lessons he has been giving us. We would have passed over Babylon's fall, we would have slighted the warnings of the resilience of evil and the constant attacks of the beast and of Satan. We would have shrugged off plagues and the suffering of both the people of God and the judgments upon the wicked, and simply focused on the glories of an unmixed portrait of the redeemed in eternity. But the book of Revelation saves this picture until last, after the end has been presented in the realistic doom of the condemned as well as the security and honor of the end millennium in Heaven. Even in Heaven, the existence in store for eternity had not begun until this moment. Now God himself will live with His people in a way He has not done before.

The Saved and the Lost (5-8)

Conclusive statements now emphasize the absolute conclusion that has been reached. God, the One seated on the throne, declares, "I am making everything new" (Revelation 21:5). Commentators spend much time speculating whether God is saying He is renewing the old, remaking the old into something new, but like the old, or indeed creating a new order of things unrelated to the old. For all the impressive arguments presented for each view, in no way can we be sure of the answer. A new Heaven and a new earth may be the words used to describe it because these alone are meaningful to a people who have only known an existence with an earth and a Heaven. A new one, however, of an entirely different order may be distinct from the basics of the old. The bottom line is that it will be entirely new. The finality of it all is accentuated with the instruction to John, "Write this down, for these words are trustworthy and true" (Revelation 21:5).

The series of statements continues with the affirmation, "It is done. I am the ... Beginning and the End" (Revelation 21:6). Now we have come to the end of the beginning God made. Furthermore, He is ready to provide to those who need it free drinks of the water that brings life everlasting. But this is only for those who remain faithful, who overcome the temptation of Satan, the pressure of the world, and the lust of the flesh. Only the ones who win out will be inheritors and counted as the sons of God.

Another list is given, characterizing the marks of the lost: the cowardly, afraid to stand up for the witness to Jesus and the gospel; the unbelieving, who had denied that God would do what He has affirmed will come to pass; the vile, who do evil of any kind to satisfy their selfish whims; the murderers, who take lives to further their wicked plans; the sexually immoral, as they fly in the face of right and wrong to satisfy their lustful desires; those who claim to have magical powers, using deceit to gain control of others; the idolaters, who make anyone or anything an object of worship instead of the one true, living God; and all liars, who deliberately falsify the truth in order to gain advantage. The concluding fate of all of these will be the second death for eternity in the fiery lake of burning sulfur.

The New Jerusalem (21:9—22:6)

The View From the High Mountain (9-14)

After the general introduction to the new Jerusalem, now a more detailed description is given of certain aspects. John has already seen the city coming down out of Heaven from God. But now an angel takes him to a special view of the city, the bride of the Lamb. Its coming is observed from a mountain, great and high. Not as though the city is getting closer as in an approach, but this is its continuing state. It is always coming from Heaven from God; but it is always shining with the glory of God. Ezekiel concludes his book, "And the name of the city from that time on will be: The Lord is there" (Ezekiel 48:35).

The brilliance is like jasper, sparkling as a diamond. The high wall encircling the city has twelve gates with twelve angels and the names of the twelve tribes of Israel. Nowhere in the book of Revelation do you have the segregation of the people of the Old Testament from the people of the New Testament. Here also they are joined together. Whereas the twelve tribes marked the gates on the four sides of the city, on the twelve foundations of the city, on all four sides, were the names of the twelve apostles.

Descriptions and Dimensions (15-21)

In Revelation 11:1, John was told to measure the temple of God and the altar and to count the worshipers there. This was for the protection of those under the promise. But here the angel measures the city, more to give a lesson from its size and planned layout of the eternal home of the saved—as in Ezekiel 40 and 41. To translate the length and height and breadth of the city into

1400 miles each way is tempting.[112] Few realize what distance is indicated by 144,000 stadia. By translating the distance into miles, we may understand more about the distance, but we lose a possible significance of the 144,000, which may be more important than the literal distance. The prime meaning is not the mileage but the presence of 12 × 12 × 1000 in the number.

The description of the city and the line up of the precious stones are dazzling beyond imagination:

Walls of jasper.

City of pure gold.

Twelve foundations.

Jasper—not opaque but crystal clear, perhaps like our diamond.

Sapphire—blue, transparent, the stone known today.

Chalcedony—word used of quartz found in Asia Minor, usually gray or milky colored.

Emerald—typically green in color.

Sardonyx—variety of agate, alternating stripes or layers of rich brownish-red and white used in making cameos.

Carnelian—flesh-red hard stone, capable of good polish, used for seals.

Chrysolite—generally a shade of green, but literally a "goldstone."

Beryl—a gem of hard lustrous mineral, sea green in color.

Topaz—the yellow topaz is used as a gem.

Chrysoprase—quartz, apple-green in color, semiprecious stone.

Jacinth—some say reddish-orange precious stone, others blue like sapphire.

Amethyst—purple variety of transparent quartz.

Twelve gates—pearls (each gate a single pearl).

Streets—pure gold.

The Glory of God (22-27)

The new city is a place of light and purity. No evil deeds associated with darkness are found in any corner of the city. Something else is missing that you might expect to find. Throughout the city,

---

[112]The measurement forms a cube, like the Holy of Holies (1 Kings 6:19, 20).

no temple is to be seen. In the earthly holy city, the temple had occupied the most prominent site of all. Even in the contemporary existence in Heaven, before the inauguration of the eternal order of things, there had been "God's temple in heaven" (Revelation 11:19); but now in the long stretch of eternity, no temple is present. Neither the Heavenly model nor the earthly copy is necessary. Actually, the temple was for a representation of the presence of God. Now, in eternity, there is no need for a representative when the very presence of God is known in the fullest way.

The sun is no longer needed because the glory of God and the Lamb give the light. Even the glory of the nations of the earth that are among the saved for eternity will be brought into the eternal city. All the priceless treasures of man in music, art, literature, and other fields may find their way into the eternal archives for "the glory and honor of the nations will be brought into it" (Revelation 21:26). But one thing is sure. "Nothing impure will ever enter it, nor will anyone who does what is shameful or deceitful, but only those whose names are written in the Lamb's book of life" (Revelation 21:27).

The Water of Life and the Tree of Life (22:1-5)

After an overview of the new Heaven and earth (21:1-8), then a more detailed description was given. One of the seven angels who had emptied out the bowls showed John the city from a distance—the pomerium: walls, gates, those excluded and those included. Now the description continues—this time from the heart of the city. The throne of God and of the Lamb is the source for all that flows forth into the city. Their presence is the key to all of existence in eternity. The images used to portray the scene are archetypal with the language from Genesis (1—3) and Ezekiel (40ff). Paradise in the beginning becomes a type of Paradise restored at the close of the earthly and the beginning of the new order.

Life is there without end. Health is there without restriction. And light is there without further source than the very presence of God himself. In a beautiful grammatical construction in the Greek, John declares there was no light from the sun and they had no need for light from a lamp, "for the Lord God will give them light. And they will reign for ever and ever" (Revelation 22:5).

The Words of Life (6,7)

The angel now makes a statement to sum up the whole of what has been made known to John. The words are "trustworthy and true." Vital to the worth of this book of Revelation is the truth of its message. The prophecies of God will come true. They will be fulfilled. The promises of God will be kept. Never fear, God will be faithful to the end and beyond in eternity. The victory of God will be complete, and He will share that victory with all His people. The words are mindful of the title of the rider on the white horse at Jesus' return: He was called "Faithful and True" (Revelation 19:11).

The reference concerning "the things that must soon take place" (Revelation 22:6) should not necessitate an application to the immediate return of Christ. The book of Revelation may well include numerous prophecies that will be fulfilled in more than one historical incident down through the ages between John's writing and the return of the Lord. Although Nero's persecution of the Christians had probably already taken place when John was writing, still more severe trials were lying ahead in Roman times and would be taking place soon. On the other hand, those who have read these words in later ages and found true application can see the timeliness of its message. In fact, it extends to our own age and will continue to have trustworthiness and truth to the end.

Application (22:8-11)

Keep the Words of This Book (8, 9)

In a conclusion to this majestic symphony of truths, the final lesson must be given rapidly, with full import, demanding fitting attention. That John again falls down to worship at the feet of an angel is doubly surprising, both that he would do such a thing when he has already been explicitly warned not to (Revelation 19:10), and that, having reported it before, he should report it again now. The message becomes double, also. John wants us to see how overawed he was at these concluding scenes to his vision, and also he wants to warn us again of the real danger of misdirecting our veneration to the wrong objects. He recognizes the need for explicit instruction concerning the false worship of lesser beings and ideas. But the positive lesson of the passage is summed up in the admonition:

(1) Worship God, and

(2) Keep the words of this book.

John urges that they keep the words of this prophecy, not that they simply hear the words. To keep the words of this book, his hearers must endure tribulation, remain faithful in spite of all pressure and persecution, and follow the Lamb to the end.

Do Not Seal It Up (10, 11)

John is instructed to leave the scroll of this book unsealed, ready for use. (Compare this with Daniel 12:4.) It should be read, weighed when making conclusions, understood, and used in encouragement for living in a way ready for the coming of the Lord. When John writes telling the wrongdoer to continue in his wrongdoing (Revelation 22:11), this is not a wish for the vile to be lost, but an extreme figure of speech warning that the time is rapidly approaching when it will be too late to turn back and repentance will be impossible. Action must be taken now or inevitable doom awaits continued resistance against God.

Invitations, Warnings, and Promises (22:12-21)

Jesus Is Coming Soon (12-16)

Soon is a relative term, dependent upon the length of time one is talking about. The important focus is not the point in time at which Jesus is coming, but that the opportunities for each person will run out by the time of his death, and Jesus "will give to everyone according to what he has done" (Revelation 22:12). In the next breath, however, one must be explicit that our salvation comes by the grace of God, and no amount of works will be sufficient for the forgiveness of one sin. The robes must be washed in the blood of the lamb (Revelation 22:14; cf. 5:9; 7:14). We are justified by the sacrifice of Jesus. But the actions of the saints have a place (Revelation 14:13; 19:8). It is important that both Christians and non-Christians be aware of the shortness of time that we have to be ready for the coming of the Lord.

"Outside are the dogs . . ." (15). Jesus gives explicit warning to those who will be outside the city. One cannot help but include in his choice as to where to spend eternity a recognition of the company that must be kept outside the walls. The "dogs" are the flagrant violators of God's revealed will, His eternal moral

principles. Some try to use occult powers, worshiping everything and everybody except the true God (idolaters), and some are pernicious liars.

The Testimony for the Churches (16, 17)

This whole book of Revelation is a testimony of Jesus given to John by an angel and meant to be delivered to the churches. Jesus is the Root (see Revelation 5:5; Isaiah 11:1, 10), the offspring of David (Matthew 5:6), and the Bright and Morning Star (Revelation 2:28; 2 Peter 1:19). When Jesus sends out His testimony through the writings of John, He wants to include invitations from others also. The Holy Spirit and the bride (the church, the community of believers) add their invitation to Jesus': "Come." Also the one who hears the message should show concern and raise his voice in agreement of life and testimony, saying, "Come." And the one who hears but does not belong to the community of believers, yet he finds himself thirsting for the water of life he has learned about—it is free for him to take of it. Let him come while he can.

Warnings and Promises (18-21)

The warnings issued here are not particularly against any scribe who might copy a manuscript and inadvertantly make a mistake or against a translator who fails to render a verbal equivalency word-for-word translation from one language to another. Rather, this injunction is against those who deny, disbelieve, or pervert the intended meaning of the inspired author—whether he is a copyist, a translator, or any interpreter of the Scripture.

Jesus closes with another promise to come soon, and John urges him, "Maranatha, Come, Lord Jesus."

Special Subject #13

The Second Coming

The second coming of Christ should be viewed as the climax of all existence on the earth. Without His first coming, however, His second appearing would lose much of its meaning. Jesus' redemptive work in His death, burial, and resurrection are the heart of the gospel. But in the fullness of His glorification, in the vindication of all His teaching and promises, the second coming stands at the climax. When challenged by the high priest Caiaphas, "I

317

charge you under oath by the living God: Tell us if you are the Christ, the Son of God." Jesus replied, "Yes, it is as you say. But I say to all of you: In the future you will see the Son of Man sitting at the right hand of the Mighty One and coming on the clouds of heaven" (Matthew 26:63, 64). This coming again, along with the other associated events—including the resurrection and the judgment—will mark the end of the old order and the coming of the new Heaven and earth. From what Jesus has taught and what the writers of the New Testament have indicated, Jesus' return will be climactic.

The writer of Hebrews states explicitly,

> Just as man is destined to die once, and after that to face judgment, so Christ was sacrificed once to take away the sins of many people; and he will appear a second time, not to bear sin, but to bring salvation to those who are waiting for him" (Hebrews 9:27, 28).

The word most often used for His coming is the Greek *parousia,* meaning presence, arrival, or coming.[113] Jesus refers to His going away, but also to His coming again. The phrase "second coming" has Justin Martyr as its earliest known source.

The book of Revelation is reputed to be the New Testament book telling us the most about Jesus' second coming. In a sense, this is true, but the event of His coming is not described until the nineteenth chapter. On the other hand, the Lord's return is put at the heart of the future events in Revelation. The book takes us through cycle after cycle of activity both in Heaven and on earth that builds up to the second coming, but each time it arrives at the threshold of the event, it recoils to traverse again the whole span from the church's beginning to the last days before the new order. Finally, in the nineteenth chapter, the second coming is described just one time, and the climax has been reached that introduced the final days and the new order of things in eternity. Only in the postlude is one convinced of the role that the coming of Christ has occupied all along. Jesus' final words affirm again and again His coming. The Spirit and the saints join in the invitation for His return. John's final invitation is for Jesus to come again.

---

[113]*Epiphany,* appearing, is another word used of His coming.

The conclusive note of Jesus' return is seen in Jesus' own instruction to His disciples. He repeatedly encouraged them and gave them assurance that even though He would be separated from them for a while, He would come back. It was the clearest note of ultimate victory. He did not know the day or the hour of His coming when He was here leaving His disciples their instructions (Matthew 24:36). This appears to be a deliberate limitation to Jesus' knowledge. But for what purpose? Indeed, this is adequate indication it is better that we do not know the day and hour ahead of time. This makes crucial the admonition to be ready for Him at any time and in every time. Furthermore, it halts any attempt to glean from His teaching hidden indications of the time of the event. He simply did not know the day or the hour, and Jesus wanted to forestall any attempts to predict the time of His return on the basis of what He taught.

Jesus did tell of signs that would accompany His return. An example of these is found in His Olivet Discourse (see above, pp. 97, 106 Matthew 24:1—25:46).

> There will be famines and earthquakes in various places [24:7] . . . the gospel of the kingdom will be preached in the whole world [v. 14]. . . . For as lightning that comes from the east is visible even in the west, so will be the coming of the Son of Man [v. 27]. . . . the sun will be darkened, and the moon will not give its light [v. 29]. . . . the Son of Man will appear in the sky. . . . They will see the Son of Man coming on the clouds of the sky with power and great glory. And he will send his angels with a loud trumpet call and they will gather his elect from the four winds, from one end of the heavens to the other . . . [vs. 30, 31]. So you also must be ready, because the Son of Man will come at an hour when you do not expect him [v. 44].

Paul had a special place in his message for the coming of Christ. As long as the Lord's Supper is commemorated, "you proclaim the Lord's death until he comes," he wrote (1 Corinthians 11:33). Then when the Christ comes those who belong to him will be resurrected (1 Corinthians 15:23). To the Thessalonians Paul gave specific information about the coming of the Lord. He will be accompanied by His holy ones (that may refer to saints or angels or both; 1 Thessalonians 3:13). His coming will be announced by the archangel, by the trumpet call of God. Those from Heaven will be joined by those caught up from the earth to meet Jesus in the clouds as He comes. They will be with Him forever (1 Thessalonians 4:17). "May your whole spirit, soul and body be kept blameless at the coming of our Lord Jesus Christ" (1 Thessalonians 5:23).

In his second epistle to the Thessalonians, Paul supplements what he had said in the first: "The Lord Jesus will be revealed from heaven in blazing fire with his powerful angels" (2 Thessalonians 1:7). Those "who do not know God and have not obeyed the Gospel of our Lord Jesus "will be punished with everlasting destruction" on the day he comes to be glorified" (2 Thessalonians 1:8-10). But that day will not come until "the rebellion occurs, and the man of lawlessness is revealed ... (2 Thessalonians 2:2-4). This one will be revealed, overthrown with the breath of the Lord's mouth, and destroyed "by the splendor of his coming" (2 Thessalonians 2:8).

Other writings of Scripture make constant reference to the coming event. Luke tells of the words of the angels to the apostles after they had witnessed the ascension of Christ. "Men of Galilee, ... why do you stand here looking into the sky? This same Jesus, who has been taken from you into heaven, will come back in the same way you have seen him go into heaven" (Acts 1:11).

Only thirty-five years later, Peter was already making reference to scoffers who had grown weary of waiting for the Lord's return. "Where is this 'coming' he promised?" ... But had they forgotten the destruction of the flood?

> By the same word the present heavens and earth are reserved for fire, being kept for the day of judgment and destruction of ungodly men.... But the day of the Lord will come like a thief. The heavens will disappear with a roar; the elements will be destroyed by fire, and the earth and everything in it will be laid bare. Since everything will be destroyed in this way, what kind of people ought you to be? You ought to live holy and godly lives as you look forward to the day of God and speed its coming. That day will bring about the destruction of the heavens by fire, and the elements will melt in the heat. But in keeping with his promise we are looking forward to a new heaven and a new earth, the home of righteousness" (2 Peter 3:7, 10-13).

Jude quotes Enoch about this coming event, "See, the Lord is coming with thousands upon thousands of his holy ones to judge everyone, and to convict all the ungodly acts they have done in the ungodly way ..." (Jude 14, 15).

James, too, adds his exhortation:

> Be patient, then, brothers, until the Lord's coming. See how the farmer waits for the land to yield its valuable crop and how patient he is for the autumn and spring rains. You too, be patient and stand firm, because the Lord's coming is near. Don't grumble against each other, brothers, or you will be judged. The Judge is standing at the door" (James 5:7-9).

One can plainly see that the Lord's return was no academic question for the theologians of the first century, but of vital concern to every person for every day.

In the book of Revelation, we come to the writing of Scripture that is most associated with Jesus' second coming. That the occasion is not described until the nineteenth chapter has already been noted. This seems to be a long time to wait. But on second thought, one is not disappointed when he looks for references to this event in Revelation. The reader has not yet reached the middle of the first chapter, just after the first doxology, when he is startled with the exclamation, "Look, he is coming with the clouds, and every eye will see him" (Revelation 1:7).

In the letter to Thyatira, Jesus commends them for doing more now than at the first, but warns against their tolerating "Jezebel." Then he adds, "Only hold on to what you have until I come." (To each of the churches except Smyrna, Jesus has some allusion to a coming.) He also promises, "To him who overcomes and does my will to the end, I will give authority over the nations." Jesus assures him He will rule with an iron scepter and He will give him the morning star (Revelation 2:25-28; cf. 22:16). The end for each individual is the extent of his life until physical death comes, but the ultimate end of the old order of things is when Jesus comes again. The promise they receive for faithfulness to each of their ends is a share in His rule.

In the sixteenth chapter of Revelation is another sudden notice to Jesus' coming. This is inserted in a description about the kings of the world as they gather for the battle of Armageddon. As a parenthetical warning, Jesus inserts the reminder, "Behold, I come like a thief! Blessed is he who stays awake" (Revelation 16:15). Three observations result from this interjection: (1) Jesus is coming again, (2) His coming will be sudden and unexpected, and (3) the Christian will be responsible for receiving Him whenever He comes (see Matthew 24:36—25:13).

Finally, in the nineteenth chapter, the long awaited coming occurs. Jesus arrives to judge and to make war (Revelation 19:11). His appearance supplements the presentation of the dauntless Christ in the first chapter. There He was the Counselor of the churches, but here He is the victorious General and the Judge. The armies of Heaven are accompanying Him. This corroborates the scene described by Paul to the Thessalonians. The picture is not simply a triumphal procession as they held in Rome some months after the battle had been won. It will not be like Jesus' triumphal entry into Jerusalem in the final week before His crucifixion. When He comes again, Jesus will face an impending battle.

The outcome, however, is sure. Action from the forces of Heaven is unnecessary. Victory is accomplished, not by a literal sword but by the very breath of His mouth, the Word of God, Faithful and True. Jesus is established to the utmost as King of kings and Lord of lords. He has been accepted as such by all believers, but now He is acknowledged by all for all time and eternity. In fact, this is at the crossroads where time ends and another stage of eternity begins.

Eternity has already begun for the believers when they put on Christ and enter the kingdom. After death, eternity continues in Heaven for the Redeemed as described in the book of Revelation to chapters 21 and 22. These last two chapters, however, tell of a new order of things, a new Heaven and earth, entirely different from the old. This occurs following the final resurrection and the final judgment. The event that starts the action is the second coming of the Lord. Not until then will the new Heaven and the new earth be inaugurated. Is it any wonder the ages stand in awe for the coming of Christ? This will mark the coming of new Jerusalem, the arrival of the new order of things, the new beginning for eternity.

The book of Revelation was not written so much to tell us of the details of Christ's coming as it is to get us ready for His coming. Its message to the believer is one of encouragement and hope, but also a challenge to faithfulness and witness. To the unbeliever, it is one of warning of doom for Satan and his followers, and an admonition to change before it is too late. To both, it is a desperate reminder in a materialistic, temporal world about the depths of one little word, ETERNITY. The second coming of Christ stands at the crossroads.

CONCLUDING NOTES

Authorship

The author of the book of Revelation gives his name and further brief identification: "John, Jesus' servant" (Revelation 1:1, 4), "brother and companion in suffering ... on the island of Patmos because of the word of God and the testimony of Jesus" (Revelation 1:9), and brother with the prophets (Revelation 22:9). He was conscious of the injunction: "You must prophesy again about many peoples, nations, languages, and kings" (Revelation 10:11). His work is closed with final assurance: "I, John, am the one who heard and saw these things" (Revelation 22:8).

Early Christian writings identified him still further as John, the apostle,[114] the disciple of the Lord.[115] In fact, early tradition is in general agreement that the author of the Apocalypse was John, the brother of James, the son of Zebedee, and the apostle who lived out his days in Ephesus, interrupted, however, by an exile on the island of Patmos.[116]

Some later questioned the identity of the author. Such suggestions as John the elder or John the prophet were given as alternatives to John the apostle. The decision of antiquity remained securely in favor of John the apostle. Still other suggestions have been made more recently because of various theories associated with literary style (see below) or use of sources. None has been

---

[114]Justin Martyr, *Dialogue with Trypho,* 81.15.

[115]Irenaeus, *Against Heresies,* 4.14.1; 5.26.1.

[116]R. H. Mounce, *The Book of Revelation,* p. 29. cf. B.W. Bacon, *The Making of the New Testament,* pp. 190, 191. Leon Morris, *The Revelation of St. John,* pp. 25-34. E. Stauffer, *Theology of the New Testament,* London: SCM Press, 1955, pp. 40, 41.

able to present sufficient evidence to replace the initial assurance that the author was the same as the writer of the Gospel and the epistles of John—in other words, John the apostle of Jesus.

This conclusion is corroborated by numerous observations. Since this particular John needed no further identification, this assures us that he is well known and not in danger of being confused with any other John at the time of Revelation's initial use. He is an individual known to the churches of Asia at the time of writing, showing a familiarity with them and having a place of authority in their lives. He has been acquainted with the land of the Jews, knows the Old Testament thoroughly, and gives evidence of knowledge of the Aramaic language.

Much material has been written pro and con concerning the apostolic authorship. When all the arguments have been accumulated, one is still assured that the internal evidence favors it and the external evidence positively indicates it—John the apostle is the best candidate for the authorship of the book of Revelation.[117]

Date

External evidence concerning the date for the writing of Revelation is strong. The last years of the reign of Domitian (died in A.D. 96) are indicated.[118] When this testimony is lined up with the conditions reflected in the letters to the Asian churches, the agreement is impressive. The churches have been in existence long enough for faith to have lost its ardor, for the inner life to have suffered. The Nicolaitan party has had time to grow up after the epistles of Paul. (It must have arisen after Paul's writings since no mention is given in them about it.) The persecution of the Christians is threatening. In fact, John is in exile because of his Christian witness. Antipas has been martyred. But the fact that more examples are lacking rather warns against putting the date for writing Revelation later when Roman persecution was rampant. Although Nero's persecution at the burning of Rome was earlier, it was short-lived and evidently confined to Rome.

---

[117]Donald Guthrie, *New Testament Introduction* (London: Tyndale Press, 1970), pp. 934-949.

[118]Irenaeus. See Henry Swete, *The Apocalypse of St John,* p. c.

The argument in favor of an earlier dating, from the time of Nero, has little to recommend it. Its strongest support was that in the second half of the last century, the Cambridge triumvirate of scholars, Lightfoot, Westcott, and Hort, agreed on the likelihood of an early date, about A.D. 66. But the grounds for such a conclusion have not found many supporters today. Although the usual wisdom of these three is recognized and respected by many today, this was not an area where any one of the three made a special study, and the weight of the reasoning has gone against their conclusions.

Further attempts to support an early date based on the interpretation of the seven kings of Revelation 17:10ff are still more precarious. One does not know whether any Roman emperor is indicated, let alone being unable to find agreement on which one would be indicated by the sixth (see above, p. 255). How can such an uncertain interpretation of establishing an unknown king be used to clarify an unknown date?

All known quantities are best met by the date in the latter part of Domitian's reign, about A.D. 96. The decided opinion of the earliest testimony, the condition of the churches, the state of emperor worship, the threat of persecution—all point to this date.

Occasion

The writing purports to be an epistle written by the apostle John to the churches of Asia during his exile. Some conjecture the writing is done on the island of Patmos and circulated immediately. Others feel John returned to Ephesus when his exile was terminated, and he then wrote the book and sent it out. In any event, it was a writing to report a series of visions seen while on the island of Patmos. The churches needed warning of coming tribulation, encouragement about the ultimate outcome, and reassurance about the return of Christ and the nature of eternity. But this was more than meeting the need of one particular period.

The wisdom of God chose to give a special revelation about things present and things to come. We should not be surprised that this book, unlike any other book in the New Testament, should be included with the rest. Rather, we should recognize how much we would be missing if this apocalyptic conclusion had not been added at the close. This is a fitting climax to all the centuries of inspired records, an announcement of the final outcome, and the introduction of the new Heaven and earth. "Write this down, for these words are trustworthy and true" (Revelation 21:5). This was to meet a need wider than one limited to a certain place and date. This need would extend through the ages to the end of time.

Purpose

The purpose of writing had several fronts. Just at the time of writing, the church was young. It was weak in face of awesome odds in a Roman empire filled with power held in the hands of unbelievers, in a world of selfishness, oppression, iniquity of every kind, when "virtues caused the surest ruin"[119] to one's worldly career. A strong trustworthy word was needed to assure the early generation of Christians that what they would see on this earth was not the end of the matter. Finally, justice would be upheld. Judgment would descend on the wicked. The grace of God and His mercy would bring salvation for the followers of Jesus. He had provided the way through the sacrifice of His own Son, and now He would lead on to victory in Heaven through the continued work of the Lamb.

But the purpose of Revelation was more than an assurance to John's own day. It must have been a word of encouragement to the first century, but it gave a strengthening word to every age to come. Not only did it bring hope, then and now, but challenge as well. The word of admonition was to remain faithful to the end.

The message did not stop with the believer. A warning was carried to the unbeliever to repent before it was too late. Judgment was coming, and the followers of Satan were doomed to the same fate as their master.

How could you write the front page of a newspaper giving a report on the news, an announcement of coming events, and advice to help improvements for the future—written in such a way that people would be reading it each day through the centuries for all posterity? This book does not tell us *when* to expect fulfillment, but *what* to expect; and it retains its freshness every day.

Form and Literary Style

The book of Revelation begins with the word *apocalypse,* meaning unveiling or revelation. Naturally, the book becomes associated with a whole body of literature labeled as apocalyptic

---

[119]Tacitus, *Histories,* I. 2, 3. See p. 184, above, footnote 54.

in its form. No other book in the New Testament is like Revelation in its style. But questions arise. Does the book of Revelation conform to a conventional apocalyptic form? Does it make use of other apocalyptic works? Why are other apocalyptic books not included among the canonical books of the New Testament?

Revelation is in some ways similar, and in some ways dissimilar, to the familiar apocalyptic. It specially has parallels to Old Testament apocalyptic passages. Some of the best examples are Daniel, Isaiah, Ezekiel, and Zechariah. These are works that have special apocalyptic portions, but they also convey sermons and straight narrative sections. Revelation is similar to their apocalyptic portions in the use of figures and symbolic language to predict coming events. The prophets of the old dispensation predicted some events near at hand, some that proved to be in the more distant future, and finally some to be fulfilled at the end of the Heaven and earth as we know them. The latter are designated as apocalyptic; the former are simply prophetic. Although no formal, cited quotation is made from the Old Testament, claim is made that more than half of the verses in John's Revelation can be related to passages in the Old Testament.[120] Whether this was John's knowledge of the Old Testament showing through, or whether this was simply similar language used to describe similar scenes, one can only conjecture. But John's work combines its apocalyptic material in the setting of an epistle, unlike Old Testament examples.

From two hundred B.C. through the first century A.D. (and following), the apocalyptic form of literature became very popular, both in Jewish and later in Christian circles. Several reasons become apparent why these were not received as part of the canon. Most of them were sent out under a false name, claiming some famous personage of the past as the source. Hope to gain notice and authority by the name was obvious. Other works were not signed at all. This is a distinct difference between John and the general apocalyptic works of his time. John wrote in his own name. In fact, this may be one reason he gave his name—in order to disassociate himself from other apocalyptic reports. Another common feature of the contemporary apocalyptic attempts was that they tended to write history under the guise of giving

---

[120]See Henry Swete, *The Apocalypse of St John,* p. cxxxv.

prophecy. Revelation is not guilty of this.[121] Because of their contents, the uncertainty of their early use and acceptance, and the subsequent insufficient proof of inspiration indicating a genuine revelation, these works are not found in the Bible. For the same reasons they are not in the Scriptures, John shows little, if any, use of these books. In contrast, the similarities between John and the Old Testament are clear and frequent.

But why was the apocalyptic form chosen for this important book? These are possible suggestions:

Past precedent in Old Testament.
> God was accustomed to use the prophetic to lead and to move His people. Figurative language was sometimes used to communicate, especially in spiritual matters.

It was a popular literary medium.
> Revelation is dramatic and timely with a timeless message, which lends itself to the popular apocalyptic style. But John took care to distinguish this work from the many pseudonymous works of the time. (See above.)

The apocalyptic was a convenient cryptic device.
> John did not want to identify too closely the things he had to say about Rome for fear officials might take hostile measures in reprisal against the Christians.

It was a necessary measure to reveal and conceal at the same time.
> If prophecy was given in a concrete form to reveal happenings of the future, it could nullify the freedom of the will and run contrary to God's program. Yet use of apocalyptic form would sufficiently establish that the future was known by God and that He would win out.

It is an expedient appeal to the mind and the heart.
> With the use of the figurative, lessons could be given to motivate both our reason and our emotions toward the desired results. Since much of the action was in a realm we have

---

[121]See G. R. Beasley-Murray, *The Book of Revelation,* p. 18.

not experienced, it was necessary to teach by analogy and simile.

Once Revelation is recognized as written in the apocalyptic form, the literary characteristics must be regarded in a new way. No other book of the New Testament is written in this form, and after this admission, who then is going to tell the author he could not be John because he writes differently from the writings of John in his Gospel and three epistles? How can anyone tell how John would write an apocalypse if he wrote one? At least, we would expect it to be of different literary style from his Gospel and epistles. So why shouldn't it be different? It would probably differ in vocabulary, sentence structure, transition habits, and manner of quotation. For example, a person might not quote sources—whether of Scripture or other works—when he is describing something he sees in a vision, in a direct revelation from God. (Revelation has no formally introduced quotation from the Old Testament, but, on the average, at least ten possible allusions can be found in each chapter.)[122]

Then too, if this is a revelation from God, the writer might well become frustrated by the conventional grammar in man's use of language. For emphasis and impression, an ingenious individual might well transcend the conventional in order to make more vivid the truth. Such are the extraordinary grammatical forms sometimes found in Revelation. The author should not be marked as ignorant or as clumsy in his peculiarities. In fact, each time John uses an unconventional way of putting a thing (not according to the usual grammatical practice), it has been noted that he makes a point of using the conventional forms either just before or just afterwards in the same passage—almost as though he is letting the reader know he is aware of the schoolroom usage. Still, he prefers to report this exceptional message in an exceptional way. This obvious answer to the frequent criticisms about the literary difference between the Apocalypse and the Gospel or the epistles of John[123] can explain how John could have written both

---

[122]Merrill Tenney, *Interpreting Revelation,* p. 101.

[123]This is the criticism that Dionysius of Alexandria made in the early centuries, and his misgivings are repeated by many today. Eusebius, *Ecclesiastical History,* 7.24-25. cf. 3.39.

even though there are differences. In fact, when one adds up the points of similarity noted between the language of the Gospel, the epistles, and Revelation, they outweigh the differences. Similarity in vocabulary and style give "a strong presumption of affinity between the fourth Gospel and the Apocalypse, not withstanding their great diversity both in language and in thought."[124]

Debate has risen as to whether Revelation is apocalyptic in form or more prophetic in form. One may ask, "What's the difference?" Certainly there are many similarities, and one writing may have the marks of both mingled together.

Marks common among the Old Testament prophets included a setting in difficult times, with hardship among the people of God, but a particularly sinful condition prevailing. Warnings would be given concerning the severe consequences of sin that were pending. A plea was issued for repentance. In the end, there was the hope of salvation through the Messiah and for the remnant. This was most often given in sermon form to meet a contemporary need.

In the Old Testament, the apocalyptic is intermeshed with the prophetic and delivered by the same prophets. It had to do particularly with the coming of the Day of the Lord, the kingdom of God. It is a time of crisis: the people of God are suffering injustice. The times are so desperate that, without some supernatural intervention, there is no hope. The promises are regularly given in symbolic language. God will bring judgment upon the wicked and will deliver His people in that last day. The apocalyptic was regularly in written form. No one knew how long it would be until fulfillment would come in the messianic age. Following the Old Testament period and a time of silence, apocalyptic works began to appear—about two hundred years after the writing of the last prophets of the Old Testament. They used the language and figures of the Old Testament heavily, but they also drew figures from other religions around them. They signed the works with names of well-known people of the past, adding both time and prestige to their own words.

So when John wrote, he had not only the Old Testament Scriptures available to him, but also the contemporary apocalyptic literature, as well as the symbolism of the myths of the gods and

---

[124]Henry Swete, *The Apocalypse of St John,* p. cxxv.

goddesses of the Roman world filling the air. Some spend most of their interpretation of Revelation on the possible sources in these three areas. John established his regular practice when he wrote the opening to his Gospel narrative. He used the word *Logos* to describe Jesus in His preexistent state. The philosophers had debated the meaning of this term *Logos* (reason, word) for centuries. John did not borrow from one of them, whether Heraclitus, Plato, the Stoics, or Philo. He simply chose to use their term so he could give them the answer they had been struggling to reach for ages. The *Logos*, who was with God and who was God, became flesh and dwelt among us (John 1:1, 14). This was Jesus. In the same way, when we read Revelation, we are not introduced to the Babylonian Marduk or Greek Apollo or Egyptian Horus, but we see Jesus, returned to His Heavenly role. When we read of His activity, we are not dependent on the Apocalypse of Abraham or the Sibylline Oracles. Although John uses symbolic language and a form that was known in his day, he gives us a carefully formulated report of just what he saw—not borrowed, not copied—but a first-hand account!

The prophetic has to do with near contemporary elements to the author or events along the way between the writer and the end days. The apocalyptic has to do with the end days, involved in the countdown at the close of the old Heaven and earth period. Both of these are present in Revelation.

Interpretation

In this commentary, a definite type of approach has always occupied the mind of the interpreter. This is true of everyone who studies Revelation, no matter how consciously developed the approach is.[125] Nevertheless, little emphasis has been placed on the underlying approach for several reasons:

1. An interpreter should not be governed by his approach, but his approach should arise naturally from the most likely interpretation of each passage.

---

[125]The main schools of interpreting Revelation have been treated above, pp. 14-17. They are not repeated at this point, but can be reviewed to make comparison with the tenets presented here. Throughout the commentary, reference to the cyclical and the end-millennial have been kept to a minimum (as well as other schools of interpretation) so as not to detract from the treatment of the specific passages.

2. The reader's attention should not be diverted from the text, the context, and the meaning for that passage originally intended by the inspired author. The approach may be helpful in some instances, but it should remain in the background.
3. The approach may be wrong or at least shortsighted, failing to see all of the implications of a particular passage. If the approach element is kept to a minimum, however, the worth of the exegesis may still prove enriching.
4. So many approaches compete for acceptance in the study of Revelation that one's whole time could be spent mastering the scheme of the approach rather than the message of the passage. The very presence of so many mainstream views gives warning against being insistent on one to the refusal of considering all others. On the other hand, when one finds fault with the major schools of approach but at times recognizes some merits in each (see pages 17-20, 294-303), both of these points should be acknowledged, as well as making plain the view that is maintained.

In order to point to leading characteristics in your understanding of Revelation, it seems better to label your tenets rather than travel under mainstream titles that are not representative of what you believe.
1. The approach used here can be identified as cyclical (see chart, p. 136). This name is used because most passages in Revelation are part of one series or another, which leads from the period present to the life of the author up to the close of the earthly period as we know it. Each time this span is covered is considered another cycle.
2. The time of the millennium (see pp. 295-303) is end-millennial, so designated because the thousand years, though a figurative number, does not include the beginning of the period from the death, burial, and resurrection of Christ to the second coming (as the amillennialist holds), but it only includes the latter part of that span (the end). Nor does it designate a prolonged extension period after the second coming (as the premillennialist holds). It occurs at the end of that period between Christ's first coming and second coming, and its own end is marked by the loosing of Satan, the return of Christ, and the judgment. This is the end of time and the beginning of the new eternal order of things.

3. The view of the prophetic is intermeshing. In the structure of the book, the number *seven* is found to be particularly important. Not only are series of sevens found frequently, but they are overlapping, interlocked, and intermeshing. The figure of cogwheels intermeshing with one another is helpful. In Matthew 24, Jesus gave teaching about the destruction of Jerusalem, which occurred just forty years later. He also foretold the signs accompanying His second coming. Several times He spoke of one and then reverted suddenly to the other. The result is an intermeshing like the cogs of a pinion fitting into the notches of the larger crown wheel. The small cogwheel represents the prophetic concerning near-contemporary events, but the crown wheel carries the notches of the apocalyptic toward the end of time. In the messages from God, they are intermeshed together. This was not only true of Jesus' teaching on this occasion, but one after another of the Old Testament prophets followed this procedure. In the case of Daniel, we found where he told us of kingdoms near to his day and following, but he also told of the Son of Man returning on the clouds (Daniel 7:13). Isaiah follows a similar pattern. His contemporary scene was the invasion by the Assyrians (Isaiah 10:33—12:6), but this is intermeshed with events centuries ahead: a "shoot from the stump of Jesse" will bear fruit (Isaiah 11:1). So the cogs of the contemporary intermesh with the notches of the Messianic kingdom. This is what happens in the book of Revelation. One time after another, the cogs of the prophetic fit into the notches of the apocalyptic, and we are brought to the point where we expect the coming of Christ to be reached, but instead the wheels stop turning and another cycle is introduced, another pinion with a new set of cogs appears.

How many ages and how many contemporary times these represent, we could never guess; but we can be sure it includes our own, and the cogs are fitting into the notches of the crown wheel, the apocalyptic. Finally, at Revelation 19:11ff, perhaps it is the sixth cycle in Revelation, the wheels continue and the coming of Christ is described. Then in the seventh cycle, the introduction goes back to begin with the end millennium and proceeds through the resurrection, the judgment, and the arrival of the new Heaven and new earth. This presents the everlasting finale of it all.

Conclusion

The sovereignty of God stands out in high relief. God will win out (virtually, He has already won out). God's people will win with Him, but not without great tribulation. This is given as the message of Revelation. But many believers accepted this before they ever opened the book of Revelation. Does it add anything else?

What strikes a reader from the opening words to the closing words of this book is the exaltation of Christ: "the revelation of Jesus Christ.... Even so, come, Lord Jesus" (Revelation 1:1; 22:20). When one reviews Revelation, this element is evident. In every section, Jesus is emphasized. The vision of Jesus predominates in the first chapter. The letters to the churches of Asia are given in the words of Jesus. Even in the throne room of God, the Lamb alone can break the seals and open the scroll. He is not only the Lion of Judah but the Root of David and the Lamb that was slain for the redemption of persons from every tribe, tongue, and nation (Revelation 5:9, 10). "Never again will they hunger; never again will they thirst. The sun will not beat upon them, nor any scorching heat. For the Lamb at the center of the throne will be their shepherd; he will lead them to springs of living water" (Revelation 7:16, 17). Revelation continues with an emphasis on the triumph of the Lamb (Revelation 17:14) and the marriage of the Lamb (Revelation 19:7). Finally comes the return of the Lord as the conquering commander (Revelation 19:11). The role of His reigning and His judgment is given (Revelation 20:1-15). We read of the Lamb's book of life (Revelation 21:27), and the new Jerusalem as the wife of the Lamb (Revelation 21:9). In the epilogue, Jesus speaks again (Revelation 22:7, 12-16, 20).

Suddenly, we are overwhelmed. The main theme must be Jesus, not God. How could this be missed in a summary? If this is your reaction, you have another step to take. We must be ready to recognize that the two, God the Father and God the Son, are One. When the throne is described, it is always singular. But it belongs to both God and the Lamb (Revelation 22:1; 22:3). At times, the singular pronoun is used following a reference to both (for example, they "will serve *Him,*" Revelation 22:3). Commentators often wrestle with who of the two is indicated? But the singular is used because the two are one. The question is raised over who will be the final Judge, the Father or the Son? Instead of answering "both," it might be more accurate to conclude, the One will be the

Judge. "The kingdom of the world has become the kingdom of our Lord and of his Christ, and *he* will reign for ever and ever" (Revelation 11:15).

The difference between the Father and the Son is found in the role of each (cf. 1 Corinthians 15:24-28). The book of Revelation gives a role description of the continuing work of Jesus after His ascension. The book of Acts tells more of the role description of the Holy Spirit on Pentecost and following for the next thirty years. Just as Jesus is present in the book of Acts, but to a lesser degree, so the Spirit is present in Revelation but to a lesser degree. John is described as in the Spirit on the Lord's Day when he received his opening vision. Certainly the sevenfold Spirit before the throne is the Holy Spirit (Revelation 1:4, 4:5). The Spirit of prophecy is a constant reference to the Holy Spirit in the book of Revelation. The whole book comes to an end in an epilogue, and the Holy Spirit adds His word with that of the believers as they give invitation to Jesus to come again (Revelation 22:17).

Besides the important roles of God, Jesus, and the Spirit, another witness stands tall in the book of Revelation. This is the testimony of the saints. "They overcame him (Satan) by the blood of the Lamb and by the word of their testimony; they did not love their lives so much as to shrink from death" (Revelation 12:11). The combination of Jesus' sacrifice and the testimony of His followers was the undoing of Satan and all his efforts.

The book of Revelation brings hope and encouragement to the Christian. It brings warning of judgment and condemnation to those who reject God. It brings challenge for the believer to remain faithful and dedicated in his course of life. One must be prepared to endure tribulation, but the promises in eternity give strength. The Bible would be incomplete without the thrilling message of the book of Revelation, but its pages cannot be understood without the rest of the Bible. Together, they are the everlasting gospel.

GLOSSARY INDEX

A

B

L

M

N

T

V

W

Y

SUGGESTED READING

The books listed below represent different points of view and come from different starting points. Those specially recommended are marked with an asterisk.

*Beasley-Murray, G.R. *The Revelation* (The New Bible Commentary). Grand Rapids: Eerdmans, 1974.

Beckwith, Ishbon T. *The Apocalypse of John.* New York: Macmillan, 1920; Grand Rapids: Baker, 1979.

*Bruce, F.F. "The Revelation of John" in *A New Testament Commentary.* G.C.D. Howley, ed. London: Pickering & Inglis, 1969.

Caird, G.B. *A Commentary on the Revelation of St. John the Divine.* New York: Harper & Row, 1966.

Farrer, A.M. *The Revelation of St. John the Divine.* Oxford: Oxford University, 1964.

*Hendriksen, William. *More than Conquerors. An Interpretation of the Book of Revelation.* Grand Rapids: Baker, 1939.

*Ladd, George E. *A Commentary on the Revelation of John.* Grand Rapids: Eerdmans, 1972.

*Morris, Leon. *The Revelation of St. John* (Tyndale Commentaries). Grand Rapids: Eerdmans, London, 1969.

*Mounce, Robert H. *The Book of Revelation* (The New International Commentary on the NT). Grand Rapids: Eerdmans, 1977.

*Ramsay, William M. *The Letters to the Seven Churches of Asia*. New York: Armstrong & Son, 1905; Grand Rapids: Baker, 1979.

Simcox, William Henry. *The Revelation of St. John the Divine* (Cambridge Bible for Schools and Colleges). Cambridge: University Press, 1898.

*Swete, Henry B. *The Apocalypse of St John*. London: Macmillan, 1906; third edition, 1909.

*Tenney, Merrill C. *Interpreting Revelation*. Grand Rapids: Eerdmans, 1933; reprint, 1980.

Walvoord, John F. *The Revelation of Jesus Christ*. Chicago: Moody, 1966.